To Renata, Hanna and Jack

There is one thing about our theatre that makes me want to hang my head in shame: its almost total imperviousness to anything happening outside these shores.
   Michael Billington from ONE-NIGHT STANDS *(1993)*

Theatres, actors, critics and public are interlocked in a machine that creaks but never stops. There is always a new season in hand and we are too busy to ask the only vital question which measures the whole structure. Why theatre at all?
   Peter Brook from THE EMPTY SPACE *(1968)*

THEATREMAKER
1974 – present

ATC LONDON
OLDHAM COLISEUM
OXFORD STAGE COMPANY
COMPANY OF ANGELS
BRISTOL OLD VIC
OXFORD PLAYWRITING

by
John Retallack

First published in 2025 by Holywell Press Ltd.

Copyright © 2025 John Retallack.
All rights reserved.

No part of this book may be reproduced, stored in a retrieval system, or transmitted in any form or by any means – electronic, mechanical, photocopying, recording, or otherwise – without the prior written permission of the publishers.

Published by Holywell Press Ltd,
16-17 Kings Meadow, Ferry Hinksey Road, Oxford, OX2 0DP, UK

ISBN: 978-1-916929-06-7

Designed and typeset by Holywell Press, Oxford.
Printed in the United Kingdon by Holywell Press Ltd, Oxford

Printed on Carbon Captured paper
Holywell Press
14039900282

FOREWORD
by Tim Crouch

Theatremaker is the right title for this book. I describe myself as a 'theatremaker' but John Retallack's title far exceeds the bounds of my own limited definition of writer, performer and director. For him, theatremaking is the collective act of everything: from creating the companies, running the buildings, managing the budgets, programming the seasons, driving the van, supporting the staff, encouraging a new generation, a new vision, being one step ahead of the funding axe – while also growing as an artist, a director, a writer and an inhabitant of the world. His book offers a fascinating insight into a balancing act between art, family and career in constantly evolving conditions. The breadth of his experience is astonishing. It spans encounters with Ariane Mnouchkine, Peter Brook, Peter Stein, the formation of ATC in 1977 (still going strong), exhaustive international touring, an Olivier Award, running a regional rep, steering Oxford Stage Company for ten years as an internationally recognised producer, the creation of a European and young people-centred model of work with Company of Angels, writing awardwinning plays, dramaturging, teaching, tutoring, mentoring, supporting. I've been privileged to have Retallack's wise counsel alongside my work from the start of my writing life. There are few people in British theatre with his depth of experience and his level of generosity in sharing it. This is a hugely practical book forged out of action not ideology. Retallack has learnt through doing and making. The presence of his diaries means that there's a vividness and immediacy to his observations.

 What do we do with the picture that he paints? It's hard not to lose hope as a contemporary theatre maker. The passage of play is not in our favour. *Theatremaker* is a book that should be read by anyone with any level of investment in the future of live performance. It's an exhortation from history to dive in, to keep going, to hold your nerve; to demand more and never settle for less; to look further than the UK for inspiration; to read widely, to watch widely, to be open to the new, to participate. The most powerful moments in this book, however, are when Retallack makes time for personal reflection. When he takes stock, thinks about his family, his partner, their children, their bills, their futures, their precariousness. Theatre is only any good if it embraces the whole of life. *Theatremaker* does precisely that.

There's a sobering record in the book where Retallack lists the productions he oversaw in his first full year as Artistic Director of the Oldham Coliseum in 1986. There were ten productions that year. Ten full productions ranging from *Dick Whittington* to Caryl Churchill's *Cloud 9* (a play which equates colonial and sexual oppression); from an adaptation of Walter Greenwood's story of working-class poverty *Love on the Dole* to a brand new musical (*Girlfriends*) which transferred to the West End the following year. Also in 1986 the Coliseum was given £100,000 for renovation from the Greater Manchester Council who were being disbanded and had unused funds which they wanted to distribute to the arts in the area.

Reading Retallack's record of that year alone is like reading about a foreign country – where 'they do things differently there'. A country where a rep theatre in a small town with a population of under 100,000 could support ten original productions a year, where local councils had 'unused funds' for the arts, where theatres were seen as an integral part of their communities, where new writing had an equal place in the repertoire, where audiences expected to be challenged as well as entertained. Retallack admits that not all the Coliseum productions in 1986 were successful and writes candidly about the pressures of keeping the building alive. He also acknowledges that there were only four channels on the TV at the time. But his book charts from the inside the gradual attenuation of UK theatre provision over the last half-century. Theatre is an inhospitable landscape in 2025 and *Theatremaker* is a fascinating personal record of a journey from the cosmopolitan potential of the late 1970s to the cultural dystopia of today.

Tim Crouch, January 2025

CONTENTS

FOREWORD by Tim Crouch — V

1. EARLY DAYS: Discovering Theatre, 1974-77 — 1
2. ENSEMBLE THEATRE: Devising with ATC London, Home and Abroad, 1977-85 — 24
3. REPERTORY THEATRE: Oldham Coliseum, 1985-88 — 76
4. TOURING THEATRE: Directing Shakespeare at Oxford Stage Company, 1989-99 — 102
5. YOUNG PEOPLE: Directing new plays for young audiences, 1991-1999 — 123
6. DIRECTING IN ANOTHER CULTURE: Reaching for new horizons, 1988-2000 — 145
7. WRITING PLAYS: Company of Angels, 2000-2011 — 171
8. LATE PRODUCTIONS: 2010-2018 Bristol Old Vic, 2011-2013 — 192
9. TEACHING PLAYWRITING: Ruskin College, Oxford, 2013–2017 and Oxford Playwriting from 2017 — 202
10. AFTERWORD — 213

PART 2: CONTEMPORARY JOURNALS 1980-1981

EUROPE JOURNAL, 1980 — 217

SOUTH AMERICA JOURNAL, 1981 — 241

Productions, Performances, Publications — 253

Acknowledgements — 260

1
EARLY DAYS
Discovering Theatre, 1974-77

DIARIES

I forget things very quickly. For this reason, I've kept a daily diary for many years.

I lost some key years – on a November flight in Brazil, I left a 1981 Guardian diary that I'd scrawled in minute lettering with a Rotring pen. I left a 1999 Rymans diary in a taxi that took me home very late at night from Piccadilly to Crystal Palace. Otherwise, I've got most years.

My forgetfulness extends to a mass of life data: historical dates, jokes, quotations from Shakespeare, numbers, key news facts, foreign languages, names of trees, which way to go round the M25 – in multiple ways, I have been greatly helped by the smartphone and the accessibility of facts.

I write a diary to make sense of my days. It listens to me as I tell it what I did – and what I thought and felt when I did it. And I can say anything I want to say, however rude or damning it is, because no one else will read it but me. This is very helpful in times of stress and uncertainty.

This intensification of consciousness apart, the diary has no practical use. Until I came to write this memoir.

From a mix of written diaries, cassette diaries, photos, leaflets, letters and reviews, I was able to piece together a period of time that I had, until now, completely forgotten. Theatre in the 1970s was thrillingly unknown territory – how did you learn about it? How did you train? Everyone told you that it was a dead end, hardly anyone made a living from it. This only served to make it more attractive, not just as a career but as an adventure.

One brief visit to Paris opened up a world to me. I saw brilliant alternative theatre work that revealed a new way of life, not just another profession. It was mysterious and I had everything to learn; but for once I felt an affinity with what I saw, that I might actually have the skills required. The great thing was this – there was no path. I had to find my own way.

I am glad now that I kept those diaries – sketchy and brief as they are, they took me back and, for the year I spent writing this, my past has become my present.

Leaving home

I failed to get to university – A levels were a mocking 'F' and 'O'.

I went to the Careers Master to ask about becoming a teacher and he said that I should simply study my subject at University and then, if I still hadn't changed my mind by the time I left, I should apply to a school – there would be no problem, no one trains to teach.

When I got two 'E's on my second attempt, I applied to a teacher training college in Cheltenham called St Paul's and St Mary's. And I had been at St Paul's School, no less, in London, because my father taught there throughout my school years. St Paul's School was right up there with Winchester for entries to Oxbridge and was always in the top three in the academic league tables. Until me, no one from St Pauls' School had ever been to a teacher training college.

Many years later, my father said he should never have sent me to the same school as the one he worked in. It certainly cramped my style and most probably his too.

My father was a stylish and sophisticated art-lover – he wrote for art magazines and was himself a good linguist and watercolourist. He'd been a major in the British Army and served at Anzio. He was renowned for his immaculate suits, silk pocket handkerchiefs and exquisite brogues. While I was at school in the 60s he was the Commander-in-Chief of the CCF. I, by contrast, wanted to grow my hair long, loathed parade, rules, uniform and found it hard to sit still in lessons. I would stare out of the window at the playing fields and wish I was a groundsman, anything to not be trapped in a classroom, bored out of my brains.

The conflict between me and my father was gruelling for us both. I felt so far from what he wanted me to be. I remember him making me cry all the time, whether with a slipper when I was young or with his devastating dressing-downs he gave me as a teenager. I failed so entirely on every level to come up to his expectations.

I played for school teams at rugby and cricket and I was able to take some pride in my achievements there. I was a good ball player and he wasn't. That was something. Despite all this, I think he loved me through my schooldays and I was touched that he did so. I loved him in return. I know this because as soon as I left home, I always wrote letters to my mother and father, long descriptive ones about the year I spent teaching and travelling in Africa. There was no rejection on either side. In fact, when he saw me off on a flight to Bulawayo in 1969, where I was to stay for some nine months, he was crying.

College

When I got to my new St Paul's, the teacher training college, the head of department took me aside and said that I might find that I would be 'well ahead of the other students'. Since I had never been ahead of anyone, I really couldn't make sense of what he said. My course was an entirely new one and I was in the first-ever cohort.

Education was at last changing. 'Schoolmasters' were out and so was the old chalk-and-talk. In its place arrived dynamic classroom leaders who would teach English through a whole range of creative means – 'presentations' of literature through acting, movement and music; the use of video to tell a story; immersive poetry walks; anything that replaced the teacher talking at the class. I went to St Paul's Teacher's Training College to do a course called *Double English* and it was designed to train future heads of English for the most go-ahead comprehensive schools. The new English teacher would be an enabler, a facilitator, a quietly inspirational figure that 'led out' creativity in every student – because, in the view of vanguard thinkers at the time, every student had unlimited creative potential.

Two great teachers led our course. One was Gordon Parsons, a radical Socialist and theatre critic for the Morning Star; the other was Brian Earnshaw, a novelist and poet, very out there (for that time and place) as a homosexual. Brian was the most original and entertaining lecturer I had ever met. His views usually shocked us. Male beauty obsessed him and made us (a very straight class) look at the world through new eyes. He found Dickens and Eliot boring; he loved Baudelaire, Baldwin and Cavafy. He turned history into scandal and culture into gossip. Brian changed our conventional thinking about culture and education because through him we learned to think for ourselves, to take a view. And so did Gordon but in an entirely different way to Brian. Gordon was idealism in action. He organised coach trips to London theatre and the RSC in Stratford; he was always at the vanguard of change in the classroom; he reported back from the Labour Party Conference. Brian and Gordon, each radical from their end of the continuum, shaped us as teachers and citizens. Even if they didn't see eye to eye, we knew how lucky we were to have a higher education course that was so personal, so focused and so eccentric.

Brian and Gordon encouraged the very opposite principle to that of St Paul's, the traditional public school in West London that I had attended. If I could believe that every pupil had unlimited creative potential, then maybe I had that too.

Everything in this experimental course centred on making the written word three-dimensional. We found ways to animate the stories that children wrote or to present prose and poetry in the classroom. It was collaborative work, very active, and we were always visiting schools to try out our ideas. Our reading list was eccentric – it included Gothic novels, Victorian poets and no drama at all, apart from what we devised ourselves.

We were encouraged to find our own passions and I spent whole days in the Alan Hancox bookshop in Cheltenham, reading randomly and widely. There was non-stop chamber music on Alan's record player. There, rather than at college, I discovered Byron, Ruskin, William Morris, the Pre-Raphaelites, Wyndham Lewis, the Vorticists, Pound, Eliot, Plath, Hughes, Sexton, e.e. cummings, the Beat Poets – and the painters and sculptors of the same era. The Double English course completely ignored FR Leavis and so I've spent the rest of my working life catching up with the literature I didn't read as a student. But during the period 1970–74, creativity was the priority of the course. This was in tune with the explosion in popular culture at the time. It rescued me and I spent four years in a state of creative exhilaration.

Teaching

My first school was called Frensham Heights, near Farnham in Surrey, and it was a boarding school in which there was nothing to do. There was no organised sport, music, drama or religion. It was an eccentric institution, part St Trinian's, part Summerhill. It existed for teenage children of liberal, wealthy and often unhappy families. Never in its history had it enjoyed the principled leadership of an AS Neill. When I arrived, it wanted to be a 'free school' – with good exam results. There were fewer than 300 pupils on site. The pupils were striking. They came from all over the world; the way the boys and the girls relaxed together was entirely new to me. They were precocious in drugs, sex and in their manners. I was the virgin teacher.

It was a terrible place in which to be bored. I lived on site in a nice little cottage but I had no driving licence. I had to amuse myself too. The only relief I found from being alone in a class with teenagers was through directing them in plays. Part of my remit as a teacher was to teach drama as well as English. Until arriving at Frensham, I had no interest in plays. I loved novels and poetry. I didn't realise until then that Double English had taught me so much about staging a play. Parsons and Earnshaw had shown us how to make the word flesh.

In my first year of teaching, I directed *The White Devil*, *The Duchess of Malfi*, *Rosencrantz and Guildenstern Are Dead* and Wilde's *Salome*, plus a revue. Frensham Heights had almost been closed down the year before I arrived because the pupils and their all-night parties had got out of control. The new headmaster approved of me immersing the students in rehearsals

Directing my first play, Webster's *The White Devil*, in 1974

and he was delighted, I think, that the school excelled in something that required time, energy and commitment.

As a result, he allowed me to stage the plays anywhere I chose in the spectacular buildings and grounds. Frensham Heights was a spooky chateau, with numerous halls, ancient fireplaces, courtyards, an empty ballroom and a massive central staircase. The site-specific locations lent themselves well to Jacobean tragedy and to the decadent melodrama of *Salome*. Soon everyone wanted to be in the plays because they were such spectacular events in the life of such a tiny community.

A performance that I remember vividly was by Sophie Parkin, daughter of Molly Parkin, a famous writer and bohemian at the time. Sophie played Salome at the age of 14 with total assurance and style. She went on to become a novelist and night-club owner but she was a very fine actor. I was as new to making productions as the pupils. In certain ways, liberal Frensham was the school that I wished I'd gone to myself.

But as an adult, I had to get out as soon as I could. I was only one step ahead of the sixth form in my life experience. The place was really the end of the line for a single teacher of 24.

Timon of Athens, Paris, 1974

While still at Frensham, I had read a rave review in *The Guardian* by Michael Billington of a great Shakespeare production in Paris. He praised the performance for being a superb example of 'ensemble theatre'. I didn't know what that was but I urgently wanted to find out. I thought that the play was *Titus Andronicus* and read it closely over the entire ferry crossing and night train to Paris. But the play was *Timon of Athens* (or *Timon d'Athènes*). It was Peter Brook's inaugural production at his new theatre, Les Bouffes du Nord, and he had directed the play in French. Despite having never read the play, its parable-like nature meant that I followed it very easily – it is the least complex plot in the entire canon.

Timon d'Athènes by William Shakespeare, French adaptation Jean-Claude Carrière, directed by Peter Brook; first performance: 15 October 1974 as part of the Festival d'Automne in Paris

(Timon makes a fortune and everyone importunes him for money until, disgusted with them and the greed of mankind in general, he goes off into the wilderness to live as a hermit. Isolated and alone, he digs in the sand with his spade and finds … gold. All the people he despises find him again and solicit his wealth once more. At the end of the play, Timon rails against mankind in a long and passionate speech of rage.)

Everything about this *Timon* was different from conventional Shakespeare production at that time. The actors sat in a circle on the floor on cushions made of hessian. When they moved, they all moved because each one of them, regardless of role, was part of the ensemble that created the world of the play. A huge bowl of golden twine represented the wealth that everyone sought but only Timon found. At one point, Timon wraps the entire company up in golden thread, a striking image of a merchant class imprisoned by its obsession with wealth. As anyone who has read Peter Brook's writings on theatre will know, this staging of *Timon* emerged from extended group improvisations with actors who, through the period of rehearsals, had developed a profound grasp of the narrative of the play and their own place in it. That is what ensemble theatre means really – all of the company in rehearsals all the time and then, in production, all of the company on stage all the time. For me, Brook was the director who lit the way ahead – and I discovered him while still directing school plays.

Shakespeare

At Frensham, dreaming of leaving, I thought up a scheme called Shakespeare Youth Theatre. This combined my new-found love of Shakespeare, my 'practical' training in Double English and a new-found disposition for thinking up schemes that were in themselves a kind of manifesto. I was very influenced by *Timon of Athens* in Paris and a book by John Russell Brown called *Free Shakespeare*.

This was the key paragraph:

Many times during rehearsals for regular productions, when the actors still wear their own clothes, and a stool represents a throne, or two stools a bed, those who watch with attention can be transported with the performer: not only that scene, but often the whole play and much else besides seems clear and immediately relevant…this power to transfigure (is often lost) when a complicated production is making its own points with irresistible effect.

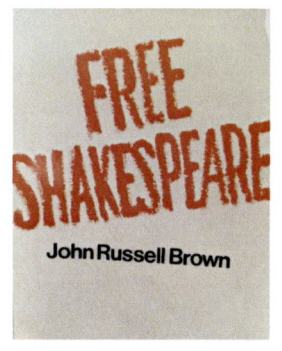

The cover of Brown's book

I didn't enjoy the productions by the RSC and, in my view at the time, its kitsch aesthetic. The more I loved a play, the more I felt the company and its directors destroyed it. This was to come to a head in 1977 with Alan Howard in the Roman plays directed by Trevor Nunn. I actually stood up in a matinee at the Aldwych and walked out, hating myself for not heckling the stage. But the RSC is like Cruft's or the monarchy, it is what it is and change has to be profound to affect it. Screaming like a reactionary from the stalls would be pathetic. I met Russell Brown soon after and I was cheered to find that I was not alone in my wish to see an entirely different approach to Shakespeare.

Friendship

I'd missed my mate from St Paul's College, David Hague, and we both applied to teach EFL for the summer at the Norrington Oxford School of English. We met up very soon after I left Frensham and quickly made friends with a third teacher who was as adrift as we were, though he was eight years older. Howard Jacobson had spent the last decade tutoring freelance at Cambridge and running a handbag stall on the market. Like us, he wanted to write. He sorted that out eventually and won the Booker Prize in 2012. The three of us enjoyed each other's company and that summer was the party that I'd felt that I'd missed over the seven years since I'd left school. We couldn't stop talking to each other in the Dewdrop, the Turf Tavern or the Kings Arms. Howard, who'd been taught by FR Leavis himself, was appalled not only by our lack of knowledge of the core reading list of English Literature but by the books that we did know; what had the Gothic Novel or Wyndham Lewis got to do with anything? 'Maybe, Howard', we'd retort, 'but where's your reading list got you?' Howard just laughed at our innocence and ignorance.

Howard, David and I were there to teach English, in various college settings, as entertainingly as possible to adult students from all over Europe. If the students were happy, then so was the school. We staged sing-alongs, poetry readings and were first to arrive at the Friday night discos in the rugby clubhouse on Marston Ferry Road. Students fell in love with us and we fell in love with students. The school had several intakes over the eight-week summer period and all three of us agreed to come back the following summer.

I got to know Howard quite well at that time and I used to visit him and his then partner, Sue Hancock, in Cambridge. He taught me a number of elementary lessons: if you are invited to someone's home for a meal, bring a bottle of wine with you; he introduced me to classical music by getting me to listen to the whole of the Trout Quintet with him after Sunday lunch; he made David and me sing in public to the students without accompaniment – I still recall my joy in getting through 'Leaving on a Jet-Plane' without hitting a bum note; he always had a suit for special occasions and made us look like scruffs, hence I bought my first decent jacket; and he told us to always find time to read, there's no excuse for not having read Conrad, James and Lawrence – or any of the other novelists in the 'Great Tradition'.

As a result of this first joyous summer, I stayed on in Oxford for the autumn and read a lot of plays – rather than novels. Despite directing Webster at Frensham, Shakespeare was new to me then. I attended lectures at the University because it was free and the speakers were so good – I heard Stephen Wall, John Bailey and, at the Oxford Playhouse, Gordon McDougall, then artistic director of the theatre, demonstrate how the text worked on the stage. I saw a very young Hugh Quarshie play Othello in daylight in the newly-built Burton-Taylor Studio and watched McDougall stop and start him through soliloquies. The student audience of around 30 asked questions of McDougall, Quarshie and Stephen Wall, who I had helped to carry up the stairs in his wheelchair. Stephen Wall was a wonderful speaker because he knew Shakespeare so well and could recite, it seemed, every line from any play. He was a very gentle person with a beautiful speaking voice, afflicted with MS from his 30s.

Howard suddenly turned up in Broad Street in October of that year. I'd parked my Morris Traveller in one of the bays that went up the centre of the street and there were two messages in the windscreen; one said, 'In the Turf – Howard' and the other was a parking ticket. He was very excited because he'd met and fallen in love with Ros Sadler and he wanted to introduce me and Dave to her. He was joyful in a way we had never seen before and she came into the pub to meet us. Dave and I were too self-centred to be really happy for anyone else's happiness. We wanted to be in his situation and we weren't. We were still dating girls and talking about it too much. That's what the three of us had done all summer long.

We were happy to see him but felt that our gang had lost its leader. Ros changed Howard – he took a full-time teaching job at Wolverhampton Poly and, as a result, at the age of 40, he wrote his first very funny novel, *Coming From Behind*.

The Shakespeare Youth Theatre was an attempt to respond to the performance aesthetic of Brook and Russell Brown – but with teenagers. Nothing came of my scheme. I didn't know how to organise such a project, who to approach or how to fund it. I wrote to a number of local authorities explaining my aim and Macclesfield offered me rent-free use of a beautiful old Methodist hall – but I had no idea what to do next. I took another job in a school.

Manchester Youth Theatre, 1976 & 1977

I went to Manchester next and taught English in a boys' grammar school for two terms. While I was there, I met Geoff and Hazel Sykes who ran the Manchester Youth Theatre. They were a glamorous middle-aged power couple who lived in a big red-brick house in Altrincham. They were famous for their rows, which often erupted in our midst. They were also an inseparable couple, both English teachers and passionate old-school lovers of literature and drama. In the evenings they loved to talk and drink and I fell under their spell. Geoff was charismatic and manly in the style of Richard Burton. He was a diabetic, who frequently rolled up his sleeves and plunged a needle into his arm, without stopping for breath. He also made drinking irresistible. He drank beer, whisky or wine with equal pleasure and I think I enjoyed drinking with him more than anyone I'd ever met. Hazel was a redhead with a taste for stilettoes. The received wisdom was 'don't get on the wrong side of Hazel'. She scared me at first but I learned to love them both – as did generations of teenagers who went through the 'MYT'.

The following summer, Geoff asked me to write and direct a show for Manchester Youth Theatre. From then on, all my energy went into writing *Backchat*, a musical revue about the English language that I wrote in Manchester's fabulous circular public library. I went there every day, after school. *Backchat* was the first show I wrote for the stage. It opened for a week in August 1976 at The Library Theatre in Manchester. Despite my productions at Frensham Heights, I soon discovered that I knew nothing of technique, of comedy, of timing or of movement. I'd written a sequence of funny scenes, many of them adapted from a most unusual book called *The Oxford Book of English Talk*. Ken MacDonald, an ex-MYT member, by then a professional actor, 'assisted' me in direction. That is, he directed it in all but name and I learnt a great deal from him. He was a funny guy in the mould of James Corden and everyone enjoyed rehearsals with him in the room. The summer of '76 was the hottest on record and we were in the attic room of a school in Moss Side, next to a big noisy pub. It wasn't the sort of place that most people would enjoy passing a heatwave summer. I was completely happy. *Backchat* was a success with audiences and, to cap it all, Howard and Dave came up from Oxford and took me out to The Happy Seasons for a Chinese banquet.

Hampstead Comprehensive, 1976-77

I didn't settle in Manchester. I took a job at Hampstead Comprehensive in September 1976. I was to teach drama, exclusively, in a school with 2,000 pupils and a well-equipped drama studio. I thought that this might be a step forward, to focus on Drama rather than English. Actually, I ended up playing lots of drama games with very young teenagers for their single period of drama every week. I really didn't enjoy it. In the second term, I caught sight of myself in the mirrors that lined one wall of the classroom while I was helping a mixed group of 14-year-olds settle a passionate quarrel over who played the parent and who played the child. I saw my six-foot bulk hovering over these children and knew that I was the wrong man for the job. If I couldn't work with grown-ups, then I wanted to work, on text, with committed older teenagers. I just wasn't interested in role-play with younger children. The head of department was gifted in this area of work. I felt completely out of place.

Camden Council offered teachers rooms to rent in a number of disused properties. I got the first floor of a Nash Terrace house in Gloucester Gate, formerly the Chinese Embassy. The front half of the building was perfect and intact. I had 18-foot-high windows and a balcony overlooking Regents Park. The back half of the building was entirely cut away. If you opened a door, woodworm had consumed three floors. There was a sheer drop to the basement. The whole building comprised three bedrooms and a vast kitchen. It was an unusual find and I stayed there several years. It cost ten pounds a week. The view from the roof was wonderful, you felt you could touch the planes. There was a lot of storage space in the basement and, over time, that became very useful.

The following summer, for Manchester Youth Theatre, I directed my new play in the same rehearsal room in Moss Side. It was called *Agog and Agape* and was about two children who lived in a circus. To me, the experience of writing and directing both productions was so much more exciting than teaching. The show got a good review in the *Times Educational Supplement* from Heather Neill, its chief theatre critic.

It was Geoff and Hazel who told me to give up teaching and become a director. They were mentors to me at that time. I took their advice and I never worked again in a school. I am grateful to them for the push.

I also remember my father coming to see *Agog and Agape* and saying afterwards, 'you show flair as a director. I'm not so sure about the writing'. That gave me confidence as a director – but I didn't write a play again for 25 years.

Mike Alfreds' Shared Experience, 1976

This was a time of loneliness and frustration and getting nowhere with anything, especially relationships. I still had the amazing balcony room at Gloucester Gate, even though I had left Hampstead School. I dropped out of teaching altogether and took two part-time jobs, one on the box office at the Collegiate Theatre in Bloomsbury, the other as a cloakroom attendant in the dress circle at the Royal Opera House. I saw Strauss' *Rosenkavalier*, Verdi's *Otello*, Donizetti's *Lucia de Lammermore* and a number of Frederick Ashton ballets. It was all new to me and I loved watching these performances multiple times over the time that I worked there.

I liked my humble role. It confirmed that the Opera House was not my world – it was a place for highly paid, highly educated bourgeois people. In truth, I was from a school in which I had the chance to be both of these things. But I was in revolt against everything about my background. Having to live inside the environment of the school from the 8 to 18 with my father as housemaster, CCF commander and Head of Modern Languages had created a deeply ingrained animosity to my own people. 'Don't deny your origins', said one friend to me. But I wanted to.

The films I loved were Jack Nicholson in *Five Easy Pieces*, Eliot Gould in *Getting Straight*, Richard Benjamin in *Goodbye Columbus* and Dustin Hoffman in *The Graduate* – all movies about young white bourgeois men who wouldn't fit in with what their parents expected them to be. 'I can't take anything seriously', whines Benjamin to Ali McCraw in *Goodbye Columbus*. That's how I felt – my school had proposed various jobs in insurance or the city and now my father could not understand why I did not want to become, for example, a 'prep-school headmaster – I'm sure you'd be very good.' Schools were definitively out for me.

But what was in? I loved it when Jack Nicholson climbs aboard the open truck in *Five Easy Pieces* and, under a sheet, uncovers a piano and stool. He starts playing, forgets where he is, the traffic frees up and he disappears into the late afternoon haze, heedless of where the truck is taking him. I wanted to be like him, more feckless than I really was, readier to let the afternoon pass in bed with a girlfriend, smoking a joint – Jack Nicholson did that, why not me?

The truth was that I lacked feckless-ness; I was too earnest to become one of the wild ones. I didn't have the existential capacity to take drugs, waste time or stay up all night and sleep into the afternoon of the following day. I wanted to be the first out of the door, I wanted to travel and to find the geniuses totally committed to making ravishing, life-changing theatre. I wanted to join them and then create unforgettable work of my own.

At last, I saw a show that was definitively great, a show that I can still play in my mind's eye, almost 50 years later: *The Arabian Nights* by Shared Experience. It took place in a daylight gym in Lancaster on an outing with the Manchester Youth Theatre. Their performance was an even greater example of ensemble than Peter Brook's *Timon of Athens*.

Mike Alfreds was a very experienced director when he started his theatre company, Shared Experience. He had run theatres in America and Israel and also had a formidable reputation as a teacher and workshop leader. He expounded a new form of ensemble that put the actor at the centre of the creative process. This is how he put it:

> *Theatre is not about plays. The art of theatre is acting.*
> *The theatre isn't there to serve plays. Plays are there to serve*
> *the actors. Plays need actors and without them, they're just*
> *blueprints. Actors, however, do not need plays. They can*
> *improvise. They can mime. They can tell stories.*

In his first production for his new company, five actors together told the most erotic and outrageous stories from the Richard Burton translation of *The Arabian Nights*. No writer was involved in the production. The lush 19th century language was projected from a place of authority and calm – yet the actors, all of them in floating purple silks, never stopped moving. They could make their bodies do whatever the story demanded. No one took the lead role because they were all the lead role. They were like a single five-headed, shape-shifting, story-telling actor that could do absolutely anything.

No lights, no sound, no set, only the one uniform costume. The show launched the company (which still thrives today) and no one in the audience had seen anything like it before. The sub-title was *Tales of Mystery, Desire and Violence*. The use of 19th century language to describe the most eye-popping erotic situations generated laughter and wonder in equal measure.

The Arabian Nights was true ensemble work.

Byron's *Don Juan*, 1977

I discovered that Byron's *Don Juan* was on the A level syllabus.

I set out to do for Byron's *Don Juan* what Alfreds had done for *The Arabian Nights*. I had no knowledge at all about how to do it. I rented the room next door at 4, Gloucester Gate and interviewed some actors. I was amazed how easy it was to find so many to choose from. I paid nothing and offered home-made cheese sandwiches at lunch-time and a promise that they could leave anytime that they got full-time work. The room was the former ballroom of the Chinese Embassy and it was necessary for the actors to be physically active because it was November and the room was unheated.

I explained that it was an *ensemble production* and that we would 'all contribute ideas.' This was because, despite having adapted the poem into a play script with scissors and glue, verse by verse, I really had no idea how to start. I kept it really simple – Byron spoke the narrative and the respective characters spoke their lines. The poem travels from the English court to the Greek islands, to a slave market in Baghdad and a shipwreck at sea to the court of the Empress of Russia. It travels from one exotic location to the next and it was a joy to devise these journeys and adventures with the actors. That is, we played all day long, physically and vocally, to tell this story with four suitcase-sized boxes.

I called the group Attic Theatre Company. I booked us a week in the Upstream Theatre

Poster for Upstream Theatre, London, 1977

just off The Cut in Waterloo. I made a poster from the portrait of Byron at the National Portrait Gallery. We staged it from Dec 6 – 10th 1977, a 90-minute adaptation. Before we opened, I thought the production was perfect and I offered free seats to everyone I could think of inviting. Later, to my relief, very few of them showed up because, watching it five nights in a row, I realised how far it was from the work of Alfreds, how threadbare the ideas, how slow the rhythm and how the 'empty space' exposed a real absence of informed direction.

What I saw in this scratch group was that the entire ensemble was not good enough in either their movement, speech or timing. Two actors excelled – but even they were only just good enough. I sat and watched and, in my head, eliminated almost every actor from further engagement. To perform for 90 minutes with only four boxes, the company had to be as electrifying as Alfreds' company. I needed to raise the bar when it came to casting and I had to plan my own direction in far greater detail than hitherto.

One person did see it and held out a helping hand: Leonie Scott Mathews who ran Pentameters, a much-loved pub theatre in Hampstead. She offered *Attic Theatre Company* a future slot there.

I then received a letter from *The Attic Theatre Company* in Winchester to tell me that the name belonged to them – would I be kind enough to choose another name for my group?

With Leonie's help and advice, I resolved to change the name – and to do Byron's *Don Juan* again, but better, the following summer.

Here is an extract from my 1977 journal:

NOTE TO SELF
HOW TO IMPROVE BYRON'S DON JUAN

Why, in good faith, adapt *Don Juan* for the stage?

The stories are wonderfully various in mood, ranging from black farce to high romance. Quite long stretches of the poem are in dialogue, and Byron had a wonderful ear for how the people around him talked.

The greatest joy, however, is the wonderful opportunity for varied movement and mime the stories afford. It wasn't written for this purpose, but it is evidence of Byron's unfailingly clear vision of things as they are: the poem is full of first-class stage directions. Byron is a talker in *Don Juan*. The poem talks to people; and if it is an epic, it's a conversational one.

Theatre in Paris, 1977

I had no money left from producing *Don Juan*, so I took a language teaching job in Paris in January, 1977. Having seen *Timon of Athens* there, I felt that this was a city where I could learn more about directing. As well as Brook's company, Paris was the home of Mnouchkine's Théâtre du Soleil, as well as several other legendary ensembles.

A CELTA qualification was not needed in those days. A BEd (Bachelor of Education) was sufficient to get me a job teaching English to bankers in Credit Lyonnais, one of the biggest French banks. All the managers that I taught had an office with a desk at the far end of a long room; to enter, you had to go through a double pair of doors, close both behind you and then walk the length of a cricket pitch to shake hands and pick up from the 45-minute session that you taught *M Le Banquier* the week before.

I found a *chambre de bonne* (a room formerly for servants, with a shared tap in the corridor) on the 8th floor of an enormous apartment building at 4, Avenue de l'Opera, next door to the Comedie Francaise and the magnificent Palais Royale.

With simple rooms like these, in buildings without a lift, Paris at that time was a cheap place to live.

Peter Brook at Les Bouffes, 1977

I went to Les Bouffes (where I had seen *Timon*) to see Brook's *Measure for Measure* with Bruce Myers playing Angelo in heavily accented French, a feature rather mocked by the French critics. The sheer energy and anarchy of the street life characters, Lucio and Pompey, delighted me. I wanted to create an ensemble in this mode.

I hung out in the café by Les Bouffes and got to know Bruce Myers and Malick Bowens well enough for them to introduce me to Brook, who then allowed me to sit in on a rehearsal of *Les Ik*. I remember Brook introducing the note session (on the rehearsal of *Les Ik*) and saying to his multicultural cast that 'English is the language that we are speaking today'. There was a fierce concentration from everyone sitting in the circle. Brook told me that his troupe toured schools in the late stages of rehearsal and that is where he could see if the 'act of theatre is an authentic one – or not'. Brook was the first director I ever heard speak with unfeigned respect for children as an audience. For him, theatre was possible in any practical space and a school dining room was as good a setting as any.

Myers and Malick told me later that 'Peter hates frivolity'. They were still relatively new to life in Paris and they asked me if I knew any girls in the city. I was flabbergasted – that was a question for me to ask them. 'Peter is very demanding,' they confided. They were intensely loyal to the maestro but they also felt burdened by the rigour of his process. Brook was the most famous and powerful director in the English language. Even in France, his authority was absolute. Hence there was a need to truant in some of his younger actors.

Despite his all-powerful position after the unprecedented success of his 1970 *A Midsummer Night's Dream* at the RSC, Brook felt it necessary to leave England and to set up his own ensemble. There were considerable disadvantages – abandoning the English language being the most profound. Brook was not bi-lingual when he arrived in Paris. His priority was artistic independence, away from the confinement of conventional English practice.

About the same time as I saw his *Measure for Measure* in Paris, I went to Stratford to see Brook's *Antony and Cleopatra* with Glenda Jackson and Alan Howard. I couldn't recognise his hand in the production – it was an operatic style of design. I remember blood thrown onto glass screens. The speaking was old-school classical and I felt as bored as I often did at RSC Shakespeare productions.

What Brook wanted to do was not possible within the flagship companies at that time. The RSC had allowed him to do *The Dream* once but that was not a sustainable *modus operandi* for future productions. It demanded a level of intensity and focus that became disruptive in a big repertory company. Brook urgently wanted to include the actor as the mainspring in the collective imaginative process of producing a play. He could see much of the great work in Europe was coming from ensembles with inspirational leaders. The old orthodoxy was that a director and designer explained their concept for a production to a group of actors brought together expressly for a single show. This is how plays are done, then and now. But this top-down approach was viewed as old hat by radical companies in the mid-seventies. Brook was part of this innovative change and he took a genuine risk to leave his country and language behind.

The context of Les Bouffes was liberating for him and he was clearly able to create sublime work on stage with a motivated ensemble.

Yet the ensemble principle carries its own directorial demands. First of all, the director has to take everyone with him when an artistic decision is made. The director cannot ride rough-shod over objections from within the ensemble. It is also necessary to have a shared principle of work (every actor works very hard all the time and he or she is present in all rehearsals for every hour of every day) and of social purpose (the actors are happy to tour school dining halls and other 'daylight venues' before the show opens to the public). All this requires a lot of discussion and devising – and weeks more time in the rehearsal space. Also, the show is always changing. The director will watch it many times and will never stop working and finessing it – which means extra rehearsal on the road.

Whenever I saw a Brook show (and I saw them all up to *The Tempest* in 1990), Brook was usually there in the audience. Deborah Warner, Declan Donnellan, Mike Alfreds, Simon McBurney and others whose work was profoundly influenced by Brook, followed him in this respect – the work of the ensemble is never finished and thus the director is present throughout long runs and tours.

Brook remains the single *best* influence on English-speaking theatre, both creatively and morally. He brought meaning to the act of theatre and he always gave full respect to the actor, the text and the audience. So many directors owe him so much.

Brook's work at Les Bouffes inspired me, and many others. It was at a physical and economic level that I recognised. He set an example I felt that I could follow with a troupe of my own. There was no set at all for *Measure*. Brook cast aside spectacle and replaced it with deeply-rooted ensemble playing. That was the way ahead.

Ariane Mnouchkine's Théâtre du Soleil, 1977

With Théâtre du Soleil (and its associated company Théâtre du Campagnol) you got *both* spectacle and ensemble. Ariane Mnouchkine's company had been resident since 1970 at La Cartoucherie, a former munitions factory near Porte de Vincennes, on the outskirts of Paris. This is an enormous post-industrial site and it was still expanding when I first visited. The vast buildings were not yet all inhabited and it was quite a distance from the end-of-the-line Metro station (Château de Vincennes) to the gates – and there was quite a lot further to walk once you'd arrived there.

When you got there, if it was warm, actors from the various companies (Théâtre du Théâtre de la Tempête, Théâtre de l'Epée de Bois, Théâtre de l'Aquarium, *et alia*) sat outside their respective theatres, on boxes and benches, chatting and smoking, relaxing before they went in to apply make-up and prepare for the show. There was something lordly about them, so at ease before the energy-release of the performance. They basked like lions on rocks. And when you went into the show, and passed through the infrastructure that supported the seating, myriad bulbs lit their faces as they changed into costume and prepared for the show itself. Everything was visible and 'de-mystifying'. Yet I've never visited any theatre before or since, that so celebrated the 'mystery of theatre' as one found it at Le Théâtre du

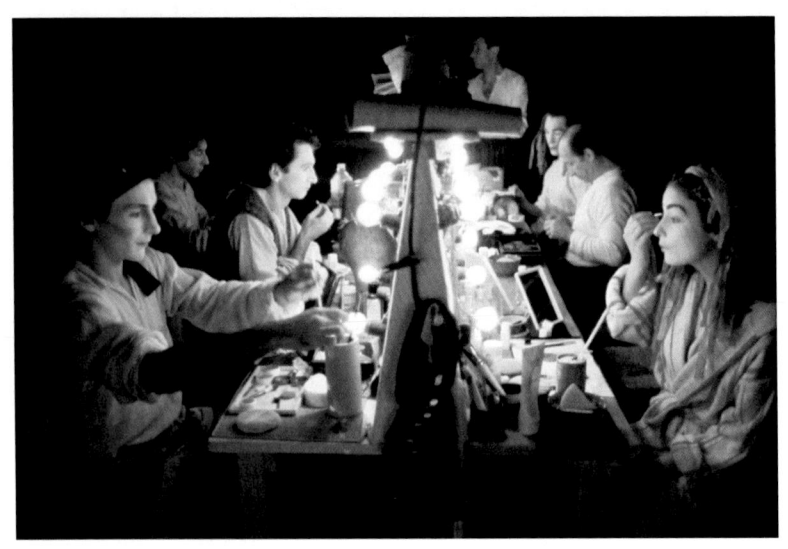

Théâtre du Soleil: the actors prepare...

Soleil. I was magicked and fascinated before the show even began. And at the *entre-acte* when you went out to buy a drink, who served you glasses of wine or cider? The actors, of course, the very actors who you had just been watching minutes before...

Le Théâtre du Campagnol: *David Copperfield*, 1977

I first got there on a spring evening to see Théâtre du Campagnol, directed by Jean-Claude Penchenat, a co-founder with Mnouchkine of the mother company, Théâtre du Soleil. Penchenat was an actor turned director and the story that he had chosen to adapt was *David Copperfield*. Because each resident company created a completely fresh playing space for each show, they could create the décor in any style, on as large a scale as they wanted. This was the most radical innovation about La Cartoucherie – all the spaces were vast disused factory floors and every new show required the building of a new theatre space to house the show.

This was the biggest playing area that I had ever seen used for a play. At both sides of the stage, some 80 metres apart, were great factory windows and much of the lighting came through vast areas of glass, creating long strips of light that worked evocatively for the beautifully studied gestures of every character and the sheer intricate detail of each costume. Because the side-light had such a sculptural effect upon the figures in this great space, it felt to me as if the novel had actually come to life. Although the audience was dispersed throughout the playing space, the production immersed itself

David Copperfield, Théâtre du Campagnol, 1977

entirely into the world of the story – there was no direct address to the audience, almost no stylised posing or theatrical display. This was David Copperfield's life and times and when it was over and I took the metro back to my studio, I felt that I had been in a great three-dimensional dream of Dickens. The eruptions of dancing and laughter surprised me the most: it felt like a fiction populated by real people.

Jean-Claude Penchenat

I was so taken aback that I contacted the Théâtre du Campagnol next day and asked if I could meet the director. I said that I was a '*metteur-en-scène Anglais*', hoping that they would not request a full CV. They invited me to a rehearsal in Châtenay-Malabry, a suburb to the south of Paris. The company had just taken the lease on a defunct swimming pool. The rehearsal took place in a very large (dry) pool with a booming acoustic. It was stone cold, just a two-bar radiator about five metres away from the director.

Penchenat was seated on the floor, smoking, directing scenes from Marivaux's play *The Legacy* throughout a Saturday afternoon. I sat next to him. He acknowledged me and offered me a Gauloise. I indicated a new pack of Peter Stuyvesant I had in my pocket and I smoked one of those instead. For the next four hours, Penchenat concentrated so intensely on the rehearsal that he never once turned to me – he just chain-smoked his way through my whole pack of Stuyvesants. The French word for rehearsals is *les répétitions* and I was astonished how many times he worked over the same scene. No one tired and there was no break. And Marivaux is difficult to break open – unlike Molière, there is subtext of the most nuanced and refined variety. It was a suspended afternoon, out of space and time. The unhurried calm and actorly compliance touched me, all the tension and restlessness sublimated into smoking. Good directors share Penchenat's capacity for total immersion in the three-dimensional exploration of the text in hand. It was another 20 years before I believed that I could direct without cigarettes.

After the rehearsal, Penchenat told me that he had spent a year rehearsing *David Copperfield*; only then did he and the company feel that they had completely imbibed the personality and inner life of Dickens' characters. It was their choice to devote themselves so entirely to the adaptation. At this stage the company was a very large fringe company, breaking into the national arena with impossibly good productions like this one – and more famously, and internationally, *Le Bal* in 1985. I had just never seen ensemble work on this scale, or a large collective enterprise of such manifest commitment. There was so much trust and loyalty involved; it felt not just a show, more a way of life. The clearest evidence that the actors were not paid is that the rehearsals that I was invited to took place on a Saturday and Sunday – they would have been at work in the week.

Le Théâtre du Soleil: *Mephisto*, 1979

I returned to La Cartoucherie two years later to see Ariane Mnouchkine's production of *Mephisto*, adapted from the novel by Klaus Mann. Klaus Mann (1906–1949) was a German novelist whose most famous work was *Mephisto* (1936). The adaptation was by Ariane Mnouchkine herself. Instead of focusing exclusively on the leading character who accepts the role of Mephisto in a prestigious production of Faust funded by the Nazi regime, Mnouchkine examines the impact of a fascist regime on an entire company of actors.

The scale of this production was even larger than that of *David Copperfield*. There were long benches for about 600 spectators in the vast former industrial space. At the beginning of the play, all the audience faced a stage with a naturalistic set at one end. At the other end was a large-scale set for a cabaret. As I sat down, I saw that the wall to my right, about 60 metres long, had a vast painting of *The History of the World* all the way along it, with a light wooden walkway stretching all the way, from end to end. Along the wall to my left was an equally long stretch of fencing with bare concrete behind it, immediately evoking a concentration camp. The contrast between the two vast side walls could not be more pronounced. The play began, set in a Berlin interior. After about thirty minutes, an actor stepped forward and invited the entire audience to stand up, turn 180 degrees, take the back of the bench they had been sitting on and push it to where their knees had just been – and to then sit down again – and all now facing in the opposite direction! It was so original an idea, and so simple, allowing the company to make the fullest use of the theatrical space. The audience could hardly contain their delight in this large-scale switch in direction – of which they had been part.

I marvelled at the skills in painting, set-building, engineering and sheer technical creativity that Mnouchkine had at her command. The play was compelling throughout (even with my limited French) and the ingenuity of the décor entirely served the play and never distracted from its central theme of artistic principle in the face of uncertainty and fear. Mnouchkine is herself Jewish and both her grandparents were murdered in Auschwitz. Her passion for this story is clear throughout *Mephisto* – but so it was in every production that I saw at La Cartoucherie.

Britain has never produced a large-scale ensemble company like Théâtre du Soleil and its associated companies. Its outlook is egalitarian and socialist and it believes in 'popular theatre', a form that it has consistently re-defined. The scale of spectacle allied to dramatic text is beyond anything we have experienced in Britain. The level of investment by government is also very high. It shows the degree to which the individual director or leader is trusted, decade after decade, to deliver work of the highest quality for his or her company. Directors, designers and actors will often stay with 'their company' for many years. The principles of ensemble have only been lived by smaller groups in this country. A company on the scale of Théâtre du Soleil has to be seen to be believed.

For anyone whose interest I have aroused, the company's website tells the story of Théâtre du Soleil in great detail, with many photographs, interviews, videos and documentary material. It is an education in itself. There is even a German documentary lasting one hour about the creation of *Mephisto*.

I didn't get to talk to Mnouchkine as I did to Brook and Stein. I have seen her often but never felt confident enough to speak to her in person. Her interviews are so clear and her intense idealism is manifest in all that she says and writes. She studied at Oxford for one year in 1963, a year before she founded Théâtre du Soleil. Recently, in 2020, she was awarded the Kyoto Prize and she spoke to a small audience at the Oxford Playhouse. It turns out that she is very fond of the city and owns a canal boat on the Isis to which she retreats from time to time..

Theatre in London, late 1970s

If the RSC had looked up around this time to see what was going on beyond Stratford, the directors would have seen a theatrical revolution going on in England – small companies were re-inventing theatre, as if from scratch. Cheek by Jowl, Joint Stock, Pip Simmons, Lumiere and Son, Shared Experience and other touring companies, like ATC, were creating thrilling *ensemble* theatre. The actor was no longer someone who simply did what they were told by a director. They were now instrumental in the creation of the *mise en scène* as they had never been before. The director expected intelligent and imaginative output from a group of actors who were present for every minute of rehearsal; they devised productions *together*. The director was no longer a figure who arrived with a pre-conceived concept and fitted the actors into it.

For his next production, to follow *Arabian Nights*, Alfreds chose Dickens' *Bleak House*. Again, no playwright or adaptor was involved. Just seven actors each armed with the door-stop Penguin copy of the book. They worked for nine months and the production lasted eight hours, split over four evenings. I saw it on tour in Highgate in 1978. The décor was seven folding chairs. I remember Inspector Bucket played by an amazing lanky actor called John Dicks – he created that furious chase across London to St Albans with nothing but his eloquent body. As with *Arabian Nights*, the rest of the company created the world of the story, whether that be the sound of carriages, storms, birdcalls, dogs or wind. The sheer length and scale of the production put almost superhuman demands upon the actors, especially as they would play all four parts on 'marathon days'. I was awe-struck. It took the ensemble approach to the absolute limit. It was brilliant – but there was so much for seven actors to do, doubling, trebling and quadrupling characters.

And Michael Billington, the pre-eminent critic of the day, reviled it:

> ... *this adaptation of* Bleak House *is undeniably done with great skill, but for anyone who can read, what is the point of it?*

But change was going on in the thinking of the major subsidised companies. Mike Alfreds had directly influenced the approach of the RSC, as became clear two years later.

I saw *Nicholas Nickleby* at The Aldwych when it opened in 1980. There were 40 in the cast. It was so different – on a proscenium arch stage, with plenty of direct address to the audience. It projected out at us to great effect. It was extremely well directed and acted. But, unlike Théâtre de Campagnol or Théâtre du Soleil, it appeared to be performed by an ensemble, rather than created by one.

Nicholas Nickleby had the attack, irresistible energy and commercial staging of a great musical. It took inspiration from ensemble companies and created a boulevard smash-hit of intense professionalism. It was as far as it is possible to be from the purist aesthetic of Shared Experience's *Bleak House* or the dream-like beauty of Campagnol's *David Copperfield*.

The works that were changing theatre from the inside were the creations of actors working closely with visionary directors. Yet Billington was as crushing on *Nicholas Nickleby* as he had been on *Bleak House*:

> *… darkly impressive and remarkable vignettes …. Yet for all that I couldn't help wondering periodically if the whole thing wasn't a waste of the RSC's amazing resources.*

To Billington, both productions offered too much illustration – and too little illumination. He was partly right – but wrong in one essential, as we shall see in the following chapter.

2
ENSEMBLE THEATRE
Devising with ATC London,
Home and Abroad, 1977-85

INTRODUCTION

By the mid-1970s I had seen some of the best new West End plays. If that was the only theatre that I had seen, I would not have become a director. To me, at that time, plays by Tom Stoppard, John Osborne, Simon Gray and David Mercer were text-fests in which actors spoke witty and well-written English to each other. A lot of cigarettes were smoked and spirits drunk. Characters expressed their complete and utter disappointment in the way that things had turned out. There was little physical movement and the only means of expression seemed to be through talking, talking, talking …

At the time (December, 1977), I wrote:

> I want a balance of movement and speech, the stage equivalent of a good novel that mixes narration (movement) with dialogue (speech). Movement must narrate what the stage can't speak. I rarely find the conventional play does this - theatre has to find a way to be real without being naturalistic …

Any number of the plays by these authors stand up well to dramatic criticism, of course – but when I used to go to London theatre during my vacations, the plays I watched seemed aimed at my parents' generation rather than my own. Theatre was like cocktail parties or car coats or *Punch* cartoons. It was for them and not for us. We had music. Our parents had theatre.

Adaptations of novels or epic poems allowed actors and directors to play together, to explore movement and mime and music as well as the words in a script. You couldn't do this with modern English plays. They were naturalistic and dominated by the fierce intelligence of the author. The plays were limiting to young actors who were longing to do all that they were capable of in terms of physical (as well as vocal) articulation.

Adaptations also said – no more armchairs and couches, drinks trolleys, tea trays full of cups and saucers and real tea, no more doors and windows, no more opened newspapers and cigarettes, no more imitation of the houses that the audience had left an hour ago. Hadn't they come to experience something different from their daily life?

Adaptations allowed stylisation, allowed the audience to imagine different worlds, to be moved as they might be by dance or by opera or by rock music or ballet because theatre is the mother form that can tell stories in any way it wishes to, in whatever way thrills and transports an audience.

Adapting stories, or novels, for the stage allowed the director and his company freedoms that they could not enjoy even with Shakespeare and the Greeks. The company had control of the text, not the author, and they were free to tell the chosen story with as much, or as little, spoken text, as they chose. Here is Stephen Jeffreys (Playwriting 2019) on his adaptation of Dickens' *Hard Times*:

> *Novels often venture into the innermost workings of the mind on the one hand, with scenes set on a riotously large scale on the other. When I was adapting* Hard Times *I learned not to be afraid of letting the actors create visual moments to accommodate both these different registers. I was stuck as to how to do a scene in which one of the characters falls into a disused mine shaft and is subsequently rescued by about two dozen people. This seemed to require more than the four actors available. Eventually, abdicating all responsibility, I wrote the stage direction, 'The company create the Old Hell Shaft.' The company fell on it in the rehearsal room like hungry animals and created a visual text much better than anything I could have written. (…) adapting a novel is closer to writing a screenplay than a play: the writer often needs to deploy a more visual style, and allow the director and actors to find a way of physicalising the result.*

Billington partly missed the point when he wrote that the key point of an adaptation is to illuminate a particular novel – for theatre makers at the time, we were interested in how the novel liberated the act of theatre and made for a whole new form of creation on stage.

Adaptations freed the stage. Actors could set up imagined worlds without décor and with their movement alone. Actors brought their skills in terms of mime and silent action to create a busy street or a desert or a coach and horses – or a mine-shaft.

Stephen Berkoff showed the way in his spell-binding poetic creations. So did Pip Simmons and Lindsay Kemp and all the other great iconoclasts of the era, each one stripping the stage of domestic furniture and the imitation of everyday life. The stage had to be opened up and the audience expanded to include younger and more diverse audiences.

Arabian Nights, *David Copperfield* and *Bleak House* (along with Brook's unusually free adaptation of *Timon*) inspired me to start my own ensemble theatre company.

I went back to Byron's *Don Juan* for a second time.

ATC Paris, Spring 1978

ATC had now become an acronym for *Actors Touring Company*. I was pleased with this neat solution to the Attic Theatre Company problem. A fresh complication occurred with the name however: because I had submitted my application to the Edinburgh Fringe from Paris, the newly founded company appeared in the Fringe programme as *ATC Paris*. I decided to accept this as a stroke of good fortune. It made the company sound exotic and I made no attempt to change it.

With the help of Leonie Scott-Mathews at Pentameters, I managed to get a wonderful rehearsal space in the hall of Hampstead Church. We took it for six weeks. Since none of us were paid, I felt that we might as well take plenty of time, more time than if we *were* paid. And since Byron's epic poem is of immense length and I knew so little about directing, we needed a lot of time. Through a friend of a friend, a brilliant young classical guitarist called

Dick McCaw, 1978

Dick McCaw joined us and stayed for the next four years, accompanying every beat of the action on a variety of stringed instruments and percussion. Dick was also a brilliant organiser and producer. He launched and managed the company until 1982.

The title role of Don Juan was played by a very relaxed and sexy Australian of Maltese descent called Edmund Falzon. He knew a lot about movement, having worked with a number of experimental directors. There were six in the acting company: Ian Frost, who took on Byron's lines; Richard Klee Leighton, a Glaswegian who looked like Frank Zappa; Ghislaine Rump; Valerie Braddell who played Haidee – and Roberta Durrant, a blonde bombshell from Cape Town, six foot in her socks.

Mike Alfreds once said in an interview:

A lot of work is done by people on instinct; they've got a hunch and a little flair. That's all right up to a point, but it doesn't carry through. The trouble is people think, 'I'll direct,' and it seems possible because the role is not defined …

I was one of those people.

Setting Up ATC

I'd set up the Byron project in a letter to each actor and company member that I'd written from my *chambre de bonne* with a very grand address; 4, Avenue de l'Opera, 75001, Paris.

It itemised a 14-week itinerary from rehearsals beginning in London on July 3rd, 1978, through Edinburgh to a series of performances in London, concluding with a week at Pentameters in Hampstead in late September. The box below shows the details, as itemised in a letter to each actor.

Previews

We previewed the show for five performances in the garden of Keats House in Hampstead. (Companies were permitted to perform five previews before Edinburgh – any more previews and they were not eligible to compete for a Fringe First.)

Audiences came along to Keats House and enjoyed it and the weather was good. Mike Alfreds also came. He was encouraging; and he gave me a lot of notes. He said the actors were not fit enough – they ran out of breath in the movement sequences. I had missed this but he was right.

The poem is in ottava rima and, in Byron's hands, astonishingly versatile. This is the chatty opening:

I want a hero: an uncommon want,
When every year and month sends forth a new one
Till, after cloying the gazettes with cant
The age discovers he is not the true one;
Of such as these I should not care to vaunt,
I'll therefore take our ancient friend, Don Juan –
We all have seen him in the pantomime,
Sent to the devil, somewhat ere his time.

In Seville was he born , a pleasant city,
Famous for oranges and women...

I had booked three weeks at The Lodge in Canongate. In those days, the festival was affordable for fledgling companies. The cost of hiring the hall for three weeks (two two-hour slots a day) was £250. We charged 50p for tickets.

It was the first time I had ever been to Edinburgh and I felt extremely nervous and small-fry with the abundance of shows that played, all day long, from breakfast to midnight. Dick knew his way around and we went to a

BYRON'S DON JUAN IN EDINBURGH

Expenses and potential earnings

<u>Rehearsals July 3rd – August 11th</u>
Daily fares and lunch
Travel

<u>August 19th</u>
Transport to Edinburgh provided

<u>Fee</u>
August 20th – September 9th
1/8 of takings; a 50% house over 3 weeks at 50p a head realises a total sum of £1100, after payment of theatre hire; = £137.50
Expenses are included in this figure, but will be advanced, if required, in part.
Private accommodation will be provided at a considerably smaller sum than digs.
If houses for Don Juan are small, the cut will be correspondingly small.
Only minimal expenses can be guaranteed against a real flop.

pub and drank halves of Guinness with Grouse whisky chasers. The actors arrived with huge suitcases that contained all their clothes for the month *and* their costumes and went off to find their digs. My newly married sister arrived with all the equipment needed for making pizzas and created a nice little pop-up canteen by the main entrance. Everyone was excited as we waited for our two-hour technical slot to run through the cues in our marathon production.

The problem was that after six weeks rehearsal, the show was almost four hours long. We played Part 1 at 12.30pm and Part 2 at 5pm every day. I knew nothing about lighting but I was the only person there who was free to operate it.

We played a preview of each part of *Don Juan* on the first day at The Lodge – and on the second day the critics came.

The following night, my sister came in to the Lodge, brandishing a copy of *The Scotsman* and read aloud the review to the company:

Like a glittering chandelier, Byron's Don Juan sparkles from every angle …

I've lost the review now but I remember that first phrase. It was a thrill to hear a 5-star rave being read aloud to us all.

And a week later, our houses full, we were awarded a *Fringe First*.

To my relief, the company became match-fit in Edinburgh through playing twice-daily. They were no longer out of breath. Full houses increased the confidence of the actors and kept my sister very busy making pizza for people who stayed for both parts. I met writers and directors who had come to see the show. The most important of these was Richard Curtis, a student at Oxford and keyboard player for Rowan Atkinson – and also his script writer. He liked the show and that was to lead to a fruitful collaboration the following year. He lived around the corner from me in London and by the following autumn we saw each other all the time as he wrote his very funny, very lyrical adaptation of *Don Quixote*, based equally on the book and ATC's improvisations in the rehearsal room.

The British Council came to see Byron's *Don Juan* too. At that time, a company of six, with a packable stage and set of costumes for two shows, was considered 'pocket-sized'. If the British Council liked our work, we were the right fit for touring to countries that had an interest in English-speaking theatre. In the late 70s, that was pretty much everywhere because the new wave of small-scale ensemble work often produced adaptations of classic texts – amongst others, Cheek by Jowl had *Vanity Fair*, Berkoff had Kafka's *Metamorphosis*, Shared Experience had *Bleak House*.

This free approach to adaptation was soon to be applied to Shakespeare by a number of companies, including ATC. The British Council became a major player in shaping the artistic repertoire of companies like Cheek by Jowl and ATC. The work that these companies produced could tour to most Anglo-friendly countries and play in any space; it was practical to mount for one night or one week; the actors were used to looking after the preparation of the set and costumes; and the ensemble playing style was original and accessible. These groups were mostly young, outgoing and very keen to travel the world. Most importantly, they responded well to giving workshops in schools and universities.

ATC Paris becomes ATC London

After Edinburgh, I went back to Paris to make back the money spent on Edinburgh and picked up my job with Credit Lyonnais. I taught a different group of middle-managers every week, from Tuesday to Friday, on the first floor of 4, Avenue de L'Opera. I would walk down the seven floors from my tiny servant's room under the roof and start at 10am. On Fridays, each group would take me out to lunch at a steak restaurant called *Hippopotamus* and they would divvy up the cost of my meal between the twelve of them. In mid-December 1978, I came back to my Regency ruin in Gloucester Gate, where Dick McCaw also now lived. Dick had worked hard on the Arts Councils of England and Scotland and we had money to tour Byron's *Don Juan* to Glasgow, Dundee and the Highlands in January 1979.

Although it was certainly easier to get Arts Council money back then (there were far fewer companies), at the time it didn't feel like that.

> There are 82 companies out there competing for 8 touring grants! If I want to set up a theatre company in England now, it's not enough, as I am learning, to simply stage a good show, sit back and expect one's art to draw co-operation and financial support from managements and bodies like the Arts Council…they expect so much more from a company!
>
> (From my diary, November 1978)

In 1978, all the information required for an application for financial support from the Arts Council could be stated in two handwritten sides of a green A4 sheet of paper.

The one thing that they questioned was the name – ATC PARIS. Was ATC an English company or a French one?

Poster for Byron's *Don Juan*, 1978   John with ATC van in Edinburgh, 1978

Since our offices were now officially at 5 Gloucester Gate NW1, I relented and Dick and I changed the company's name once and for all.

From January 1979, we became **ATC London**.

My father and Dick McCaw's father acted as guarantors on the purchase of a white touring van. We went up to Scotland equipped with snow chains and toured *Don Juan* to the Traverse in Edinburgh, The Strathclyde Theatre Club in Glasgow and then further north. I drove the van and I learnt to operate the stage lights in the numerous village halls and black box studios in which we stopped for the night. Dick had organised the digs for everyone at every point of a long tour – this was unusual, because in most companies, actors were expected to arrange their own accommodation. We felt, as a mini-management, it was both kinder and more efficient to do this ourselves. We wanted the actors to give their attention to the show and to enjoy the tour – not be in phone-boxes trying to find a bed for the night.

The Scottish tour led to our first English tours, subsidised by the Arts Council and fees from the venues. At this stage, although we only received our money from tour to tour, there was an abundance of willing bookers and we were able to keep the company together for months without any lay-offs.

Sometimes I had to 'go on' for an actor. I went on for Russell Enoch in Brighton because he'd been taken ill by eating oysters – I borrowed trousers from Jack Ellis and when I bent over, they split right down the back. Loudly. The company melted down with suppressed laughter. Fortunately, professionals that they were, they worked it in.

I was very much part of the company's life on the road, whether in this country or abroad. Touring mixed the practical and the aesthetic in a way that I enjoyed, despite all the things that made it a crap experience. In the early days the only food you could buy at 6pm was a greasy take-away or fish and chips. Pubs didn't do food like they do now. Other things for which I feel no nostalgia at all are the nylon sheets in the B&Bs, the steaming heavy breakfasts served invariably by the 'man of the house' (with Radio 2 coming from the kitchen) and the tip-toeing around the newly formed 'touring couples'. Worst of all (without GPS) was attempting to find the venue once you'd actually arrived in the town, most of the company impatient for a pee or a phone box or a cigarette.

The stone-cold moment of the touring day was getting out of the van around 4pm and stiffly opening the back doors to unload the set, the flight cases full of costumes and numerous instruments – and then carrying them up three or four flights of stairs. And there might be a luke-warm welcome from a techie dressed in black, impatient to know how you want to play the show, as he has to leave in the next ten minutes.

Then the show happens and the audience really respond to the company with great warmth. It turns out there is a pub open down the road and when we've re-loaded the van with all the things we took out of it six hours before, there is a welcome as we walk into the bar. There are folk in there who saw the show and they go over the top in praise, which is pretty welcome after a very long day; we all accept a drink and sit down and light up and, as we finally relax, we agree that it's all worth the effort.

And the next day, the van leaves at 10am for somewhere 110 miles north...

ATC carried a very simple set for its first shows: a floor cloth that could be expanded or contracted depending upon the size of the playing space; and an especially designed metal structure that could be telescoped out to 20 x 20 feet or reduced to 15 x 15. We boasted that we could create theatre in any space, for any audience. As well as schools, church halls and studios, we played in a hotel lounge, a boxing ring for riggers in the Shetlands, a pub garden, a camping site, a canal barge and, when on a British Council tour, in actual theatres with a proscenium arch.

The actors did all the stage management work and looked after the cleaning and ironing of their costumes. Over time, tasks fell to specific actors; some were called in for the heavy lifting, others for sewing. As the vans got bigger, and the company more established, we took on a full-time touring manager who took over the driving, the lighting and the day-to-day management of the tour.

The most important thing was to get a nightly group warm-up before a show. Without this the actors were still, in effect, travelling; at least, they were a very long way from the state of mind needed to play a demanding classical role in which they created the entire story-telling experience for the audience. I made the warm-ups part of the contract. No one was signed up for a tour unless they agreed to participate.

As director, I saw the show every night for months, right through the English tour of 1979 to three weeks on a second (and more profitable) visit to the Edinburgh Fringe. Edinburgh 1979 was a marker – we had survived an entire year as a company.

I learnt how to direct by watching *Don Juan* 150 times. Deborah Warner, then director of Kick Theatre, was the first director that I asked to direct a show for ATC. She turned me down because she didn't want to direct a show that went out on tour – it was simply not possible to keep full aesthetic control in the way that a director could in a fixed space. She was right. But, at that stage of my life, I loved the stimulation and variety of touring: it was my directing school.

THE GUARDIAN, OCTOBER 21ST, 1978
ATC LONDON/BYRON'S Don Juan

HOW IS IT that when a group of actors comes rhubarbing and tumbling on in one of those open stage studio productions, one knows at once whether it is going to be any good? Some groups generate instant electricity, others fall like lead, an effect easier to recognise than to analyse. A company called ATC London, touring a remarkable adaptation of Byron's Don Juan, are brilliant. Byron's satirical mock-heroic doggerel, with its occasional lyrical interludes, is marvellously spoken. The script consists entirely of Byron's actual verse, distributed among the characters. The mime is superb: I shall not soon forget Alfonso's jerky, gymnastic death throes, or the horrifying end of Don Juan's unfortunate tutor. There is some lovely dancing too. All six of the actors are excellent, vital and energetic, controlling with conviction their lightning changes of pace and part. Director John Retallack has imposed a consistently effective style on the disparate elements. The production is simple, adapted for touring: music is one guitar, set is four small rostra and a chair or two – a studio type production which really works. If it tours your way, don't miss it.

At this very early stage of what I hoped would be my career, I learnt the craft of directing through repeated and patient observation of nightly shows.

Dick McCaw continued to create music for the company but he slowly handed management responsibilities over to a new producer as he went off to found Mediaeval Players, a very successful company in its own right. The new producer behind ATC was a dynamic American called Eric Starck. Eric had trained as an actor at RADA and I'd met him at Riverside Studios one afternoon when we'd both turned up to watch Dario Fo. We got talking and ended up working together for five years. Eric had commercial flair and was especially responsible for making our regional tours such a success. He made an *event* out of our arrival in any small town; people turned up to see what the fuss was about. He really maximised the impact of print and worked the telephone ceaselessly to get the venue host active and engaged with ATC. He also operated very well with our overseas tours and brought real professionalism to life on the road, taking the company to Edinburgh for almost a month every year. He was switched-on, a great companion and never bored with the detail.

DON JUAN AT AVIGNON, July 1979

The company toured around England and Scotland with Byron's *Don Juan* through winter, spring and summer of 1979. A Paris-based company (whose theatre was a barge moored permanently on the Canal St Martin quayside) saw our *Don Juan* the previous year in Edinburgh and had invited us to bring the show to the Avignon Festival. They sailed the barge from Paris to Avignon; I drove the company van from London to the festival city, an unforgettable journey through the regions of France to the swelteringly hot mooring occupied by *La Peniche* on the banks of the Rhone. We played in the early evening as the day began to cool and were able to create the lighting by moving the sliding panels that formed the adjustable ceiling of the traverse theatre space. The audience was on two sides and the central playing space was in the belly of the floating barge. The acoustic was very good and it made a charming and unusual studio space for about 100 spectators, enjoying the evening breeze as it came off the Rhone and into the indoor/outdoor ambience of the performance.

The big event of that year's festival was *The Conference of the Birds* by Peter Brook's company. I re-introduced myself to Brook on a quiet café terrace and invited him and his company to our show; he said he'd try and fit it in (he didn't) but he also invited all of my company to his.

It was thrilling to go as a group, though we were divided on that show: half of the group adored its beautiful allegorical simplicity and the manner in which Brook's actors created each bird; the other half announced (as companies will) that 'our show's a lot better than that!' Brook was kind to us all and sought our response as we left and promised to come if he could; he was in an African phase at the time and wore a patterned Nigerian shirt that greatly emphasised the whiteness of his skin. Yet he looked completely at home in this festival ambience and was sought out constantly by fans, wanting his advice or his autograph or both.

What impressed me most was the company of actors that Brook had brought together over the years. They came from all over the world and were of every ethnicity and nation. You could see that there were some larger-than-life personalities there too, certainly not men or women who would be afraid to voice their opinion to Brook, or to disagree with him. I especially remember a giant white American actor called Andreas Katsulas (1946-2006) who took your eye first in a number of shows; as a director myself, I thought that he looked quite 'difficult'. I was probably right. But you realised that Brook's vision was so clearly articulated to his actors – and so came from his brilliant heart and mind – that the actors would do anything that he asked – including becoming a very earth-bound bird with enormous wings.

French poster for Byron's *Don Juan*

***THE PROVOKED WIFE*, August 1979**

Early in 1979, we chose *The Provoked Wife* as ATC's second show. Vanbrugh, great architect and playwright, said, 'I write as I speak'. This was evident in his play and it is something he has in common with Byron. I've always been drawn to the vitality of the English language in different eras. It gives the actor the chance to revive the living tissue of people who died centuries before. Vanbrugh's play is from the end of the 17th century. The characters speak directly to the audience to express their vexation or their desire. Language like Vanbrugh's provides a whole range of physical gesture in its rhythm, texture and earthiness. Women are as outspoken in the play as

Valerie Braddell as Lady Brute in *The Provoked Wife*

men. And their emotions and dilemmas are more richly explored. Here was a play we all wanted to perform.

This is Lady Brute confiding with the audience about her husband at the very beginning of the play:

> *Who knows how far he may provoke me?*
> *I never loved him, yet I have been ever true to him;*
> *and that, in spite of all the attacks of art and nature*
> *upon a poor weak woman's heart*
> *in favour of a tempting lover.*
> *Perhaps a good part of what I suffer from my husband,*
> *may be a judgment upon me for my cruelty to my lover.*
> *Lord, with what pleasure could I indulge that thought,*
> *were there but a possibility of finding arguments to make it good!*
> *And how do I know but there may?*
> *Let me see--what opposes?*
> *My matrimonial vow--why, what did I vow?*
> *I think I promised to be true to my husband.*

Well; and he promised to be kind to me.
But he hasn't kept his word--
Why then I'm absolved from mine-
Ay, that seems clear to me.
The argument's good between the king and the people,
why not between the husband and the wife?

The play did well at the box office. Dick McCaw created the music and this brought a sensuality and depth to the entire performance. Valerie Braddell was beautiful and provocative in the title role and she featured on the (oft-stolen) poster. All the company had leading roles and it played well in tandem with *Don Juan*. It was still possible to play both shows in one venue and that gave us a chance to stay in a town for two nights. We were on our way to becoming a 'repertory company on wheels'.

We played *The Provoked Wife* in a wide variety of venues; on an oil-rig in the Shetlands where the audiences drank up to twelve pints with whisky chasers; in the lounge of a smart Scottish hotel near Wick; in a school at nine in the morning – and, not least, in a tin-rooved village hall near Fort William during a sustained thunderstorm. We also played some theatres. At the time, the company had very little money to pay for the set and costumes. One morning, I went out in the van very early on a Sunday morning and stole two large painter's platforms from scaffolding erected as part of the restoration of St Pancras station. These formed the basis of the set that we used over a period of two years. When the show was finally over, never to be played again, the platforms were too big for the company to store and I drowned them in the Thames – my shameful solution to their disposal. These were hand-to-mouth times until the British Council began to book us for foreign tours on a regular basis. We were fortunate that Byron's *Don Juan* remained so popular – we would never have managed on *The Provoked Wife* alone.

THE YOUNG VIC, (Assistant Director to Michael Bogdanov) September-December, 1979

I was, for three months in the late autumn of 1979, Michael Bogdanov's directing assistant at The Young Vic. I was part of an Arts Council Director's Training Scheme and it was intended that I remain at The Young Vic for one year.

'Bodger' (as he was affectionately known by everyone in the theatre) was a very astute director and he didn't waste time on overlong rehearsals

Michael Bogdanov

(like I did) or fuss over detail very much (like I did a lot). He was a genius at the bold stroke, the killer interpretation, as in the famous opening to his RSC *Taming of the Shrew* in 1979 when Jonathan Pryce's Petruchio tore down the entire set in the opening five minutes of the show; he was also a very good company leader and he enjoyed sustained loyalty for some years from a talented and irreverent group of actors.

Bodger knew how to work fast; he was very strong technically, especially on sound and light. As his assistant, I learnt a lot from him on *The Rime of the Ancient Mariner* and *Rosencrantz and Guildenstern Are Dead*; he and Tom Stoppard would talk together all the time through the rehearsal, the writer as willing to modify or adjust as if it was a premiere, not the *n*th revival since the play opened in 1967.

The key thing I got from Bodger was to know occasionally when to stop – every Tuesday, whatever was going on, however pressured the day, he would walk through the café at 4pm holding a cricket bat and go off to the Oval with Victor Glynn, his then assistant, to have his weekly nets – and that was the end of his working day. But the rest of the time, he was a workaholic. Only a titanic energy like his could have achieved what he did with the English Stage Company – and then write an excellent book about it.

Assisting a powerful director like Bogdanov is good for a two- or three-show stretch but it becomes tedious pretty soon. An assistant director has less status than anyone else in the rehearsal room; I spent the day trying to think of something clever to say to the director. As it happened, my tenure at The Young Vic turned out to be a much shorter experience than planned.

The theatre got into serious financial difficulties before the Christmas of that year and closed for an indefinite period. Having worked with Bogdanov on *Rosencrantz and Guildenstern* and his own adaptation of *Hiawatha*, I was abruptly left with an unspent bursary.

I was glad to get away from The Young Vic and return to my own company. About this time, through the influence of John Russell Brown, I was offered the chance to become an assistant director at the National Theatre. I turned it down. I felt that my assistant directing career was over.

THE LIFE AND DEATH OF DON QUIXOTE
Part 1, January 1980
Part 2, April 1980

Part One (The Life)

I had been working on a stage version of *Don Quixote* with Richard Curtis since I first met him in Edinburgh in 1978. We both lived in Camden. As everyone now knows, Richard is a brilliant once-in-a-generation scriptwriter. I spent a lot of time in his house with other of the 'Camden Boys' who either lived there, camped there overnight or just came round for good company. It was noisy and witty. I was a little older than them all and I hadn't been to Oxford. I felt out of place but Richard was motivated by the theatrical challenge. We got brief passages of time without interruption to talk about the approach to Part One of the book. Hard as it was to get Richard's attention for long, here was a brilliant young man who grasped the point of adapting an impossible novel. And I had a very good group of actors who could improvise many of the 'un-writeable' scenes; scenes like Don Quixote charging the windmills that the ancient knight believed to be giants.

Cervantes was born in 1547, a few years before Shakespeare – and both died on the same day, April 22nd, 1616. Cervantes was to the novel what Shakespeare was to stage drama. *Don Quixote* is seen as a founding work of literature, and is referred to as the first modern novel, a tale with both tragic and comic elements. Don Quixote is the ancient figure who believes in the chivalric stories of heroic knights-errant; Sancho Panza is the realist, an illiterate peasant who agrees to be his squire, with no idea of the surreal adventures ahead. Most famously, Don Quixote attacks a group of hill-top windmills, believing them to be giants. Of course, he ends up suspended on the sails of the highest windmill…

Part One of the Cervantes novel provides an opportunity for broad slapstick and physical comedy. It seemed to me an inherently theatrical story. After all, it had been turned into a ballet, an opera, a film, a comic book – why could it not become a theatre piece? And a theatre piece with broad appeal, the sort of physical show that would play very well on one-night stand performances in village halls as well as on more professional city stages.

Part One is the most difficult section to bring off – it took hours and hours of rehearsal time to perfect the night-time farce in the inn where the ancient Quixote believes that the inn-keeper's daughter is a princess that he must save because she is in love with him. It was full-on farce, using only mime and movement, with a chase through an unlit inn in which every character cannot see where they are going. Richard would write it and rewrite it. It was a brilliant sequence but more rewarding for us to devise than for Richard to write.

The key to the success of Part One was the extraordinary musicianship of Dick McCaw. He had provided the scores for Byron's *Don Juan* and *The Provoked Wife* – this show offered new opportunities for classical guitar and a range of stringed and percussion instruments. Dick was with us throughout all the rehearsals. His brilliance was to be able to unite the broad physical comedy with the romantic idealism and yearning that lie beneath Quixote's humiliating mishap.

The drive to make theatre of this book (that few read anymore) came out of a wish to stage epic stories about an 'Everyman' character. (Byron's Don Juan is another Everyman.) Quixote is beloved for his innocence and preparedness to believe in the impossible. His is a simultaneous triumph and defeat of the imagination. Without Quixote there is only fact; fact tells us that very little can be achieved or experienced in as dusty, dry and dull a world as La Mancha. Quixote sees it differently. The world is full of possibility if only someone has the vision and the self-belief to change it. That is what Quixote, aided by the exquisitely unimaginative Sancho Panza, sets out to do, bolstering them both by his literal readings of chivalric tales. The more he is defeated, the more the reading public of Spain fall in love with him, until he becomes the most famous man in his country. He is a secular comic alternative to Jesus Christ, a man whose capacity to suffer is limitless.

Part Two (The Death)

The writer came into his own on Part Two of the book, a second full-length show that toured with Part One, creating a two-night spectacle called The Life and Death of Don Quixote. In this book-length section, Don Quixote, the gullible ancient who believes he is a true knight of an earlier chivalric age, is now famous all over Spain. Wherever he travels in his country, he is recognised. A bored aristocratic couple decide to host him and Sancho in their ancient castle. They create a series of 'reality' scenes in which they can observe and tease the 'knight' into even greater levels of delusion. Curtis was liberated to write a sublimely surreal and witty script in which Sancho Panza becomes a judge on an imaginary island and Quixote falls desperately in love. In the end, when the chivalric pair escape the cynical games played upon them by the Duke and Duchess, they travel and, for the first time in their lives (coming from Le Mancha), they reach the sea. I could never watch the following late passage of Part Two without being moved by the simplicity and depth of Richard's comic writing.

NARRATOR
Outside Barcelona, is the most beautiful of hills. It seems to be drawn in strips of colour, first, the red line of dust blown from the drier plain below, then, as they rode higher, the short strip of light green grass, washed by continual breathing of fresh sea air. And finally, at the peak, a little cap of yellow, where the winds have blown impatient sand to catch a glimpse of the city below. And up this rode the intrepid pair, Don Quixote and Sancho Panza, and one would have thought, achievement of beauty enough when they reached the top. But, no, their questing eyes looked forward once more.
(THEY BOTH WALK DOWN TO THE BEACH IN WONDER)
SANCHO
The land's run out.
DON QUIXOTE
I believe, Sancho, that is the sea.
SANCHO
It's enormous.
DON QUIXOTE
Yes. For the first time I pity the Turks, having to cross such a vast expanse of blue.
SANCHO
And there, sir, is that the edge of the world?
DON QUIXOTE
Possibly, Sancho. Although there is a new theory being put about, that the world is round. Like an orange.
SANCHO
That's stupid.
(SANCHO GOES DOWN AND COMES BACK)
It's coming closer.
DON QUIXOTE
That, Sancho, is the tide. Ruled by our sister, the moon – patron of Dulcinea.
(SANCHO TASTES THE SEA. SPITS IT OUT.)
SANCHO
It's full of salt.
DON QUIXOTE
Of course, Sancho.
SANCHO
I pity the fish.

What is so beautiful about the entire novel, to me, is that without the madness that drives them, Sancho and Quixote would never have found the sea – in fact, they would never have left La Mancha. There is such human mystery behind this comic tale and our production went from the very simplest slapstick to a powerful and surreal parable of human existence.

The show itself went through many changes as it toured. The British Council picked up the production for a lengthy tour of South America; the long-winded title The Life and Death of Don Quixote became simply Quixote (no exclamation mark) as the show was compressed from two evenings entertainment to one. This was a major edit to make but the resultant two-hour show worked successfully wherever we played it.

MEASURE FOR MEASURE, MAY 1980

ATC rehearsed Shakespeare's *Measure for Measure* at Battersea Arts Centre (now BAC) in May 1980 and opened the production there. We played it in the traverse, (ie, like a tennis court) very long, maximising the scale of the former council chamber that was then the main theatre in the building.

Michael Bogdanov came to the opening night. He told me that *Measure for Measure* was 'very stylish'. That doesn't sound very much writing that today, but I was delighted. Three years later, when ATC received Revenue

Ray Sawyer as Angelo, Valerie Braddell as Mariana

Funding, he agreed to become a trustee and he was extremely supportive when the company was faced with difficult decisions over its future.

Difficult Rehearsals

I found *Measure for Measure* very difficult to direct and perhaps that is why any word of encouragement went a long way. It wasn't the text so much as the two actors who played the Duke and Isabella. They really fell in love. That sounds a happy story but it wasn't. The two expressed this in a singular way – they behaved as if no one else in the room existed. There was at least a 25-year age gap between them. They simpered and mewed and giggled and whispered all day long, both on the rehearsal floor and through every break. Soon it became clear that they had their favourites in the group, and others of whom they shared a negative opinion. The poor actor playing Angelo found it hard to keep Isabella's attention – and the ending of the play between the Duke and Isabella became so schmaltzy that it was hard not to gag. The curtain call became like Maria and Baron von Trapp in *The Sound of Music*.

Each of the other actors on the cast had come to me individually to say that they were intensely pissed off with this situation, with the implication that they would leave the moment this tour was over. Every director of a theatre company has been here. The company of actors can't do anything to solve an impasse like this one; their priority is to make the show work every night. They look to you. Without speaking, the question is in their gaze: 'What are you going to do about this?' and 'When are you going to do it?'

It came to a head when the loving pair were no longer talking to the rest of the cast – except on stage. ATC were playing in a village hall in Sussex and I took each one of the lovers aside individually and fired the bullet. I gave each one notice that their contract would end with the final performance of *Measure for Measure*. Despite my dread in advance of doing this, I'd discussed it with Eric Starck and I was ready for any flak I got from them or from the rest of the company who still might have decided to support the right of these actors to continue working. I told the Equity rep in advance, so everyone knew. In the end, they stayed to the end of the tour and no one mentioned the future.

The two actors concerned left the company after the final performance of the English tour of *Measure for Measure*, after which there was a timely break. The rest of the company stayed on for the next production, which was to be Richard Curtis' adaptation of Cervantes *Don Quixote*, Part Two.

The process was formal and respectful to all concerned. Later, we revived *Measure for Measure* for a further season at the Oxford Union – and we re-cast the roles of the Duke and Isabella.

Keeping the Company Together

By the spring of 1980, Chris Barnes was just one of the actors I wanted to keep in the company: he was highly intelligent, a fine performer and a brilliant clown, a wind player with a beautiful singing voice and a veteran of Michael Bogdanov's company in Leicester and the Young Vic.

As Eric Starck and I planned foreign and international tours, we didn't really stop to think that the actors might not be available when we asked them back to the company.

Then Chris said, 'If you stop work for the summer, how can I say I'll come back with you in September? I've got to work. I'm a company actor, but what happens to ATC shows if I can't come back?'

At the time it seemed normal to be seasonal – all the other groups did that. But having got this far with actors who were now in *Measure for Measure*, *The Provoked Wife* and *Don Quixote*, it would have been suicidal to chuck away all the work that they had contributed.

The penny dropped: ATC, the Actors Touring Company, needed its *actors* if it was to develop into an exciting ensemble. What was true for Chris Barnes, was true for the rest of the company.

In the UK, at that time, the actor had always been essentially a freelance artist – he or she seldom belonged to a single company. It just wasn't the way the business worked. This is why I believe Brook had to leave and go to mainland Europe where a more expansive, more experimental model of theatre could receive funding.

High subsidy from government leads to companies with lasting ensembles who work together, year in, year out. Low subsidy from government leads to an elevated (or depressed) status for the individual artist. He or she has to 'make it in the business' or to give up – there are few companies who will provide professional shelter for longer than three or four months. We now understood that we wanted a company that worked in the European tradition – but within the UK funding system…

That required keeping a company performing or rehearsing for 47 weeks a year.

'Summer in Oxford', 1980

In March 1980, Eric Starck visited the Oxford Union building in St Michael Street, spoke to the administration there and secured a favourable rental for July and August in the famous Debating Chamber. They agreed to allow us to set up our own bar on the lawn, so it became a pleasant retreat from the city to come early and have a glass of wine. We had exclusive access to the Debating Chamber and could therefore rehearse in the day-time. For several

The Oxford Union Debating Chamber

weeks, we had our own theatre and rehearsal studio right in the centre of a city. We trusted that tourists and locals alike would come to watch one of our productions in the evening.

We re-arranged the chamber so that we had a large playing space, part-thrust, part end-on. We put up as much black cloth as we could find to define the playing area because the biggest challenge was the booming acoustic, a feature of a Victorian building intended to give the nation's future leaders maximum amplification and power.

The actual chamber was designed by Alfred Waterhouse in 1879, and opened in 1880, precisely a century before; I didn't know that we marked the centenary and I felt that neither did the Union administration. The whole feel of the place, despite its centrality, was sleepy and forgotten. This was no doubt how Eric was able to secure it for ATC. It was a brilliant catch. We brought energy and activity in the dead summer months. There was nothing like as much cultural activity in Oxford vacation time as there is now.

During the summers of 1980-1982, we played in Oxford till the first week of August and would go on from there to York, where, for a week, we played in The Treasurer's Garden in the shadow of the Minster – and then, further north still, to the Edinburgh Fringe for three weeks, with a Scottish tour to follow.

We played *Measure for Measure* with a cast of six. Jack Ellis moved from Claudio to The Duke, Ray Sawyer remained as Angelo and Chris Barnes did a range of clowning on Lucio, Pompey and the Provost of the jail, armed with a machete and a watermelon to demonstrate his skills as an executioner. Diane Katis came in as Isabella and Valerie Braddell played Mariana and Mistress Overdone. The stage manager was the young Clive Mendus (Théâtre de Complicité) and he doubled as Claudio.

The box office was sufficient at the Oxford Union to pay the company throughout the summer. That, after all, was the central aim of the enterprise; that, and ample time to rehearse the next production.

From 1978 to 1983, the company paid every member the same weekly wage, whether actor, director, producer or stage manager. It reflected the ethos of the company and, given that we always operated at just above Equity minimum, it was simple to administer.

From this time, it became the company's boast that we were the only permanent touring ensemble in the UK: 47 weeks of rehearsal, workshop and performance throughout the year – with five weeks holiday.

We are used now to very long lists of names in programmes for the 'creative team', everyone from the director to the choreographer, via lighting, sound, vocal coach, designer, workshop leader, participation and so on. A small

Chris Barnes as Abhorson in *Measure for Measure*

company like ATC, an ensemble of seven, had to find all these resources from within the company. Ray Sawyer did the movement, Chris Barnes did the singing, Jack Ellis did accents because he could imitate anybody, Valerie Braddell advised on costume, make-up and acted as interpreter in Spanish, French and Portuguese, Christine Bishop was the literature specialist and Russell Enoch, a veteran of great companies, discreetly taught the group to act.

The skills of each actor were important. What was also necessary was both a readiness and a confidence to take workshops, whether with a group of OAPs in a village, a class of teenagers in a school or a whole drama department as was the case at Lancaster University. When we toured overseas the workshops became ever more important: these mattered as much to the British Council as the shows themselves. Wherever we were, the actors normally paired up and, after a group meeting to agree who was doing what (and that the spread of work was reasonable and fair), everyone got on with it. I sometimes took workshops in the company of another actor, as did Eric Starck, the producer. Eric and I took them ourselves if the actors simply had too much on.

The crucial warm-up took place an hour before every performance and this was entirely the private ritual of the actors. Leading the warm-ups got passed around but everyone was there and they could not start until everyone was present. After the 30-minute warm-up, came the 'half'; everyone put on their costumes, make-up, wigs, beards – whatever was required. All seven actors often shared the same dressing room.

I only know the buzz in those collective build-ups to performance from dropping in to give some late note, always knocking on the door with ostentatious politeness. Directors are not meant to be anywhere near the dressing room and I always went into a diplomatic cringe when I entered the intense ambience that preceded a performance.

Free days on tour were cherished, especially if we were somewhere exotic. Since we were very often in places that were not in the least exotic, it was as well to be busy.

ACE-funded European trip, October – November, 1980

In the summer of 1980, I talked to the Arts Council about what I could do with the rest of my unspent bursary; the remaining eight months that I was due. I proposed to Andrew McKinnon at the Arts Council (he was the officer responsible for my case and a theatre director himself) that I use the rest of the money to go off to Europe in October to watch theatre and meet directors in France, Germany and Poland. This was such a fantastic idea that I could not believe that he would agree to such an alternative to sitting in a rehearsal room in Waterloo. But he said yes. I was overjoyed and immediately set to working out my journey and establishing (by snail mail) who I should meet, what shows I should see, where I could stay en route with friends or contacts, anything to stretch out the money as long and as far as possible. I've always felt in debt to Andrew McKinnon for this life-changing opportunity to see and meet great directors and companies.

In October 1980, I left for Paris, the beginning of a month of theatre-going and meeting theatre makers in mainland Europe.

A detailed journal of the trip follows in PART TWO – Europe Journal.

BERLIN/BERLIN, March 1981

I came back to London from Berlin and Warsaw feeling politicised. Stein's obsession with democracy, my sudden grasp of what the Berlin Wall actually was and the passion I observed for theatre in Warsaw – despite no food in the shops – these and many other meetings and images had changed my sense of what a theatre company was for. Theatre was a good night out, but wasn't there more to it than that?

After Berlin, I drafted a play inspired by Robert Musil's 1933 novel, *The Man Without Qualities*, called *Berlin/Berlin*. It involved the same characters as those in the novel but the likeness stopped there. The play was set in modern Berlin, in and around the Wall, the political cabaret scene and also the sexy peep-shows that you could drop into for a German mark on your way home from the office. The composer Paul Sand was in the process of writing a dozen songs for *Berlin/Berlin*.

West Berlin was a strange and eerie place before the Wall came down in 1989. It seemed empty. There was a zoo at the centre of the city and at night you could hear the cries of caged animals. There were many elderly people, particularly old ladies, and young singles – property was very cheap and you would routinely see six individual name plates at the door of one of the vast apartments. There was a lot of money available for cultural activity that authorities wanted to show that democracy was alive and well in Berlin. This was the time the city authorities built Peter Stein a new theatre, which I saw for the first time when we returned there in 1982 with *Berlin/Berlin*.

Berlin/Berlin centres on a West Berlin academic called Ulrich who has stepped aside from university life exclusively to read the newspapers:

> *My daily reading time for all the German dailies is now down to three hours. My personal life is inseparable from outside events. I see it all through my window.*

His sister Anna, whom he has not seen for twenty years, comes over from East Berlin to join Ulrich for the funeral of their father. We see the life of the city through her eyes.

*Look at me here/All things in disorder
Deciding between/A wall and a border ...*

The difference between the two zones of the city is very marked and she is astonished by the level of fear that exists in the western part – especially fear of nuclear attack.

She meets peace activists, fund-raisers and intellectuals. Into this mix comes a character called Moosebrugger, a prisoner who has been released after ten years inside, and who is traumatised by a visit to a Berlin peepshow. He kills the girl who performs for him. He walks into the Café Einstein where Ulrich's group is gathered and demands to be arrested, claiming he is a 'terrorist'. Ulrich is fascinated and, to the dismay of all those close to him, arrests Moosebrugger, taking him home for the night before he turns him in.

ULRICH: My father died on Monday. May he rest in peace. So many people can be moved by the death of one person. But if 500 are killed we don't feel it 500 times as much. By the time you get to the really big numbers, we have very little response at all.

Valerie Braddell as Mia & Russell Enoch as Dr Kortner in *Berlin/Berlin*

The play deals with the widely held view in West Germany that the massive build-up in the East of nuclear weaponry posed an immediate existential threat to its cities. Since the contrast between East and West was so marked in Berlin, this city becomes the epicentre for a kind of apocalyptic neurosis. The play finishes with a suitably insane act of destruction by the now very unstable Ulrich.

The final song goes:

Oh you know what will happen
Oh you know what will come
Most of us will not believe
It's happened when it's done.

I hadn't written a play since Manchester Youth Theatre. And the company had never done a musical play before. I say that I wrote *Berlin/Berlin*, but in rehearsals it got torn up by the company and put back together again on a daily basis. At times, the interior panic I felt became extreme. I would go home (or back to my digs) to re-write it for the next day.

About 4 am, I'd think I'd got it. I'd go to sleep to the sound of bird-song. I would go in early to the theatre to put my handwritten re-writes through the Roneo machine, turning the handle until I had ten copies. In rehearsals, my re-writes were frequently met with a stony silence. Sometimes the silence was friendly. Sometimes no one liked the changes. Because I had stayed up all night, I had to try very hard not to become defensive. As director of the company, I felt enfeebled not to have a 'great text' to depend on.

In fairness to the company, and to myself, we were united on the script by the time we opened it at the Nuffield Studio at Lancaster University in March 1981. It was helped by the fact that the Drama department had invited the company to come and work with their students for a whole week. With them, we worked around the themes of the play and even staged a workshop version with a cast of fifty. This got us all to look

Denise Black as Lina in *Berlin/Berlin*

outwards and to feel some pride in the issues and themes with which the play was dealing: nuclear war and the particular vulnerability of a divided Berlin.

The play was freighted with issues: nuclear disarmament, the Wall, the nature of the right-wing press, the hypocrisy of the charity sector, the ineffectual nature of the left, terrorism. It could be described as a naïve play with good music.

The 'cabaret' mix of styles and the individual performances of the ensemble brought wit to the show. It played well and, if audiences liked it, it was because they also wanted to grasp a sense of Europe at that time. The production looked great, using a combination of lighting and mobile Venetian blinds; the songs brought detachment and irony.

But I learnt a lesson – don't write a play *and* direct it, unless you are very sure of the quality of your writing. Certainly, don't write it *while* you are directing it…

I didn't do the fatal double again for another twenty years. The demands of being both director and writer are very great because they are entirely different functions.

We were joined for this production by Denise Black, a very talented singer and pianist who also played Miranda in *The Tempest*. Chris Barnes and Valerie Braddell both played keyboards. Everyone sang, some better than others. As well as the songs, there was a spoof cabaret set in the real-life Café Einstein. The movement in the show was helped greatly by Ray Sawyer who had become our resident coach in all aspects of gesture and physical expression.

Berlin/Berlin went to the Edinburgh Fringe Festival in 1981, having opened at Lancaster University. Nele Hertling, Director of the *Akademie de Kunst* came to see it in Edinburgh and invited us to perform in Berlin the following May. This was a thrilling result and yet another example of why playing Edinburgh had become so essential.

THE TEMPEST July 1981

It was important to keep this company together – and the play that found us was *The Tempest*. It suited our desire for a powerful allegorical narrative laced with magic and elements of the fantastic – and for Shakespeare's verse which the actors wanted to learn and to get into their bodies.

Valerie Braddell had joined ATC in 1979 and took over the role of Haidee in *Don Juan*. She played the leading role of Lady Brute in *The Provoked Wife*, Dorothea in *Quixote*, Mariana in *Measure for Measure*, Prospero in *The Tempest* and a variety of roles in *Berlin/Berlin* and *Ubu*.

Christine Bishop as Ariel and Valerie Braddell as Prospero in *The Tempest*

In the early eighties, it was a novelty to have a female Prospero but it was in tune with the zeitgeist – Churchill's *Top Girls* came out the following year. The mother and daughter relationship between her and Miranda was affecting to watch. There was also playfulness and wit in her match-making with Ferdinand.

There were only seven in the cast and the set was a large yellow floor cloth. There was nothing else except the movement and the music. *The Tempest* is one of the most musical of Shakespeare's plays and the theatrical styles of the play move from broad physical comedy to some of the most lyrical and poetic in the canon.

The doubling with a cast of seven proved effective. A small ensemble can control the beats of a story like *The Tempest*: it has a feeling for how the dynamic of the play is working at any given point in the performance. The same play, with a full cast, can feel sprawling and episodic. The central meaning can easily be lost because the play has so many metaphors on the go at the same time. The 'seven-headed storyteller' helps to impose upon the diverse styles and moods of the play. It centres the text upon the action and history of Prospero and her relationship to every other character.

Our reading of the play was a healing one. The production implied that Prospero, as well as Alonso, had learned something chastening and profound in the course of the action. It was a huge gain to have an actor who could have played Prospero himself, no doubt very well, in the role of Alonso.

Prospero is then alone on stage; she calls Ariel and frees her:

PROSPERO: *My Ariel, chick,*
That is thy charge: then to the elements
Be free, and fare thou well!

In our production, Prospero watches and waves to her liberated spirit as she flies off into the blue, both sad and ecstatic to see her spirit set free; and the body of Ariel collapses to the floor, her human body now superfluous, a discarded husk. Caliban enters and, with great gentleness, carries it off.

It was a wonderful play for an ensemble to rehearse – it broke down into so many discrete scenes, that the actors who were not with me could be working alone or in pairs in different parts of the building.

All the actors came together for Prospero's final soliloquy to the audience.

Now my charms are all o'erthrown,
And what strength I have's mine own,
Which is most faint: now, 'tis true,
I must be here confined by you,
Or sent to Naples…

The speech that follows is both part of the action of the play *and* refers to the two hours itself that the audience has passed watching the performance. As Valerie spoke to the audience, removing her cloak to reveal a 'classic' modern two-piece and court shoes, the company entered from every corner and lifted the yellow floor cloth and folded it over upon itself. As they exited and Prospero finally departed, only the great ball of canvas was left upon the stage; it appeared to breathe, as the air slowly left it, and to have a life of its own.

It was as if now only the island was left – and that soon would disappear into the sea.

The Tempest opened in July 1981 at The Treasurer's House in York (in association with the National Trust) and then went on to play at the Oxford Union for the summer, before a month at the Edinburgh Fringe in repertoire with *Berlin/Berlin*.

In September, 1981, ATC were invited to tour South America for two months with *Quixote* and *The Tempest* in repertoire. This was a breakthrough for our scale of theatre as the following extract from *The Times* makes clear:

THE TIMES
September 1981

The Actors Touring Company (ATC LONDON) sets off this month for one of the longest tours of South America ever arranged by a British group. They are being financed to the tune of £45,000 by the British Council, the Government funded organisation which promotes our educational and cultural role in foreign parts, and visit Venezuela, Peru, Chile, Argentina and Brazil in the course of eight weeks. The repertoire is an adaptation of their version of *Don Quixote* and *The Tempest* with Prospero played by a woman.

The facts are not in themselves remarkable. But only three years ago they would have been unthinkable. The British Council used to promote staid, unadventurous stuff. This has changed. The Glasgow Citizens, unconventional and outrageous, have twice toured with hosannas from the Council; the Actors Touring Company are far from the theatre establishment and already have been to Greece, Israel and Yugoslavia.

The change is attributable to the British Council's Drama Director for the last two years, Robert Sykes, a youngish member of the Council's career service who is not in the usual mould of desiccated bureaucracy. He inaugurated the change of emphasis, after a diligent survey of the available companies.

A detailed journal of the tour follows in PART TWO – South American Journal.

On return from South America, we were soon back in the ATC van. The company embarked on a six-week tour of England, including a fortnight in Lincoln and Humberside with *Berlin/Berlin* and *The Tempest* in repertoire. In early 1982, the company toured *The Tempest*, *Quixote* and *Berlin/Berlin* all over Scotland, Northern Ireland, Eire, and the Borders. *The Tempest* had a short visit to Italy before opening the 1982 Berlin Festival with *Berlin/Berlin*.

Berlin/Berlin in Berlin, May 1982

In Berlin, the show played at the prestigious *Akademie de Kunst*, just along from the Brandenburg Gate. It was well attended and the critics came up with a number of explanations for the play and the puzzlement it caused: in brief, that it left an audience not sure how to react, that the play was too lightly played to be really serious – or that there were too many themes. This last was true. Nele Hertling, who remains the director of Performing Arts to this day, talked about it with me a lot and said that the play had 'puzzled,

The new SCHAUBÜHNE on Kurfürstendamm, 1982

May 1982 Journal

The new Schaubühne on Kurfürstendamm is like a chic hospital, dazzlingly white, with a very smart restaurant and bar, girls in jeans pouncing on you not to smoke. Downstairs it is an unending mirrored corridor of 12-inch wide lockers for your coat. The toilets are so extreme, they cry out for blood on the walls. Even the urinals reflect an austere intellectualism for all those brainy cocks. It's an extreme anti-fringe statement and more snobbish than any theatre I've ever seen. A blend of ironed denim and high-mindedness realised to a chilling extreme. I hope it does not set a trend. An ordinary citizen just wouldn't like it. It's what the theatre has been trying to get away from for years.

---

fascinated and eluded audiences' and that I should continue to experiment with theatre in this way.

The audience in the city was so open to experiment, so serious in the best sense that it was a privilege for the company to find themselves there. Through playing *Berlin/Berlin*, it dawned on us that German art is fiercely pacifist, in all art forms, not just in theatre. The Parade of the Allied Armies took place while we were in West Berlin:

> It's a very hot cloudless day. The French, American and British armies begin with a 12-gun salute from the Tower of Victory. There's a lot of smoke and the crowd lining the parade jump at the noise. Here it all is, the concept of an Allied Occupied Zone exactly as in 1945. Before the great tanks and the weapons, the British officers file past holding swagger sticks, then the French looking both relaxed and snazzy, the Americans cool and armed and then the Germans...with beards and long hair, crushed under caps, looking the very antithesis of any military tradition, let alone a Prussian one. You wouldn't be surprised to see one playing a flute or with a shoulder bag from Greece. No belts, no guns, no angles. A peace chant starts in the crowd and the German military officers laugh and blush, embarrassed.

Playing this show, the company saw that the history of Germany is writ large on everything in Berlin; nothing had really settled yet since the war despite the efforts of the culture to come to terms with its past. If the military expression is self-consciously soft, it goes the other way in the theatre. I went across to East Berlin to the Volksbühne Theatre, the most iconic of all Berlin's theatres, on Rosa-Luxemburg-Platz, the central square of the then DDR. I saw the 1974 production of Heiner Muller's play, *Die Schlacht (The Battle)*, still in repertoire.

> A terrible butcher hacks up a joint. Cleaver, axe and chopping block. Bloody apron, swastika, very fat. Sexy, vulgar old wife, also gross. He takes off his vest. Puts on his brownshirt. Nightmare scenes of bloody violence and sex. Loud music, chiselled images, all perfect, angry, grotesque, accurate. Adolf Hitler dances with his bride, poisons the German bear. The fear, the horror, the waste, all made up in this modern German aesthetic. Yet they don't feel like clichés at all. I cannot imagine ever seeing something like this in England. The actors appear dead to each other and the audience but the writer's view is compelling and original.

Work like this (and *Die Schlacht* is the most extreme of a number of expressionist works playing in Berlin at the time) is a long way from the adaptations of Dickens that had so ignited me in Paris and London. Here there is absolute control by the director and the writer. The actors are not there to 'contribute' any more than the soldiers I had watched earlier in the

UBU, June 1982

We had spent time before and after South America talking about and workshopping Jarry's *Ubu Roi*; we were due to open the play in August 1982 at the Oxford Union, prior to Edinburgh. Our time in Argentina and Chile had fed into this process. The actors had all seen first-hand the fear and the damage that a dictatorship brings about. They'd talked to people non-stop throughout their tour of South America and everyone had something to tell these very receptive actors. With Reagan in power since January 1981, leading a massive build-up of nuclear weapons, and Gorbachev cautioning that Russia and the US stood on the brink of a nuclear war, *Ubu* was a response to the madness in the air. We were several weeks into the Falklands war and Mrs Thatcher appeared to us as a new despot – much supported by Reagan who she, in turn, revered.

We adapted Cyril Connolly and Simon Watson-Taylor's 1968 translation of *Ubu*. Their version captures the casual brutality of the main characters, Ma and Pa Ubu, better than any other. Their translation is as funny as the original, something like an obscene version of *The Goons*. Because the plot

Chris Barnes as Pa Ubu, Susan Colverd as Ma Ubu

Jack Ellis, Head of Espionage

loosely follows *Macbeth,* here was an outrageous satire that the company clearly understood. The actors also felt free to improvise upon the text and to draw upon their recent experiences of touring to such a range of republics, democracies and dictatorships.

And the rhythm of the dialogue was just made for a delirious form of physical theatre:

> CAPTAIN MCNURE: *Duke of Transylvania, Arch-Duke of Kracow, Duchess of Gdańsk –*
> UBU: *Guilty! Guilty! Guilty!*
> *What's eating you Ma?*
> MA UBU: *You're so bloodthirsty, Pa Ubu!*
> UBU: *I'm getting rich aren't I? Read me what I've got, M'nure.*
> CAPTAIN MCNURE: *That's the lot.*
> UBU: *What do you mean, 'that's the lot'?! Round up all the nobles and, since I don't intend to stop getting rich, execute the lot and confiscate their revenues!*
> *De-brain them and keep the cash!*
> MA UBU: *That's ridiculous, Pa!*
> UBU: *Shut your gob, clownish female! I wish to change everything!*
> MA UBU: *You're insane, Pa! They'll throw you in jail!*
> UBU: *You're making fun of me! Shoot all the judges as well as the nobles, M'nure!*
> MA UBU: *Come, come Lord Ubu, you're butchering the whole world!*
> UBU: *So? Pschitt!*
> *Fear nothing, my sweet child.*
> MA UBU: *My darling...*
>
> (UBU AND MA UBU, DANCE A FEROCIOUS TANGO.)

The political clowning and the physical knockabout struck a chord. Chris Barnes' two great roles for the company were Sancho Panza and Pa Ubu. Chris was a gifted clown who could incorporate text and character into an extreme physical performance. Sue Colverd was a late entrant to the company, replacing Denise Black. Sue joined us a year before the 1983 Warehouse season and took on the incredibly diverse roles of Miranda in *The Tempest,* Lina in *Berlin/Berlin,* Ma Ubu in *Ubu* and Lady Fanciful in *The Provoked Wife.* For this last, she was nominated for the 1983 Olivier for

Valerie Braddell, Chris Barnes, Jack Ellis

Best Comic Performance (Griff Rhys-Jones won the award). Sue was a truly brilliant serious *and* comic performer with a great singing voice. I think that a small company like ATC was able to give an original talent like hers a chance to express itself in a way that is more difficult to achieve in a big company. Our company centred around the individual actor, as well as the ensemble, and it suited every one of its long-standing members – they had a true say in what the company did and how they did it.

However, the freedom that the actors enjoyed to create work that they felt fully invested in came at a personal price. They were away from home for many weeks in a row and, when in the UK, they stayed in B&Bs and they travelled together in the company van. When Justin Savage joined ATC as company manager in the summer of 1982, he upgraded the van to a very large Fiat with the company's name and logo all over the sides. It was the best yet – but it was still a van and everyone travelled in it together. A number of the company smoked so the stops were longed-for 'smoke-breaks' before clambering back in for another 50 or 100 miles. Smoking was very common then, even in the rehearsal room.

Everyone was given a single room wherever we stayed. But because everyone is away from home for such long periods of time, actors often tended

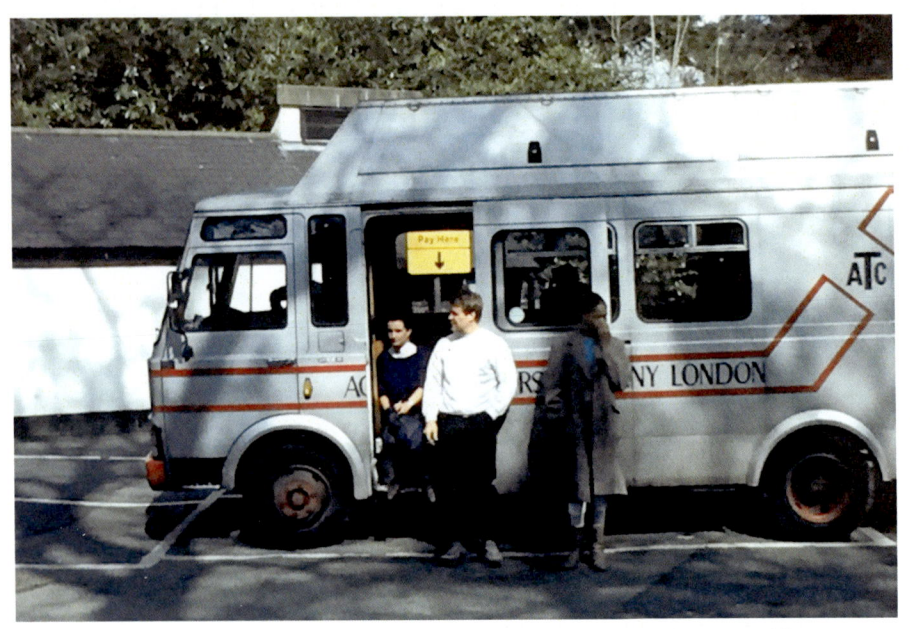

Renata, Terry John and Clare Benedict taking a breather from the new Fiat van, 1984

to create a 'home away from home'. Eight single rooms were booked but only four or five would be slept in. On-road partnerships would emerge and be lasting – for the length of the tour. When one company manager responded by booking doubles, and thus saving money on the unused rooms, I had to point out that everyone had a right to a single room and where they chose to sleep was entirely up to them. People had relationships at home too and we could not make adultery a condition of touring, even if it might have saved us thousands of pounds. It was essential that the refuge of the single bed was always available. There were romances and there were explosions; anything was acceptable as long as, in their actions, each actor acknowledged that by the time the 6.30 warm-up was called every night, the group loved each other equally and respectfully. We were all in this together – without unity we were sunk.

Theatre was much better attended in small-scale regional venues than it is now. There was no internet, less on TV, less of everything. Many venues ran an all-the-year-round programme, often able to offer us more than a single night's performance. Publicity was about posters and leaflets, backed up by word of mouth. Marketing was infinitely less complex that it is now and there was less competition.

We never stopped touring. My diary reads:

April 29th, 1982

Sitting at home, out in the back garden, the sun shining and I'm back home for that rare week away from unending group life on tour – let's think...since January...

Northern Ireland & The Republic (3 weeks)

Kent & Sussex (2 weeks)

Lancaster (2 weeks)

The Scottish Borders (1 week)

Cork (1 week)

Paris (1 week)

Oxford (1 week)

Glasgow (1 week)

Edinburgh & Nairn (1 week)

I had 4 days at home between Cork and Paris and this week.

That's 11 days out of 13 weeks.

And I'm off to Berlin in a fortnight.

No wonder my mother says, in the future, it will be hard for me to settle down.

BACK ON THE ROAD

And here is the tour sheet for rest of 1982, after Berlin, and after a further six weeks in Oxford and three weeks in Edinburgh, right up to the Christmas before we opened at The Warehouse in January, 1983:

TOURING SCHEDULE – SEPTEMBER – DECEMBER 1982

DATE	VENUE	PRODUCTION	TIME
Sept 20	MALVERN Malvern Hills Centre for Adult Education Tel: 06845-67856	PROVOKED WIFE	8:00

THEATREMAKER

DATE	VENUE	PRODUCTION	TIME
Sept 21	NR. TELFORD, WELLINGTON Centenary Theatre, Wrekin College Nr Telford Tel:0952	P/WIFE	8.00 + W/ shop
Sept 22-23	BIRMINGHAM Midlands Arts Centre, Cannon Hill Tel:021-440 3838	P/WIFE	7.30
Sept 26-	SWEDEN – SKÖVDE Stadsteater, Trädgardsgatan	QUIXOTE	3.00pm 6.30pm
Sept 27	VÄXJÖ Växjö Teater, Västergatan		7.30pm 7.30pm
Sept 29	STOCKHOLM Södra Teater, Mosebacke Torg 3		7.30pm
Oct 1 and 3	SUNDVALL Sunvalls Teater, Köpmangatan		7.30pm
Oct 4	ÖSTERSUND Störsjoteatern, Residensgränd		7.30pm
Oct 6	KARLSLOGA Karlaskoga Stadsteater, Kungsvägen		7.30pm
Oct 7	VÄNERSBORG Vänersborg Teater, Kyrogaten		7.30pm
Oct 10	KALMAR Konserthusteatern, Stortorget		7.30pm
Oct 11-12	Kalmar Teater, Larmtorget		7.30pm
Oct 13	KRISTIANSTAD Kristianstads Teater, Tivoliparken		7.30pm
Oct 14-15	MALMO Stadsteatern, Lund, Kiliansgatan		7.30pm
Oct 18	YUGOSLAVIA – LJUBLJANA National Theatre	BERLIN/ BERLIN	
Oct 19	National Theatre	P/WIFE	
Oct 20	SKELJE National Theatre	BERLIN/ BERLIN	
Oct 21-22- 23	ZAGREB National Theatre	P/WIFE OR BERLIN/ BERLIN	
Oct 25-26	SARAJEVO National Theatre	P/WIFE OR BERLIN/ BERLIN	

ENSEMBLE THEATRE

DATE	VENUE	PRODUCTION	TIME
Oct 27-28	SKOPJE National Theatre	P/WIFE OR BERLIN/ BERLIN	
Oct 29-30	BELGRADE	P/WIFE OR BERLIN/ BERLIN	
Nov 1-2	GREECE – THESSALONIKA Katerina Theatre	P/WIFE	
Nov 4-6	ATHENS	P/WIFE	
Nov 11-13	OUNDLE, NR. PETERBOROUGH Stahl Theatre, West Street	P/WIFE	7.45pm
Nov 16-17	WEST MIDLANDS KIDDERMINSTER Rose Theatre, Chester Road.	UBU	7.30
Nov 18-19	DROITWICH Droitwich High School, Ombersley Road	P/WIFE	7.45
Oct 20	SKELJE National Theatre	BERLIN/ BERLIN	
Oct 20	SKELJE National Theatre	BERLIN/ BERLIN	
Oct 21-22-23	ZAGREB National Theatre	P/WIFE OR BERLIN/ BERLIN	
Oct 25-26	SARAJEVO National Theatre	P/WIFE OR BERLIN/ BERLIN	
Oct 27-28	SKOPJE National Theatre	P/WIFE OR BERLIN/ BERLIN	
Oct 29-30	BELGRADE	P/WIFE OR BERLIN/ BERLIN	
Nov 1-2	GREECE – THESSALONIKA Katerina Theatre	P/WIFE	
Nov 4-6	ATHENS	P/WIFE	
Nov 11-13	OUNDLE, NR. PETERBOROUGH Stahl Theatre, West Street	P/WIFE	7.45pm
Nov 16-17	WEST MIDLANDS KIDDERMINSTER Rose Theatre, Chester Road.	UBU	7.30

DATE	VENUE	PRODUCTION	TIME
Nov 18-19	DROITWICH Droitwich High School, Ombersley Road	P/WIFE	7.45
Nov 20	OSWESTRY Croeswylan School Hall.	P/WIFE	7.30
Nov 22 – Dec 4	LONDON	UBU AND TEMPEST	7.30
Dec 6	SOUTH EAST ARTS – EWELL North East Surrey College of Technology, Reigate Road	UBU	
Dec 7	SOUTHBOROUGH, NR. TUNBRIDGE WELLS Royal Victoria Hall, London Road	UBU	
Dec 8-9	BRIGHTON Brighton Pavillion, New Road	UBU	
Dec 10	BROADSTAIRS, KENT Hilderstone Adult Ed. Centre, St. Peter's Road	UBU	
Dec 11	South East – T.B.C	UBU UBU AND TEMPEST	
Dec 13-18	SOUTH WEST AREA		

    In Zagreb, the company was invited to an English-speaking school and asked to 'give some examples from your repertoire'. It was in a large school hall and most of the pupils were present, about 200 seated on the floor. All of us were there for this one. I was the compere and I told the audience something of the life of the company and how we created our repertoire. As I got to each title, I turned and asked the actors in question to perform an extract for maybe five or ten minutes. We started with *The Provoked Wife*, then *Berlin/Berlin* and *The Tempest*, next *Quixote* and last of all, the wildness of *Ubu*. It was the first time that it actually sunk in: this group of seven actors could perform five plays. If they had the stamina, they could turn up at a market-place and perform all five in a single day. I recall walking into the late October sunshine and feeling intensely proud of the company – and how it was always abroad, rather than at home, that you sensed a feeling of real achievement.

JR, van driver, with Valerie Braddell, on a Caledonian MacBrayne Ferry, 1981

The open roads of England exerted a powerful draw on us all. Yes, it was frequently draining to play small-scale venues in a region; when, for example, we returned from South America, we went almost straight into a tour of Lincolnshire and Humberside for a fortnight. England was so dark after the two months that we had just experienced. One night in Lincoln, I could not get warm in my single room and I pulled down the curtains and used them as blankets. The actors were quite tough and endured periods of drabness, bad weather and small audiences without complaint. Getting to the pub after the show was important and so was a warm reception from someone – a group in the audience, a welcoming venue manager or just a round of the drinks brought to the dressing room after the show by the director.

Our favourite tours were to Scotland. Joyce Macmillan joined us on a tour of the Highlands and Islands in 1982 and wrote a long piece about it for *The Guardian*:

THE GUARDIAN
Joyce Macmillan

The Actors' Touring Company of London arrived at Strontian in a drenching West Highland downpour, their van ploughing its way through sheets of rain to the door of the smart new community centre. Strontian is a small, scattered community of only a few hundred souls, and ATC were there – courtesy of the Highland Regional Council – to perform their epic stage adaptation of Don Quixote, first put together early in 1980, at last year's Edinburgh Fringe Festival.

The members of the ATC – 7 actors, musician, director and road manager – arrived at Strontian damp and dispirited after a difficult drive from Skye. The weather was shocking, the advance publicity had been poor and, said my landlady, some people in Strontian resented the idea of the Highland Region sending professional companies into that expensive new hall "when we used to have a perfectly good amateur dramatic of our own."

In the end, the village mustered an audience of exactly 18 people, including three bashful schoolboys who had to be home by ten o'clock, and a couple of confused souls from the old people's sheltered housing. Nevertheless, ATC turned in an immaculate performance, bawdy and literate, humorous and lyrical; and afterwards I found at least half of the audience sitting in the hotel bar, with a shining wistful look in their eyes.

John Retallack, ATC's director (and, for the purposes of this tour, stagehand, lighting operator and long-distance van driver) was particularly pleased that the company had given a good performance in such depressing circumstances; and the next day the company rolled into Fort William at lunch time, in bright sunshine and high good humour.

ATC's roots are in the English literary tradition on one hand, and in the continental concept of intense, creative ensemble theatre on the other; and although the company as a group finds itself increasingly interested in political ideas – "when you travel together, live together, read the papers together, and then work honestly together, it's inevitable," says Retallack – it has absolutely no pretensions to a working-class perspective.

The secret of ATC's success seems to lie in their relentless pursuit of a few basic artistic values: skill in performance, sensitivity to the audience's response, complete honesty and integrity in making aesthetic decisions. Last week, among the honest, open Highland audiences, it seemed increasingly clear to me that ATC's values are absolutely essential to any genuine achievement in the theatre.

THE DONMAR WAREHOUSE, January–April 1983

Paradoxically, ATC was about to come not only to London but to the West End. We had one particular backer (amongst a number of smaller ones) who came forward with enough cash for the company to take over the Donmar

Warehouse with a repertoire of five shows for a period of 12 weeks from January 24th to April 16th, 1983. The winter of 1983 was extremely cold and there was a lot of snow. London had regular tube strikes. The numbers of people attending events across central London were down considerably. For an unknown company called ATC LONDON, with five shows, our hopes were pretty low from the outset.

The Donmar Warehouse was our biggest challenge. It was then a large studio theatre in Covent Garden with seating for 250 that had been in regular use by the RSC since 1977. It was a chic venue for a touring company to hire and Cheek by Jowl and Shared Experience had both had runs of individual plays there. Later it was to become a small-scale producing house led by Sam Mendes and it has remained as such until today. This 1983 season was intended to provide an overdue London run for the work that we had put together, and honed, over the last four years. The actors wanted to be seen. I wanted the productions to be seen – and to be reviewed. All the usual reasons that companies want to play in central London after years on the road.

After always 'moving on', we were in the critical spotlight. Everything was different from our normal working lives: there was nowhere to travel to, so we were free in the day-time; the audience was on three sides and the acoustic did not require much projection; every actor's family and friends could come and see them on stage (when they were used to being far from the scrutiny of home); reviewers from the national papers came in clusters; we had five opening nights in the West End in as many weeks; all the relationships in the company were coming to an end. With one more tour (this time to the Britain Salutes New York Festival), no one knew what was coming next. None of us could even see beyond the Donmar Warehouse.

Even an actor with the coolest temperament would find all this stressful. There was one punch-up in the dressing room; one actor got pissed on stage (for the first and last time) on the very night we were auditioned for

ATC brochure January 1983

ATC London just before the Warehouse, January 1983

a documentary by a leading arts programme; another stalwart collapsed of exhaustion on a Saturday matinee and was rushed to hospital – he recovered; sometimes actors performed on a diet of antibiotics and steroids, whatever was needed to keep the flu and burn-out at bay for another performance. And the reviews often praised one actor and destroyed another – it was the reality of performing on a metropolitan stage. Audiences fluctuated. The biggest surprise to us was that *Ubu* and *Berlin/Berlin* created more interest than *Quixote*. We knew *Quixote* was a great show but we couldn't bring it to life in the Warehouse – somehow, however much we prided ourselves on our flexible staging, it lost its heart in that particular place.

The Warehouse exposed us as a barn-storming ensemble, full of invention and ideas but happiest *performing* rather than acting. Over the course of the 12 weeks the energy and style of the company began to suit the two-tiered space and the sophistication of the audience. The company became stronger in its individual performances. The actors learned not to push so hard or to project so far. After all, the audience was right there before us, you could sit on their knees in the front row.

I went back to *London Theatre Record* recently and found dozens of reviews of the Warehouse run. As I read them all, almost 40 years after the event, my body temperature shot up and down depending upon if I was being trashed by Robert Cushman or over-praised by Giles Gordon. In all that time, I have never read them end to end like that. In fact, during the run, I insisted that no one bring any review into the theatre, a command bluntly ignored by our stage manager, Renata Allen, when we got a rave in the *Evening Standard* for *Ubu* – she walked into a note session and read the whole thing out to the company. It cheered everyone up enormously. Jack Ellis was so excited that he took all his clothes off. *Ubu* turned out to be the most popular of all our shows.

In late 1983, I wrote the following for *Drama Magazine*, who voted ATC *The Most Imaginative Touring Company* for that year:

> Playing in the Warehouse proved an exciting period for the company. After working so hard with so many terrible acoustics, or sight-lines, or tiny box stages in school halls–all in themselves interesting and rewarding problems to be solved at the time–it allowed us for the first time to work uninterruptedly upon acting, pure and simple. In the same place for months, we could actually address ourselves to such things as emotional balance, the precision of tone required or the exact meaning of a gesture, in a way that is impossible when your stages are changing week by week or, often, night by night.
>
> What keeps the standards of touring theatre high is the inspiration of adverse conditions (or, just occasionally. wonderfully favourable ones). A new space, a new audience, means the actor has to be on the ball, alert to revised entrances or reversed exits ('downstage left tonight, not up right'). Touring a fixed set could solve a lot of these problems, but then you might as well tour a theatre too. It is a stimulating discipline to create more and more circumstances for intelligent actors to have to think their way around a new space together.
>
> The company, by late '82, was getting too good at this. At an hour's notice, they could have staged *Ubu* in a sentry box. Our London season has shown us that a blend of residence and touring is desirable if we are to go on developing artistically. We could become in danger of 'formula' if we were to continue an endless cycle of touring with no beginning or end. Touring is exciting, whether it's South-East England or South-East Asia; its danger is that a company develops a performing style rather than an acting style. That distinction annoys everyone; for a start, what does it mean?
>
> A performer overtly 'works' an audience, an actor does so covertly. What can happen in continuous touring is that an overall 'out-front' style develops which blurs these distinctions. These performances are often highly effective on tour, and are backed by a lot of energy. It is a touring style that perforce creeps up on many actors–the

> practical demands of that night do utterly outweigh the subtleties of interpretation. The more magnanimous and 'engaged' the actor is, with the particular 'event' of that night's performance, the more he or she may do it. The joy of working at the Warehouse was to see our actors finding subtler and more discreet means to persuade an audience. The opportunity was overdue.

NEW YORK, April – May, 1983

On the 23rd of April, 1983, we flew out to New York and presented *Quixote* and *The Provoked Wife* at the Perry Street Theatre in Greenwich Village as part of the *Britain Salutes New York Festival*. The small theatre was elegant and the weather outside was hot. The intensity of these final performances was matched by the emotions of the company, the majority of whom had been together for four continuous years. It was the first time that this company had no future and they were anxious about how they would feel when they returned home – and stopped touring. Only Russell was eager to get back to his new wife, Ettaline, a radiant Brazilian doctor he had met on the South American tour and who was now living with him in London. Jack Ellis stayed on and married his fiancée Christine at Coney Island; Valerie returned to her native Portugal; Ray went back to his home in Brixton; Christine back to her home and family near Lewes; after a break, Chris Barnes continued to tour with the company. Nearly all of us had children in the next few years, as if we needed to compensate for all the years away from a stable home. My world, too, was soon to be turned upside down; at the time, however, my chief concern was what to do next with the company.

The 1980-83 ensemble was a great one and a lot of tears were shed towards the end. Everyone had both had enough and didn't want to stop.

And I couldn't work out a way of life that would keep this particular company of actors together.

ATC brochure in New York, 1983

Peter Brook was in New York at the same time as ATC. He invited me to take breakfast with him at his hotel. I asked him if there was space for me to create a company in his style outside England. He retorted with a long speech in praise of the infinite versatility of the British actor, their capacity to do almost anything that they are asked to do and how much more difficult it is to find that level of skill in a language other than English; the British actor's capacity for give and take; their receptivity to new ways of working; their wit, speed and musicality. I felt naive for having asked the question. I also knew my fluency in French was nowhere near his. It was instructive to hear Brook, the exile, praise the country he had left behind and its actors. Though I was later to direct overseas as a freelance, I took his advice and abandoned any romantic notion of becoming a fellow-exile.

In January 1984, I learnt that I had won an Olivier award for *Quixote* and *The Provoked Wife*. The award was for the *Most Promising Newcomer*. I couldn't be there at the ceremony because I was on tour with the new ATC in Hong Kong. My mother sent me a telegram saying "Well done darling. I always said that you were a late developer".

A NEW ENSEMBLE, 1983-1984

The Olivier didn't really sink in for several months. This was partly because I wasn't fully aware of the significance of such an award and partly because I was deeply in love with one of the actors on tour. My doting had started in

Clare Benedict, Richard Henry, Terry John, Michael Mears,
Edmund Falzon, Renata Allen

rehearsals for the 'new ATC' that had entirely replaced the veteran company that had played the Warehouse and the Perry Street Theatre in New York. We had run long auditions and finally recruited an ensemble of six actors to perform Molière's *Don Juan* and Shakespeare's *Twelfth Night*. We rehearsed *Don Juan* in a large school gymnasium in West London through a hot August.

About three weeks in, after being immersed in rehearsal all day, I went home, fell asleep early and dreamt all night about one of the cast members. By the time I walked into rehearsal the following morning, I was in love with her. It was as if Puck had sprinkled the fairy dust in my eyes because I didn't feel responsible for this feeling and neither could I overcome it. However much time I spent with the company on the road, my emotional and sexual life had always been outside the sacred circle of the acting group. A director, like a doctor or a psychiatrist, is allowed an intimacy in his dealings with an actor that are only otherwise permitted to someone who is very close. Even if my directions were unreliable, I wanted to be trusted by the actors as a human being. I didn't want anything non-professional between myself and an actor in the company when I wanted to overhaul a role – or just had to give very critical or difficult notes.

HONG KONG, AUSTRALIA AND NEW ZEALAND, JANUARY-FEBRUARY, 1984

The woman I had fallen in love with was Renata Allen, who had been Assistant Stage Manager and the female understudy in all five plays at the Warehouse. She was bright, independent and a very funny mimic. I asked her to play Olivia in *Twelfth Night*. The play is about the way love erupts and won't go away, however inappropriate and impractical the circumstances. It is a play that celebrates the power of love to prevail over rules, gender and mundane day-to-day reality. I was suffering under an 'excess' of love myself and this did not make me a better director of the play. I longed for my past directorial detachment. I lost a stone in weight. I felt professionally helpless as I watched our performances of this inexhaustibly fascinating play. Feste's song about "*Journeys end with lovers meeting*" touched me most.

Renata took on Viola's philosophy:

O time, thou must untangle this, not I.
It is too hard a knot for me t'untie.

The tour of *Twelfth Night* and *Don Juan* began in Glasgow and then toured all over England and Scotland. The affair between Renata and me had begun during rehearsals but we both thought that the rest of the company had no idea of anything going on between us. When we began a tour of Hong Kong, Australia and New Zealand in early January 1984, I twigged that our closely guarded affair was an open secret. Justin Savage, the production manager, was leading the company along an open hotel corridor in Perth, Western Australia and allotting rooms – "number eleven, Terry, number 12, Ed, number 13 Janet, number 14, John and Renata…". I was flabbergasted. The whole company just laughed at us for thinking they hadn't noticed our relationship over the last few months.

I felt enormous relief. After this 'outing', I enjoyed the tour. Renata and I spent a free week in China after playing Molière and Shakespeare at the Hong Kong Festival. We got to know each other a bit. Because Renata had been the acting ASM at the Warehouse, she knew a lot about the 'old company'. We went to Gwelin and took an open boat along the River Li. The weather was bright and numbingly cold. I bought the largest woollen Mao suit I could find in the local Government Store. There were hardly any cars to be seen in 1984, just a million bicycles and very primitive conditions everywhere. The villages were extremely long and the streets were packed with men, thousands and thousands of them stretching out into the distance, all dressed in identical blue. The barber doubled as a dentist and had an operating chair that was used for teeth or hair. There was no glass in the windows and people would stand around and watch teeth being extracted without anaesthetic. We ate fish and rice outside at stone tables; the below zero temperatures appeared to affect no one but us. Everywhere we went children threw bangers and rockets at very close range. The hotels all had thermos flasks full of hot water and we warmed up on Nescafé and local brandy. In the market places, they sold a range of small furry animals we had never seen before – including dead rats that old ladies picked up and inspected, as if they were in a supermarket choosing between steaks on the open shelves.

It was a different world – and the first experience that we were able to share together.

Both *Twelfth Night* and *Don Juan* became outstanding shows, exemplars of the ATC style that had been achieved since 1978 – but it took a lot of performances to get there. This was a group of actors all new to each other who took three months to cohere into a fluent ensemble. When the productions opened, the actors were tentative and some regular fans of the company deplored the lack of style and force that they had enjoyed in the old ensemble. But these are elusive texts, none more so than the *Don Juan* of Molière. Edmund Falzon (who played the title role in ATC's long-

Terry John as Sganarelle and Edmund Falzon as Don Juan in Molière's *Don Juan*

running production of Byron's *Don Juan*) became very strong as a world-weary street-wise cynic who must seduce every woman that he meets, and Terry John excelled as his morally appalled servant Sganarelle. Like *The Tempest*, Molière's *Don Juan* has an episodic character that a small ensemble can integrate and master with flair and understanding. I had always been fascinated with the way that this 'morality comedy' both condones and condemns the appetites and behaviour of its central character. By the time, the production reached Hong Kong, it was a stylish and virtuosic international show that used, yes, five large laundry baskets to create different places, different states of mind.

Terry John as Sir Toby and Clare Benedict as Maria in *Twelfth Night*

Twelfth Night was a very funny production. Though I am not unbiased, Renata's interplay as Olivia with Michael Mears' Malvolio became a central feature of this production. By the time the show reached the Bridge Theatre in Battersea for an extended run in April, 1984, Mears' Malvolio had grown into a fragile monster and his performance deserved the rave reviews that it received from the national press. The performances that I still cherish are the open-air matinees at the Globe in Perth University where the dimensions of the stage (and the full houses) perfectly suited our production. The late Terry John was a most natural Sir Toby; his relish for the role was infectious to the rest of the ensemble and was part-responsible for the success of this *Twelfth Night*. He and Clare Benedict's Maria generated a lot of energy together.

The tour ended in New Zealand with a fortnight in Christchurch. I proposed to Renata on the flight back to London in early March. To my intense relief, she accepted.

Of course, everything changed from this moment. I had been on the road now for eight years. Over the course of the next few months, I decided that I wanted to give up working with the company that I had created and, while remaining in the theatre and working as a director, move on to pastures new. I was 33, Renata 26. I wanted to be with her.

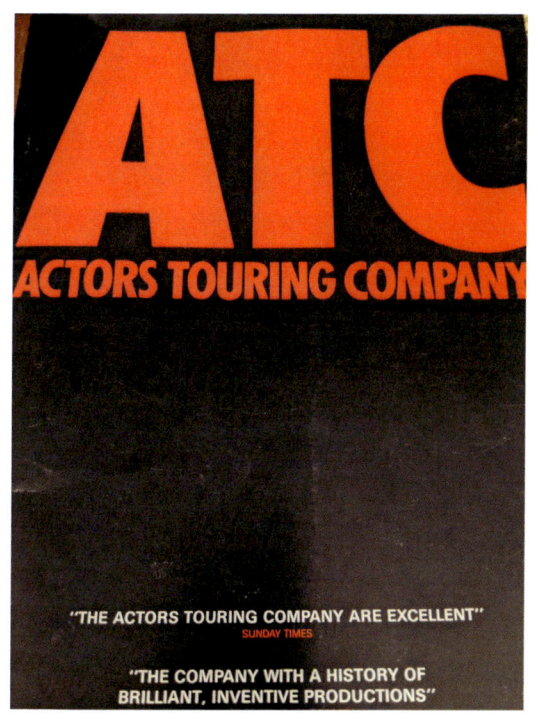

ATC's London brochure

3
REPERTORY THEATRE
Oldham Coliseum, 1985-88

Renata and I married at St Stephen's church in Shepherds Bush on July 6th, 1984.

It didn't make Sense for either of us to disappear on tour again. We needed to go on working in the theatre but in one place. It dawned on me that such a place pre-existed my aspiration – and that it's called a 'rep'. A rep produces all kinds of plays; the sort of plays I'd never read. It was time to catch up on something other than Shakespeare, Vanbrugh, Molière, Byron and Cervantes… In late 1984, I applied for the role of Artistic Director of a producing repertory theatre, advertised in *The Stage*.

OLDHAM COLISEUM 1985-88 – FIRST IMPRESSIONS

I could have applied for Salisbury or Chester or Watford; they were all up for grabs around this time. They were towns far more sympathetic to my kind of repertoire, ie Shakespeare, the classics, adaptations and the occasional new play or devised work. But I was fascinated by this late 19th century theatre with the most unlikely and colourful address: Oldham Coliseum, Fairbottom Street, Oldham. The theatre had been a circus once upon a time and Charlie

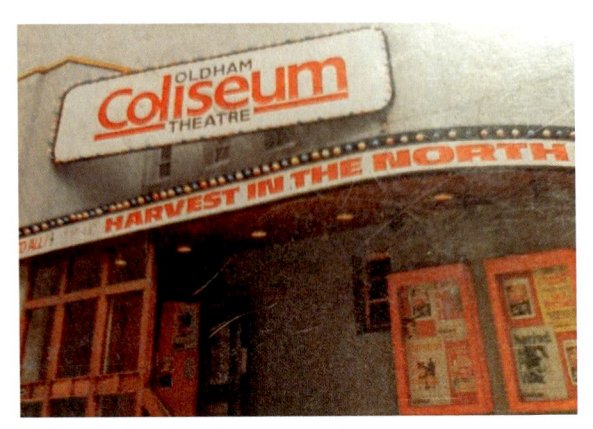

Oldham Coliseum, 1986

Chaplin and Laurel & Hardy had played there – so had Joan Littlewood and the stars of Coronation Street. It was famous for its pantomimes that all agreed were the best in the region. Oldham was near to everywhere too – Bolton, Sheffield, Manchester, Liverpool, Bradford, Leeds. There was a lot to do, a lot of theatre to see at the Exchange, Contact, the Library Theatre, the Octagon, the Crucible – and that meant that there was a whole network of actors who lived nearby because the north-west was a regional home to Granada, the BBC and Channel 4. The post offered a fresh start.

I knew the flavour of the region from teaching in Manchester in 1976 and also my two summers with the Manchester Youth Theatre. I liked the Lancashire voice in real life and on the stage – it was like an alternative form of RP ('received pronunciation') and Albert Finney and Ian McKellen made it the basis of their classless Shakespeare performances. There were good directors around to call up and meet for a drink – John Adams (the founding director of Paines Plough) ran Bolton Octagon and Tony Clark (later artistic director of Hampstead Theatre) had made Manchester Contact a wonderful centre for fresh interpretations of classics like *To Kill A Mockingbird* and *Blood Wedding;* Bridget Larmour directed the first production of *My Mother Said I Never Should* at the same address and Glen Walford was delivering smart and very popular work at the Everyman in Liverpool. In short, Oldham seemed a much more interesting prospect than an equivalent town in the south.

Oldham, 1985

My predecessors were Kenneth Alan Taylor (1978-82) and Pat Trueman (1982-85). Kenneth was very popular in the area and known to everyone through Coronation Street (he played Cecil Newton). He was a brilliant panto dame and also an extremely versatile actor who had been working at the Coliseum since 1962. He was married to Judith Barker, a superb actress who I worked with twice at Oldham. They had been married for 30 years and were living proof that a family and a theatre could live together co-operatively, even harmoniously. Their children had often sat in the stalls during rehearsals – Judith told me on my first visit to the theatre, "when they were babies, we just put them in the box-office for the afternoon. Jean and Sue were lovely with them". Jean and Sue were still working there. I took Judith at her word.

Being Artistic Director of ATC was a very different job to being Artistic Director of Oldham Coliseum.

Artistic Director of ATC meant hands-on skill in terms of driving, lighting, leading workshops and managing a group of actors who I was always urging to go further, be better, work harder. We were all in the same van, or plane, or hotel most of the time. There was minimum separation between us. Though I was the boss, the practical day-to-day work minimised the difference in status between us. And we were all paid the same wage every week.

In a repertory theatre, it's different. Everyone goes to work in the same place every day. There is an actual workforce: box office, admin, bar management, production manager, stage managers, marketing department, head of design, design assistants, electricians, carpenters, lighting team and wardrobe, to name the key players. At this time, it was normal for theatres to make their shows in-house. Every set and every costume was constructed and made in the theatre workshops and cutting room. Nothing was out-sourced.

In a conventional rep, like Oldham Coliseum, the artistic director and the executive director are at the top of the tree. They spend a lot of time talking to each other, even when the artistic director is directing a play for the theatre. The success of this partnership is crucial to the functioning of the whole operation. Whatever their differences, they have to be as one when they bring the whole theatre staff together every week or fortnight for a company meeting to catch up on all the latest developments. The permanent staff was 36 – plus the actors currently performing and rehearsing. Actors came in for a season of plays or just for one individual production. An acting company might stay for three plays in a row and that saved money; they could rehearse in the day-time and perform in the evening. It also produced better performances overall as the company got to know each other's rhythm and approach. There were breaks in the days, laid down by Equity; nevertheless, it was a demanding work schedule if you lived in Manchester and couldn't get home for a sleep in the course of the working day/evening.

I was fortunate that the executive director was a very smart, very competent and calm individual – Chris Moxon. He'd been there already for seven years and I was his third artistic director. He really knew the ropes and he helped me to learn them too. Chris was precise, always in a suit, kind and fair to all, yet firm when he had to be. He was the sort of untheatrical person who really loves the whole operation and spectacle of theatre. His partner, Philip, was a regular at opening nights and I got to know more of the off-duty side of Chris through him. They lived in a large rambling Victorian house in a residential part of the town with some trees and grass around it – one of the town's few leafy areas. Chris really liked the Coliseum and the town. This came out most vividly when we travelled together to faraway meetings – for example, the annual conference of the Theatre Managers' Association (TMA). The first one for me was in Plymouth, six hours from Oldham. He not only talked all the way there but (when I might have gone to sleep at the wheel) all the way back. He was a great driver's companion and, on these long drives, I learnt much from Chris about the theatre and the people who worked there.

Chris always walked around with a large sheaf of papers under his arm. Nowadays, he'd have a Mac and a mobile; then it was all about paper and land-line phones that you could sometimes hear from the auditorium in a quiet moment on stage. He had the tiniest office in the building, basically a windowless cupboard with a sliding door. 'Why don't you move upstairs Chris, there's space there and you won't be so cramped!' 'Yes', he replied, 'but this office is in the middle of the building, close to the stage, the box office and the bar – I can actually *hear* if there's a problem or if something is not right. And everyone knows where to find me.'

He was right. But I wanted an office that was bigger and where people *couldn't* find me, so I took over a distant room in a till-then unused outbuilding overlooking some semi-destroyed back yards. As it was cleaned up, more and more habitable space emerged and the design team moved in too. It became a good hub for readings and model boxes and production meetings about each show. The shows seemed to come hurtling at us at an unstoppable rate. No sooner had you got past the first night of one, than the whole building threw themselves into the countdown to the next.

At the start, I was seen as an existential threat to the Coliseum. The day after I was appointed, the technical director went to Chris and said that his team were very alarmed because 'John Retallack doesn't like sets – he does everything on a bare stage! We'll lose our jobs!' Chris called me (I'd just got back to Shepherds Bush) and said that I needed to come back up and reassure the technical team in person. I went back up the next day and explained that I had taken the job in order to use décor and lighting in a way that I couldn't on the road, with only a van to hold all the set and costumes. The team was relieved – if not convinced.

My first show was a double bill of *Bouncers* by John Godber and *Clowns on a School Outing* by Ken Campbell. The technical team were alarmed because these two plays are very much bare-board shows. As it happened, it gave the technical and lighting teams a lot to do. Chris Bond, the lighting designer who was to stay throughout my time at the theatre, got a chance for some stylish and flamboyant lighting. But it proved a challenge too far for the technical director, the very one who had objected to my appointment. During the first preview of *Clowns on a School Outing* an open-topped comedy sports car was 'driven' onto the stage to polite applause from the audience. It turned the full circle of the stage and then couldn't get off to the wings because it was too big. The Oldham audience loved this and duly rocked with laughter.

What was clear in these first two shows was the talent in the local actors – they were spectacular as the four (Oldham) bouncers. On Friday nights, Oldham was rammed with young people out on the lash and no matter how wet and cold it was, they all wore only short sleeved sports shirts without pullovers (the boys) and mini-skirts without tights (the girls). Because the actors knew the Friday night scene so well, I was able to bring a lot of movement to *Bouncers*.

Clowns was altogether more strange, even bizarre; afterwards the Chair of the Board took me aside and asked me if *Clowns* was – he lowered his voice–'political?'

At the end of a very positive review the *Guardian* said:

> If Oldham does not turn out for Bouncers *it is legitimate to ask how much the town wants a theatre.*

The next production was Molière's *Tartuffe* and the *Manchester Evening News* said:

> This production deserves to play to full houses from now until mid-November, and if it does not, we don't deserve good theatre in Oldham.

REPERTORY THEATRE

Stuart Golland, Clive Duncan, Jeff Longmore & Barry McGinn in *Bouncers*, 1985

Julia Ford and Jeff Longmore in *Clowns on a School Outing*, 1985

The theatre was attended by a white middle- and working-class audience. Theatre plays, as well as local media, made much of its white working-class past and the solidarity of local communities who lived cheek-by-jowl in row upon row of two-up two-down terraced housing. YouTube has many home-made movies and photo-montages of Oldham's twentieth-century past.

On the occasions that the theatre was full, you saw row upon row of middle-aged couples, dressed up for a good night out. At that time, I saw nothing unusual in the make-up of the audience – most of the work that we put on played to this demographic. After all, if it didn't play to them, there would be no one in the theatre at all. The only time that the audience was visibly different to the regular one, was in the schools' performances and workshops that we ran in the auditorium. There was an ethnic diversity visible that was not reflected in our repertoire at that time, or in our audience.

When I arrived at the Coliseum, rehearsals lasted three weeks with an additional 'technical' half-week to put the show onto the stage. A three-week rehearsal period meant an approach to theatre-making that was completely foreign to me. Three weeks (15 working days) is just enough time for actors to read a script and to learn the lines and the moves – they must be able to perform a run-through of the entire play without being near the script itself in that time. An occasional prompt is acceptable but no more. On the 16th and 17th days the actors will do 'the technical' in their brand-new costumes. They will have all their moves calibrated to work with the lighting plot so that they memorise the precise positions where they will stand, move or sit. On the Wednesday morning, at the latest, they will have a first Dress Run in which all their moves, words and precise orientation are put together for the first time. In the afternoon, the technical team will adjust, re-paint, mend and fix whatever needs doing. At 7pm that same day, the actors will receive their first half-hour call and then perform for the Free Dress audience at 7.30pm! As the Director I had to give a speech in advance to the audience warning them that an actor might forget his lines or that 'we might have to stop the show if we hit any technical glitches'.

(In Oldham, *three-weekly rep* was seen as a recent luxury; before that, in the seventies, it was *fortnightly rep*; and until 1968, believe it or not, it was *weekly rep* – but back then the theatre was more exciting than television and the 'patrons' would come every week, whatever was playing. What weekly rep meant for actors was that they performed the current play in the evening and rehearsed the one for the following week in the day-time!)

Once directors and actors are used to the rep system, the actors will often prepare and learn lines even before the rehearsals start. For directors, if they are experienced, they will know that there is very little you can expect from actors in such a short time. The key to repeated success in a 'twelve-show-year' is to imagine each entire show in a model box, and on a storyboard, long before the first day of rehearsal. The concept, and the set, dictate what the actor does. The intelligent actor will quickly respond to the clear instructions that he or she receives from the set itself and the director. In ATC, the actor came first; in the very short rehearsal time afforded by a repertory theatre, the actor comes last.

Seen from 2022, it is astonishing how well-funded theatre was in the mid-eighties. In my first year, I took on a company of nine actors to perform

REPERTORY THEATRE

Lighting designer Chris Bond in the picture. The auditorium has 524 seats.

Clare Ferraby's design above the proscenium arch, 1985

three major shows before the panto – all of these shows had fully designed sets that were trashed or re-cycled after the closing night. After the panto, there were a further six shows until the final one, a full-scale musical, played its last show in mid-June. The orthodox way to run a rep at that time was to have between four and fifteen actors on stage over a twelve-show year, with only the pantomime having a run of longer than three weeks. The only two-hander play that did the rounds of the reps was *Educating Rita*.

I asked Annie Castledine, a brilliant director of naturalism with a track record at the RSC and the Royal Court, to take over on the next play, Peter Whelan's *The Accrington Pals*. Annie, born in South Yorkshire, was a formidable director and seemed the perfect choice for this play about the relationship between two women at the time of the First World War.

Annie was very much into a form of expressionist theatre at the time. That meant that the acting was realistic but the set wasn't – it was a sort of hill that represented a lot of things; the war, the trenches, the coal-heaps, the absence of opportunity or beauty in the lives of these women. This led to a lot of confusion amongst the technical staff as to exactly how to build and light the set, created by one of our two designers, Sal Crabbe. Sal was excited by it and so was Annie but it was quite hard to capture the intimacy and reality of the play in the shadow and bulk of the abstract hill. Audiences didn't like it. As I stood at the door playing 'the vicar' (saying good night to everybody as they filed past to the street), the comments that I heard were not encouraging. Their shoulders were bent as they walked past, as if they did not want to look me in the eye and say what they really thought. Of course, some did; 'sad', 'negative', 'dark' is what they said.

I remember when I arrived at the theatre and first talked to Chris Moxon and Sue Stonehewer, the box office manager, they told me the following:

'The Oldham audience want to be entertained. They want to enjoy themselves. They don't mind sad. They like to be moved. But they do not want negativity. The name of the writer makes little difference to them. They want really good characters. And if there is humour – all the better!'

I learnt how difficult it is to employ a director, even one as good as Annie Castledine, to do a show. You want to look after your technical team and acting company as well as give full support to your visiting director. To do both these things is sometimes not possible. In a three-week rehearsal period, it is always too late to change very much. I also realised that after the first night, Annie would be gone for good. A priority for freelance directors has to be their *next* show – in a different theatre.

In that first season, I saw how good it felt to play to a full house on a Friday or Saturday night – and how depressing when the show aroused no interest at all and only 25% of the seats were filled over an entire three-week run. Both *Tartuffe* and *The Accrington Pals* received good reviews – but that didn't fill the theatre in Oldham. The worst thing was that whatever the box office percentage on the opening night of a show, you could almost predict the final box office figure, certainly to within 10%. Therefore, the cast knew in advance that they would play to semi-empty houses for a whole three-week run.

I had taken on an ensemble company for that whole first season and there were some fine actors; Barbara Martin, Sally Edwards, Jenny Howe, Julia Ford and Stuart Golland all came from the north-west. I brought the brilliant Barry McGinn from London with the plan that he might become associate director the following year. Barry was a powerful, funny and very versatile actor, fully capable of charming a full house on a Saturday night – and a good director.

Sally Edwards came to me towards the end of the season to say that I should get to know the acting company better – I was too remote. That shocked me – I was so used to being close with a group of actors. But I think that, at the time, I was only just staying on top of my job. I had a lot of lessons to learn after my first season.

PANTO SEASON – AND ESCAPE TO LONDON

The mood in the theatre changed completely at the beginning of December – it was panto season! Everyone knew what to do and there were smiles on the faces of the box office as they prepared for the massively pre-booked six-week run of *Aladdin*. Chris Moxon was among those putting up theatre decorations in the foyer and the auditorium. Box office was at over 80% already and we hadn't even done our first preview. Everyone was flat out: the technical team had to build the many sets and the wardrobe hundreds of costumes; the Sheila Carter School of Dancing was going through its professional-level

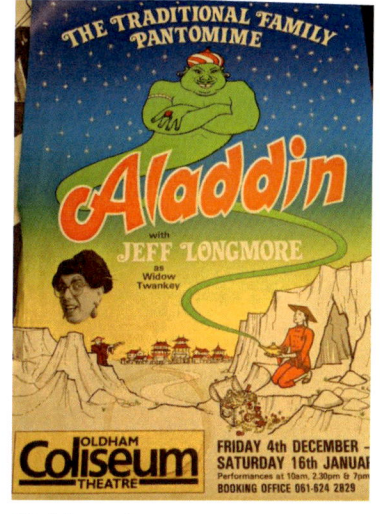

Aladdin poster

routines; Jeff Longmore, the Dame, flounced into the foyer during the technical rehearsal in one of Widow Twankey's extravagant creations and the ladies at the box office squealed in delight. The friendly message to me was: 'Leave it to us – it's going to be great!'

This was actually a blessing. We had moved into our house in July, our first child, Hanna, was six weeks old and we had experienced very little time together. This was a chance to consolidate at home in Oldham.

But it wasn't to be.

I had agreed to direct an adaptation of Purcell's opera *Dido and Aeneas* by Howard Goodall for The South Bank Show over the Christmas period. Just as I wanted a break, this opportunity arrived. We moved to Goodall's flat in Muswell Hill for a month and he moved to his girlfriend's flat nearby. The project was especially interesting because it was an all-black cast starring Debby Bishop and Peter Straker. I went to work every day in Vauxhall. I often felt out of my depth (my first opera, my first show for TV) but the creative team was outstanding and the resultant production went out in early 1986.

On New Year's Eve we were in the midst of recording the opera and Renata and I (and Hanna) were together in the glass fronted studio. There was a phone call to the studio for me. The voice of our neighbour in Oldham came through – 'I'm so sorry to bother you but there's a cascade of water coming out from the bottom of your front door. I think you or someone needs to come up and do something about it.' I couldn't leave the studio or abandon the recording. Renata took the keys, and Hanna, and promptly drove the 200 miles up to our house. Five hours later she called to tell me that she'd got the fire brigade in and they'd stopped the flood from the burst tank in the loft. Everything was completely under water or sodden. As a result, I came back two days later and we moved into the house of a neighbour while the insurance company carried out a comprehensive drying and disposal of almost every item of furniture. The silver lining to this was that, two months later, we got a far better decorated house than the one that we had moved into. But there was little rest over Christmas.

SPRING 1986

This season was a mix of dire failure and dramatic success. *Me Mam Sez* by Barry Heath is a slice-of-life about a family of ten who live in an Oldham two-up two-down in the early days of WW2. It's very funny, sentimental and the theatre was packed out. This is what the audience wanted to see on the stage and every time we presented a stylised view of a Northern past (whether humorous or romantic or political) we had near-full houses.

The children, all played by adults, are aged from 7 to 21 and they are held together by Mam, played by the incomparable Judith Barker. The oldest boy Jimmy was played by Ralph Fiennes in his first professional job. Ralph had auditioned for me and Barry McGinn in London. When Ralph left the room, Barry exploded with delight; 'That is the best audition by a student that I have EVER seen!' Ralph brought four separate pieces to the audition and he had learnt all of them. Most student auditionees just read from a script. Ralph wore solid brogues and corduroy trousers and a thick Celtic sweater. He looked different. He was impeccably modest with beautiful manners. He completely wiped the floor with all the competition. At that age he had a kind of coltish awkwardness. In *Me Mam Sez*, he was a Naval recruit who had to go off to fight after basic training. His reunion scenes with his family – and especially his mother – were very affecting. When I stood at the door to say goodnight to the audience, I twigged that a good cry is as transporting as a good laugh. Any play that we staged at the Coliseum had to have one of these ingredients. With this simple and touching play, they had both.

Until *Girlfriends*, the last show of the season, we had three flops in a row. All three plays *(The Mad Adventures of a Knight, Cloud 9, The Kiss of the Spider Woman)* were either too literary or too political to persuade more than a small number of devoted patrons to buy a ticket. I felt that I

Renata Allen, Ralph Fiennes, Barry McGinn, Christine Cox in *Mad Adventures of a Knight*, 1986

should have forecast the terrible box office percentages from the titles alone. I swore I would do better in the autumn. It took a long time for the penny to drop that anything that is too abstract, too ideas-based, too foreign or just too wordy-without-action will die the death with an audience that seeks real blood sweat and tears – plus a few good laughs.

I got it right when I went out of my own repertoire and into an unfamiliar genre – a musical, or a comedy, or a powerful working-class saga of family life.

The experience of *Girlfriends* was a case in point. It was composed by Howard Goodall with book and lyrics by (among others) Richard Curtis. The musical tells the story of the women who joined the WAAFs in WW2 and who provided essential ground support for Bomber Command. Howard had a major success already with his adaptation of Melvyn Bragg's *The Hired Man* and won an Olivier after its transfer to the West End in 1984. This was my first musical and it was absolutely thrilling to hear his songs, with Howard at the piano, sung by the cast of twelve, ten of them women. Howard had the very best of the rising musical talent at that time: Maria Friedman, Jenna Russell and Clare Burt all had matchless voices and the group spirit within the cast was comparable to the WAAFs themselves. It was a joy to direct and the audiences loved it. By half-way through the run, there were no tickets left. I do not exaggerate when I say that by the last week, there was an immediate standing ovation every night. Chris Moxon would come out of his office just to see it.

THE GUARDIAN
Francesca Turner

'Absolutely beautiful', spluttered the man sitting in front of me as the interval lights came up. 'Bloody marvellous'. Oldham Coliseum has certainly pulled off a theatrical coup in premiering Howard Goodall's new musical. GIRLFRIENDS is about 10 wartime WAAFS – there are only two men in it – and how they cope with everything from their scratchy blue uniforms and parachute packing to death and sex. It's set on a north-east Bomber Command base between January and August 1941 when only one in five airmen survived their first tour of missions. With a theme like this, it could easily have dribbled into sentiment but it never did. Rarely is it appropriate to mention everyone involved in a production. But Girlfriends tempts me to do just that, however boring a list of names might be. Somehow, the whole team from John Retallack, director, to Sheila Carter, choreographer, seems to come together like notes in a chord.

The Oldham cast of *Girlfriends* with Howard Goodall (in cap), 1986

It was the most exhilarating moment at the Coliseum. Judith Croft, the designer, had designed a stylised NAAFI canteen, with wooden panels and piano in the corner that evoked both time and place perfectly. The canteen adapted very elegantly to an RAF runway with the two pilots, Andrew C Wadsworth and Gareth Snook, returning home safely, guided in by the Flight Officer, Tina Jones. It was one of those rare occasions where all the facets of a show hang together. The representatives of Howard's agent, Noel Gay, were astonished at the brio and finesse of the show on its opening night, as were Howard's friends, family and numerous supporters, some of whom came up from London in a car almost the length of Fairbottom Street itself. Afterwards the cast, crew and supporters filled every table in our local Italian. There was much talk of whether it might 'transfer' (go to the West End) or not. De Wynter's, the graphic design company who were responsible for most West End posters, footed the bill for the entire meal to the dazed gratitude of everyone lucky enough to be there.

There was an offer from the Old Vic in London to stage it immediately, that very summer. Everyone was free and I was surprised when Noel Gay decided against accepting the offer.

It did transfer to the Playhouse Theatre in October 1987 in a radically revised production, a new cast (Maria Friedman replaced by

Hazel O'Connor), a new designer (William Dudley) and an orchestral score, the actors now all in wigs and with radio mikes. There was an ominously dark lighting plan from Mark Thompson. It was a thing of beauty to look at but it bore no relation to the show that we had mounted in Oldham, even though I was once again the titular director. Even the piano that had dominated the chamber orchestration so successfully in Oldham was no longer evident. Looking back, it was an epic production of a chamber piece and it misfired on every count. It was a massive disappointment to Howard. The music was so fantastic and he deserved great success. Notices were bad and *Girlfriends* closed within five weeks.

MAIL ON SUNDAY
25 October 87
Kenneth Hurren

GIRLFRIENDS (PLAYHOUSE)
Almost criminal that this fine theatre has been out of use for so long. Worse that it should be reopened with this drearily tuneless Howard Goodall musical about the wartime WAAF. Hazel O'Connor stars but doesn't shine and David Easter co-stars. Worse theatrical things probably came out of the war but I can't think of any.

There were enforced cast changes by the management in order to get some actor-recognition from London audiences. In all respects, this really was a case of a show being 'improved' by producers, trying to turn it into a 'proper West End show', not the simple and straightforward musical that had entranced the notoriously hard-to-please Oldham audience. Actually, the style of the original production caught the texture and camaraderie of the time and place that the musical is about. The producers felt they knew better.

AUTUMN 1986

The *Loving and Working* season was a major step forward for the theatre in its planning and we began to announce thematically linked plays in batches of two or three, instead of the indigestible announcement of six plays over half-a-year. (The first thing a punter would do with these heavy brochures was to work out what they were *not* going to see that season.)

Paul Elkins joined the staff as Associate Director; he had been my assistant at ATC and also the company manager on all our overseas tours.

Brochure for *Loving and Working*

I decided upon a 'themed' season that reflected upon Oldham's past and the values of the audience's parents and grandparents. Two of the plays were Northern classics (although *Love on the Dole* was rarely done) and the third was a discovery from the works of James Lansdale Hodson. Hodson was a native of Bury in Lancashire who had written a series of drama for Granada Television in the sixties. *Harvest in the North* was his major (unperformed) play.

THE GUARDIAN
Robin Thornber
HARVEST IN THE NORTH by James Lansdale Hodson

As a work of art it is sentimental, melodramatic, and clumsy compared, inevitably, with Walter Greenwood's simple tale, LOVE ON THE DOLE. But as a journalistic period-piece with the power to move an audience, it is a classic of its kind which deserves revival. This is still a powerful play reflecting the way that people see their world – as the first-night audience's enthusiastic response demonstrated. It wasn't just because of a stunning performance by Fenella Norman, as the working mother beset by bother. Or the telling set designed by Phil Swift. It was because, 50 years on, the Oldham audience was saying: "Yes, this is true."

I learnt later (from Joan Littlewood herself) that she had acted in *Harvest in the North* – at the Coliseum – in the early 1950s. The play is a gritty and well-characterised drama and it brought good performances from the ensemble of actors that we had brought together for this season of Northern plays. I directed *Harvest* (and *Spring and Port Wine*) but it was Paul Elkins' production of *Love on the Dole* that was the hit of the season. For this production he invited Lez Brotherston, a brilliant young designer who had served his apprenticeship under Philip Prowse, one of the triumvirate of directors at the Citizens Theatre in Glasgow. The beauty of his vision was striking and its impact upon our audience was immediate.

It was the first time I saw how design can lead the way in attracting audiences to a monthly repertory theatre. Paul worked out the majority of his production in the model box itself. He 'blocked' (ie, choreographed) most of the moves in advance with the designer. The design becomes the leading element to the production. Rehearsals are relatively straightforward because so many decisions have already been made by the time the actors turn up for the first day. The key thing remaining is to be clear about the characters – who they are and what they want in the play.

Love on the Dole exploded all predictions. Sheer visual beauty worked on this tried and tested classic. Brotherston created an expressionistic décor that incorporated close interiors and the panoramic nature of the Pennines. The set spread out from the stage and out into the auditorium itself. Everyone told their friends about how beautiful an experience the play was – and how moving they found the play. The increase in attendance was very much more than usual after the opening night – it looked set for 40% but that figure doubled over the course of the three-week run.

The picture (left) is the only one surviving from this production and Brotherston's set managed to integrate interiors and the walk that Sally and Larry take in the Pennines. As Philip Prowse is renowned to have said, 'There is no play that can't be done on a single set'.

Meriel Schofield (Sally) and Kevin McGonagle (Larry) in *Love on the Dole*, 1986

The final play of the season, *Spring and Port Wine*, was a more conventional production and the audiences came, partly because they had enjoyed *Love on the Dole* so much. Like all the plays in the season, it received excellent reviews.

SPRING CENTENARY SEASON, 1987

Chris Moxon said to me at the end of *Spring and Port Wine*, 'You need to see this theatre when it's really packed, not a single ticket to spare'. Apart from the end of *Girlfriends*, I hadn't seen it like that, certainly not for several weeks in a row. And what Chris meant was, 'It's about time that you gave this audience what they really want, which is some great comedy. And it's January and folk need a break from the rain and the sleet and the snow.'

Chris didn't intervene often so I took this as a gentle but steely hint. I'd heard via Kenneth Alan Taylor of a writer called Frank Vickery, a Welsh writer in his thirties known as 'the Ayckbourn of the valleys'. That was a misnomer really because Frank wrote very funny working-class comedies that were hugely popular with amateur and professional companies alike. He was a bus driver at the time of *Night on the Tiles* and did not take up writing full-time until 1989. Like Barry Heath, he had a perfect ear for dialogue and the rhythm of language. By 2006 he had written 28 plays and said he wanted to write "28 more – an audience that can't stop laughing is like a drug for me – I just can't get enough of it."

Brochure for *Comedy at the Coliseum*

You get the flavour and mood of the man in the picture below of the cast.

> *Drunken Grandpa, Mum and Dad, warring sons and pregnant wife (not to mention the nosey neighbour) struggle to keep peace in an overcrowded household – where the only solace to be found is the outside loo. (from the play brochure)*

I can still remember the first Saturday night and coming out of the door nearest to the stage and walking up the central gangway and marvelling at how packed the entire theatre was ten minutes before the show began.

Frank Vickery (in striped top) and the cast and creative team of *A Night on the Tiles*, 1986 (Note the designer, Judith Croft, on the extreme left.)

The expectation! The excitement! The sheer din of everyone chatting at full blast with a drink in their hand! The pressure to shape up to expectations was intense. The actors could feel it backstage as much as I saw it as I strode up the aisle, nodding, presidential-like, to friends and neighbours that I recognised.

The audience loved it. It did a super-high percentage. It was fun to rehearse and the actors cottoned on very quickly. And they kept their concentration up, they didn't miss laughs, they built them. I loved doing 'the vicar' on these nights because I took the bouquets of praise on everyone's behalf.

CLASSICAL CENTENARY SEASON, 1987

The two comedies filled the theatre and everyone was happy about this. Box office percentages impact greatly on the general mood of a working rep like Oldham. Two hits in a row were a tonic for everyone. But the Coliseum is a theatre subsidised by the Arts Council and other funding bodies. If we could be full all the time with sentimental comedies about working class family life, the theatre wouldn't need a subsidy. Artistic directors are appointed to bring something new to regional stages. I had been longing to do something popular and classical, just to see how the audiences took it, especially after their positive reaction to *Love on the Dole*. I really loved the proscenium arch stage in Oldham. It was big enough for brilliant visual performances and yet intimate in its relation to audiences. I wanted to show our audience how beautiful a play could look and sound up there. So we made a flyer that advertised:

> *The most popular English Comedy –* **The Importance of Being Earnest**
> *The most popular English Novel –* **Wuthering Heights**
> *The most popular English play –* **A Midsummer Night's Dream**

Brochure for Centenary season

I wanted this very particular audience, for the centenary of its theatre, to enjoy some classic works on its beautiful stage. We would do our utmost to make all three pleasurable for their entire families. And it was the work that we could do best. We invited Kenny Miller and Lez Brotherston to design – Kenny was also fast becoming, alongside Lez Brotherston, a leading European theatre designer who had served his apprenticeship at the Glasgow Citizens. Kenny succeeded Prowse as Head of Design there. I directed *The Importance of Being Earnest* (with Kenny) and Paul Elkins did *Wuthering Heights* with Lez. Phil Swift, our own Head of Design, was the designer on *A Midsummer Night's Dream*.

We brought together a very strong ensemble of actors for these shows; most of the actors were in two of the plays, some like Steve Halliwell and John Jardine (both local actors) were in all three. We also brought in Jack Ellis from ATC, Sadie Shimmin from Cheek by Jowl, Peter Leabourne and Rebecca Stevens from Cliffhanger in Brighton. These were all witty and creative actors, accomplished in movement and text. There were also two actors who had already done a season with the theatre, Meriel Scholfield and Malcolm Scates, two extremely versatile and creative actors.

Meriel and Malcolm embodied all the qualities of the best ensemble actors. Original in what they had to offer to the performance – and always alert and responsive to the rest of the cast. Both merry and unstressed, they put everything into their work and were rewarded with a string of brilliant roles.

Malcolm Scates and Meriel Scholfield as Lysander and Helena in *A Midsummer Night's Dream*

Malcolm Scates and Meriel Scholfield as Gwendolen and Jack in *The Importance of Being Earnest*

Steve Halliwell and John Jardine were both highly accomplished actors and also delightful men. John had been director of the Coliseum for a short time in the seventies and he knew far more about how this proscenium arch theatre worked than I did. He would say, 'Would you like me to go upstage at this point?' I'd say, 'Ah yes, John, why not, good idea', grateful to him for having solved a tricky bit of stage composition while I was under pressure. He played Quince to Steve Halliwell's Bottom. Steve, who did ten shows for me in the first two years at the Coliseum, embodied a kind of warm ruggedness and honesty, both gentle and wry. John Jardine, in addition to his impeccably elegant Lady Bracknell, brought intelligence and high energy to every role he played. Like Judith Barker, he was the real deal – the consummate repertory actor. John and Judith were both over 60 and they could play panto, family dramas, northern comedies, Shakespeare, Miller, Pinter, you name it. It is almost impossible for a young actor today to enjoy an apprenticeship as rich and diverse as theirs. For me, it was a pleasure to direct actors like this because they were still so open and engaged in rehearsal. Lots of laughs, sometimes at my expense which, of course, relaxed everyone. And their suggestions were invaluable. Here are Steve Halliwell and John Jardine in the moment that Bottom rejoins Quince and the rest of the mechanicals in Act IV of *A Midsummer Night's Dream*.

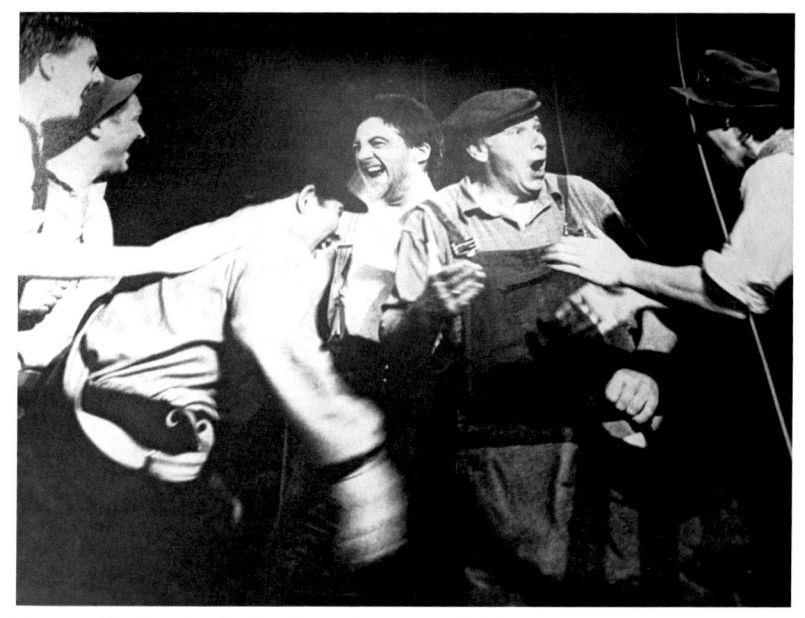

Steve Halliwell and John Jardine as Bottom and Quince

BOTTOM: *Where are these lads? where are these hearts?*
QUINCE: *Bottom! O most courageous day! O most happy hour!*

All three plays looked fabulous and the quality of the design was very high – the Glasgow Citizens designers had really transformed the look of the Coliseum stage. The ensemble of actors collaborated very well and we earned extra-long rehearsals for *Dream* because the actors worked in the day while they played *Importance* in the evening and they got a further three weeks during the run of *Wuthering Heights*.

The additional fortnight of rehearsal time allowed so much more detail and experiment than usual. *Dream* was a sumptuous and sensual production and I loved it. Believe it or not, this is a rare feeling amongst directors about their own shows. Normally, we see only the faults. But this was the kind of joyful, collaborative work that I used to make with ATC. Except this time, I had the full resources of a 500-seat theatre, a large cast and an excellent creative team behind me. For a golden moment, I really thought that I had not only learnt a lot over the last two years about every aspect of theatre production but that, judging by the response of the first-night audience, and then some great reviews, I had finally won over the local audience to the kind of work that I wanted to do.

Wrong. *Dream* did 37%. It lost money for the theatre and it didn't interest the local audience. And *Importance* didn't do very much better either. Next season, it would be time to start again. Again.

Renata was eight months pregnant with our second child during rehearsals for *Dream*. With Puck (Beccy Stevens) she had choreographed a dozen local children as the fairies. Oberon (Jack Ellis) and Titania (Aletta Lawson) looked like gods as they moved amongst them.

Carole Sobers as the artist's model in *Importance*

Renata and I worked together quite a lot at Oldham – she wrote three of the pantos, acted in a couple of shows (including the Widow Quinn in Synge's *Playboy*) and directed *The Steamie*. Because of Kenneth and Judith bringing up their own children over their years at the Coliseum, the theatre was used to a working theatre partnership like ours. If we turned up with

Renata's homecoming with baby Jack

a child in a pram, Jean Maiden or Sue Stonehewer at the Box Office would offer to sit with the pram for an hour or so. The people of Oldham, to a couple of southerners like us, were the friendliest and warmest people we had ever met. Our neighbours in Springhead (ten minutes from the theatre) were in and out of our front door all the time we lived there. One family in particular were incredibly fond of our infant children and would play with them every day. It was a very traditional set-up there too: their dad insisted on having the kitchen curtains shut if he did the washing up – he didn't want his mates to see him. Yet his children were adorable – see them here with Jean their mother and their own painted sign to welcome Renata (Nina) home from Tameside Hospital with Jack in her arms on June 19th, 1987.

Our son Jack was born on June 18th 1987, the actual day of the theatre's centenary. I went from the hospital to the Coliseum to enjoy the celebrations (full evening dress, live bands, food and drink) and then returned three hours later to Renata and Jack in the hospital, still dressed in dinner jacket and patent leather shoes, a very unfamiliar outfit in Oldham.

The author and daughter Hanna aged 5 months, 1986

The plan in coming to Oldham had been to integrate work and family. From that point of view, Oldham was a great job; our two children were born there and we both kept on working. Renata also wrote and directed a play for Manchester Youth Theatre. But in the end, I grasped the fact that I wasn't the right artistic director for the Coliseum. My tastes were too classical, too literary. I did a final season but I was much caught up in the London transfer of *Girlfriends*. My remaining three shows for the Coliseum were *Twelfth Night* (less engaging than *The Dream*), *The Playboy of the Western World* (a great show but it failed to bring in audiences) and *Educating Rita* which of course went very well. I'd never directed a two-hander before and I found the play very good but (so it seemed to me at the time) there was almost nothing to do as a director except help the actors remember their lines.

I was on the lookout for a new company to run and, in the spring of 1988, I was appointed Artistic Director of Oxford Stage Company, a national touring company to audiences that actually wanted to see – amongst other things – classic plays.

The new job was to start in January 1989 and so we left Oldham in July and we went freelance for the autumn.

OLDHAM COLISEUM: POSTSCRIPT

I programmed 36 plays in the course of three years. I learnt that the play that can be adequately rehearsed in three weeks does not interest me as much as more complex dramas that take longer to realise on stage. My preference for longer rehearsals and the longer runs I'd known at ATC became even more pronounced by the time I left Oldham. That's why I applied to a touring company – there is time to continue working on a play in the course of the normal eight or ten-week tour. I loved to see overall and individual performances grow over time and to remain active as a director in making that happen.

Over the time at Oldham, I felt that there was something antiquated about the whole rep system – why did theatres at this time still expect to run every show for three weeks?

It seemed a relic of the pre-television age to expect enough people to turn up every week from Monday to Saturday. It meant that one had to programme box office hits every night for ten months of the year. Theatre must be more various and be in a dialogue with an audience who respond to a variety of genres, or else it should be programmed less.

Yet the experience of doing so many plays in three years was a very important one. As I've got older I've thought how much I would like to return to programming a rep season, especially one that is themed like 'Loving and Working', or a season of new plays, or a brace of plays on climate change with talks after the shows, or a double-bill of classic comedies, or one company performing *Hamlet* and *Rosencrantz and Guildenstern Are Dead* in repertoire – the list of possible exciting combinations is an endless one *if* you have an audience on your side and you know that you will break even every playing night.

Every time the Press Night was over for a show that I had directed, the staff descended on me – there would be decisions to be made for the next season because the brochure was overdue, casting decisions on the play after next, answers needed on a variety of issues that had piled up while I was directing and trying to get everything in place for the opening night. If anything, the work became more intense and diverse after opening a show. Peter Hall in his diaries says repeatedly that rehearsals were a 'holiday' from running the National. He's right. Even the Oldham Coliseum took it out of you.

In writing this now, I realise what a time this was – ten to twelve shows a year and up to fourteen actors on stage for a five hundred-seater in a small town outside a major city. I didn't imagine at the time that all this would pass and what we took for granted would one day evaporate.

Francesca Turner of the Guardian put it another way:

Seeing The Steamie *reminds me of golden times when visiting Oldham Col gave you a warm glow like eating pie and mushy peas after a blizzard on the moors ...*

May, 1988

4
TOURING THEATRE
Directing Shakespeare at
Oxford Stage Company, 1989-99

INTRODUCTION

We sold our house in Oldham for £29k and bought a terraced house in East Oxford for £78k on a 100% mortgage. Financially speaking, we hadn't been clever to leave the South-East in the first place. Over the next ten years we paid our monthly mortgage at rates of, or close to, 15%. The mortgage was usually over £1,100 a month and my salary began at £17k. Both of us worked and took on extra work whenever it turned up and from 1994 Renata taught drama part-time in schools and from 1998, full-time.

The house remained in 'negative equity' for nine of the ten years we lived there. (Only between 1988 and 1989 did it abruptly go up in value, allowing us to buy a flat in London.) Fortunately, the house we bought in Oxford was next to the gates of Florence Park, and we had neighbours with children of the same age. The garden was long and looked out onto a huge area of allotments. It was a ten-minute cycle ride into the centre of Oxford. The river was closer still. I was born in Oxford and felt very happy to settle there. There is a civic Oxford of canals, fields, parks, allotments and public space that was ideal for a young family like ours. Renata's family lived in Shepherd's Bush and my father lived near Chipping Norton, so we were equidistant from parents.

The offices of Oxford Stage Company (OSC) were on the top floor of the Oxford Playhouse. It was in the centre of the city but the theatre had been closed for some time and it was miserable to go down to the abandoned foyer and theatre, locked up in time. It should have been the official 'home stage' for Oxford Stage Company.

When I arrived in January 1989, I wasn't made welcome because the then Executive Director had also applied for my job; he wasn't happy that I, and not him, had got the job. Nor were his supporters in the office, and I was blanked on arrival. I just stood at the office door as if I was invisible. I didn't know anyone there and eventually, after an agonising wait, I was introduced to the staff of eight. Since no one knew me at all, I decided to carry on as if

I hadn't noticed the hostility. I had my pride. I felt that if I did great work, all would come good.

It was a difficult start, even though the board, under the chairmanship of Rupert Rhymes, offered me full support. There was no theatre in the city for us to play and the company staff were disaffected. All was drab. Where would we rehearse, where would we play?

The difference from ATC and Oldham was that Oxford Stage Company had twice as much money to spend on half as many productions. This meant that I could go out and search for an exciting space to rent for the summer, both to rehearse and to open shows.

AS YOU LIKE IT AND *KING LEAR*, 1989

We found the Newman Rooms, opposite the main entrance to Christ Church Meadows, just off St Aldates. This was the Catholic Chaplaincy, a vast interior stone-flagged space with a good acoustic, ideal for rehearsal and big enough to bring in seating for an audience of 250. The Newman Rooms allowed productions much greater freedom in their use of space than the stage of the Oxford Playhouse. We called it the Rose Theatre because it was in Rose Place and the Elizabethan Rose Theatre had just been discovered in London.

I chose *As You Like It* as my opening production, to be followed by *King Lear* played by the same company. Deborah Findlay played Rosalind to be followed by Philip Voss as Lear. The company would be made up of 13 actors and for *King Lear* it rose to 14 when Philip Voss would join after we had opened *As You Like It*. The plan was to rehearse *Lear* from the

The Rose Theatre – 4-sided set for *Measure for Measure*, summer 1990

time that *As You Like It* opened on July 25th to September 20th in Lincoln, a period of eight weeks. *As You Like It* had rehearsed for four weeks, so we gave double the time for *Lear* rehearsing 'under' the evening show.

The first part of the programme was successful. The company of *As You Like It* were extremely good and they got on well and attracted excellent audiences throughout the run. Deborah Findlay was a luminous Rosalind. The Newman rooms became a semi-Elizabethan theatre with the audience of 250 in a horseshoe around the large open playing space. Drinks were served in the foyer and smokers wandered out into the little mews that faced Christ Church Meadows. And the reviews were fabulous.

It was the second half of the plan that didn't work.

I was happy that the first of the two Shakespeares had gone so well but I was very tired by the time the Press Night was over. And the first read-through of *King Lear* was scheduled on the Friday of the opening week. Philip Voss arrived, fresh and impatient to get started. His text was marked heavily throughout and he had a lot of questions. My head was not yet in *King Lear* and nor were those of the cast.

Mistake one: I ought to have included Voss in *As You Like It*. In that way we would have all got to know each other and he would have been a continuous reminder of the fact that opening *As You Like It* was only a mid-way point in the programme.

Mistake two: the company themselves were already performing a long play eight times a week – it is hard to schedule them for the kind of substantial rehearsal that the actor playing Lear seeks.

Mistake three: the biggest one of all was that moving my family into Oxford and dealing with the unhappy staff at the office, had left me little time to think through *King Lear* before I started *As You Like It* rehearsals. I was doing it all on the hoof with a well-known actor playing the lead role. He saw through me very quickly. Voss felt neglected and it frustrated him deeply how *short* rehearsals were – the actors who performed in the evening had to start later than him and finish earlier.

I never recovered my energy. Voss tried to be helpful but he wasn't happy with some of the casting. He hated the lighting and he really got the thin end of the wedge when we opened the play, mid-tour in Lincoln – only two reviews for his Lear. In Oxford, Deborah Findlay had a dozen national papers sending their first-string reviewers. Rehearsing 'under' another play works in a fixed repertory theatre but it is a disorientating addition to a long weekly touring schedule.

I became completely drained and my diary entry for Wednesday September 20th, 1988, the night we opened in Lincoln, reads as follows:

> I'm absolutely fed up with working such very long hours, on one unrelenting thing – SHAKESPEARE – and not seeing my wife, children or having any other interests or distractions. Try as I might to prevent it, I feel that I've submerged my identity into theatre and I desperately lack other interests. I smoke and I shouldn't, I've got a bad cough and I'm starting to put on weight through having to eat out all the time. I'm utterly fed up with watching these mesmerisingly long Shakespeares. *King Lear* is put together so fast that it's a simple no-nonsense version, in various non-specific costumes, not nearly thought out enough. It's a miracle that it stands up at all in the few interrupted hours we've had in a dozen different rehearsal spaces; it's a tribute to the company's professionalism and harmony that it works at all. It's been made under duress. I can't bear to work on it any longer.

But I found it impossible to stop working on it. Directing is an unhealthy and compulsive occupation.

Yet after this difficult first season, I remained loyal to Shakespeare. Once again, I was so fortunate to be in a place where I could audition and cast his plays with outstanding actors and, with OSC, not scrimp on the company size or production values. Once I began directing his plays, however painful the experience of *King Lear*, I couldn't look back. The fascination of every text occupied me throughout the months leading up to rehearsals – and, perforce, I learned better how to prepare each play. I always spent the summer holidays after each Shakespeare production thinking about what the next one would be the following year. (I write in closer detail about certain Shakespeare productions later in this chapter.)

Deborah Findlay as Rosalind, 1989

OXFORD STAGE COMPANY

In 1988, when I applied to OSC, the company was part of a touring 'matrix' of companies that all shared a similar brief; to tour for 32 weeks a year (Oxford weeks were included) with four plays per year. OSC was one of three national touring companies, the other two being Cambridge Theatre Company (CTC) and Century Theatre, based in the Lake District. The Arts Council allowed us to tour to Scotland, Wales, Ireland and indeed the rest of the world, but we all had to tour the minimum 32 weeks in England.

I felt that Oxford was a good home for a company but many disagreed – the Oxford Playhouse ('ugly but necessary'- *The Telegraph*) had been closed for some time and it always had a reputation for poor audience attendance. In my interview for the job, I didn't know if the Playhouse would ever re-open.

To Oxford's good fortune, Tish Francis and Hedda Beeby were appointed as artistic co-directors in 1990 and the theatre was opened and run mostly as a receiving house (that is, a theatre that programmes touring work). This led to the theatre doing far better than it ever did as a traditional repertory theatre. After they were appointed, we opened all our productions at the Playhouse, including long runs for Shakespeare in the summer. The Playhouse became a desirable touring theatre for all the companies that played 500–800 seaters ('middle-scale'). Tish and Hedda oversaw a total refurbishment in 1996 and we played *Hamlet* in the Rose Theatre that summer, thus sustaining the Playhouse audience a mile across town. The busy programme at the Playhouse, of which OSC was very much part, changed everything about the cultural scene in Oxford for the better. Oxford had for too long been dominated by the University and the arrival of Hedda and Tish was the beginning of a sustained push-back by the city that lasts till this day. Now the Old Fire Station, Pegasus Theatre, the North Wall, the New Theatre and the Story Museum contribute to a thriving scene that no one would have foreseen in the late 80s.

I conceived four threads of work for OSC: an annual Shakespeare production; a new work for children and young people; a contemporary classic; and a devised/adapted work from another source than a conventional play. I also committed to living and working in Oxford so that the company would become part of the local scene.

I liked the opportunities that OSC provided to create well-planned and well-rehearsed shows that ran for at least two months, on tour. It also made it possible to take on outstanding freelance directors from the UK and overseas. The company produced 40 productions during my tenure, of which I directed 26. Guest directors included: Mike Alfreds (who went on to run Cambridge Theatre Company/Method and Madness); Stephen Unwin (who went on to run Century Theatre/ English Touring Theatre); Antonio Fava (commedia dell'arte maestro from Italy); Alexandru Darie (artistic director of the Bulandra Theatre in Bucharest); Barney Simon, (co-founder of the Market Theatre in Johannesburg); Mark Dornford-May (founder of the Isango in Cape Town); Irene Brook (later artistic director of Théâtre National de Nice); Dominic Cook (later to become artistic director of the Royal Court).

From OSC it was also possible for me to freelance. In spring 1993, I was invited to direct Shakespeare's *Comedy of Errors* by the Shakespeare Theatre in Washington DC and I returned in the summer of 1994 to re-stage the production for an outdoor setting. In the autumn of 1994, the Tokyo Globe invited me and my assistant director, Karl James, to direct *Romeo and Juliet*. My own OSC production of *Romeo and Juliet* toured to the Globe at the same time as we opened the Japanese version and the two productions played in tandem throughout December of that year, in Osaka and Tokyo.

The board of OSC was formidable and deeply experienced; it was difficult not to feel nervous on the days that board meetings took place. Rupert Rhymes was Chief Executive of the TMA (Theatrical Managers Association) and other trustees included Colin Tweedie, Chief Executive of ABSA (Association of Business Sponsorship for the Arts), and the late Andre Ptaszynski, soon to become Chief Executive of the Really Useful Company. Later us 'officers' (as the management are referred to in board papers) would go to the bar of the Randolph Hotel around the corner for a convivial drink. These quarterly meetings took a lot of preparation and discussion between me and the Executive Director. I always found it hard to relax after them. Powerful and supportive as the board were, I was always relieved when those evenings were over for another three months.

The company remained in the black throughout this time and our core ACE funding increased by 40% in the period 1989-1999. OSC also won substantial awards from Trusts and Foundations; Sainsbury's awarded us £50,000 in 1995 and The Vivien Duffield Foundation £50,000 in 1996. We gained significant additional income through touring overseas, especially to Japan – half of our Shakespeare productions played at the Tokyo Globe.

PRODUCTIONS OF SHAKESPEARE AT OSC

OSC gave me the opportunity to develop my work on Shakespeare to another level. We nearly always rehearsed in the Oxford Newman Rooms, which, when not doubling as The Rose Theatre, is an enormous stone-flagged interior hall with low ceilings. It was a thrilling location to explore a play. In the first week of each rehearsal, we would improvise a free and complete walk-through of the play that ranged across the entire space. Of the twelve Shakespeare plays that we produced, I directed ten and from these there are six that I want to mention in more detail.

AS YOU LIKE IT, 1989

Returning to *As You Like It*, my first production for OSC, there are certain key ingredients that influenced most of the Shakespeare plays that I worked on over the decade that I was artistic director of the company.

The composer, Howard Goodall, was always exacting in the questions that he asked about each Shakespeare play. In my first conversation with him on *As You Like It*, his interrogation helped me to get the balance between court and forest and what each location represented. Out of these discussions, Howard produced very melodic versions of the songs.

Music is a starting point for me, it comes even before the design of the play. Visually, I always want the actors to have space to move and to create telling and beautiful physical compositions. I have never liked the designer to create a décor that defines place or time. I want text, music and movement to combine and release the play in as fresh a way as possible to a complicit and increasingly engaged audience. I love the 'musical' plays of Shakespeare best of all – *As You Like It, A Midsummer Night's Dream, Twelfth Night, The Tempest* and *A Winter's Tale* for example, not just for their songs, but because their structure invites the director to think of them in a musical frame.

Poster for *As You Like It*

With music, movement arises in the most natural way. The suspension of speech is arresting in a Shakespeare play, that continuation of action through other means than text. On the other hand, when actors are speaking verse, it is usually better to have no music at all

As You Like It is a dream, as transporting as *A Midsummer Night's Dream*. The difference is that there is no magic. It is a dream that a lonely young woman could have lying in a field in summer. Given the reality of Rosalind's life, it is a very joyful dream that keeps getting better. And it is not only her exile with which the play in concerned, it is the exile of her father's court. They find comfort, and even joy, in being so close to the elements, as well as in the comradeship of their fellow exiles.

Howard Goodall was able to link both the longing for home and the longing for romantic love into his music. He brought a vivid narrative meaning to a play that often feels disconnected and episodic.

OBSERVER/ Michael Ratcliffe

John Retallack's exhilarating Oxford Stage Company production of *As You Like It* is fresh, lucid, funny and textually consistent. The pattern of eight lovers is meticulously interconnected through a series of questions, prescriptions and games, and the play once more revealed as the great comedy of passion, instinct, imagination and art.

THE TEMPEST, 1991

I returned to *The Tempest* for a second time in 1991. I had an excellent cast very clearly led by its Prospero, Richard Durden. He was enthusiastic about warm-ups, he was full of praise for the mostly young cast and he accepted all the direction that came his way, however demanding he found it. Prospero is a very difficult role to bring humanity and love to: his character is a contradictory one, both cruel and kind, emotional and suppressed regarding his daughter and her relationship with Caliban, and vexed, too, in his own love for Ariel. The island is a place both with and without definition, a liminal space between a real world and an imagined one.

So elusive is the play's own poetic reality, I don't think our production was ever 100% 'right'. But the spirit of this company is illustrated by their reaction during an outdoor performance in Lincoln in August, 1992. A torrential downpour occurred in the middle of the Ferdinand and Miranda

Caliban (Femi Elofowuju jr) and Stefano (Patch Connolly)

Miranda (Juliet Aubrey) and Prospero (Richard Durden)

Ferdinand (Ray Fearon) and Ariel (Diane Parrish)

scene. The linen costumes of Juliet Aubrey and Ray Fearon were wet through immediately. I checked with the Lincoln Theatre's production manager that there was nothing happening on the stage of the theatre that night. Having briefly consulted the cast, I announced that the play would continue at the theatre in 20 minutes if the audience would like to join us there – where it would be dry. 400 people followed the cast through the streets (I can still see that in my mind's eye, an unending column of umbrellas) and once the last spectator took their seat, the play continued from where the rain had stopped the action.

The cast were on an empty stage they had never seen before until now. All were thinking how to improvise their rehearsed moves on a bare space without décor. In the event, the music (by Howard Goodall) re-centred all of them on the ugly black bare space; they sustained their concentration by focusing closely upon the character with whom they were in dialogue (and not worrying overmuch about the space). Yet as the performance continued, they began to use the large unfamiliar size of the space to move more freely. Ariel (Diane Parrish) opened up more and more as she sang and Caliban (Femi Elofowuju Jr) bounded across from one proscenium to the other. There is a liberating genius in a play as fantastical as *The Tempest* – and Prospero held the centre, bringing meaning to the stage cliché that 'stillness is strength'. It was an experience that proved very positive for the production as the cast sensed how fully they grasped the play when all the carefully prepared design and physical composition were taken away from them.

THE COMEDY OF ERRORS, WASHINGTON DC, 1993

The Shakespeare Theatre in Washington invited me, on a freelance basis, to direct *The Comedy of Errors* with their permanent company. By chance, I was already scheduled to direct *The Comedy of Errors* for OSC in the summer of 1993, in conjunction with *Pericles*.

The Shakespeare Theatre had a very different company culture to any group I had ever met before. The actors were very good textually. Witty and versatile, they could catch a wide range of nuances from a funny line. The actors who played Antipholus and Dromio (Floyd King and Philip Goodwin) were comedy veterans. In early rehearsals, they stood there and traded banter – and then they stopped and looked at me. Their faces said, silently and politely, "What do you want us to do now?" I felt panic. I had no idea to offer. I never worked out all the 'blocking' in advance. I had ideas but it was far too early to say, turn to your left, walk to the right and then stand still. In my productions, I *evolved* all these things with actors. I would set up whole scenes and improvise them this way and that, I'd talk about it with them, then start again from the beginning and a composition would emerge through 'play', that is, playing together with the meanings and the actions of each scene.

This wasn't on the cards here. I was expected to be more like an opera director, with a set and a storyboard and clear moves already set in my head. I wasn't meant to walk in and ask a few intelligent *questions* about

Floyd King as Dromio, Philip Goodwin as Antipholus

a play. I was the guy with the answers. So I set the play in New York's Little Italy in the early 20th century. I stayed up for nights in the first week and worked out 'the moves.' As soon as I did this, Floyd and Philip came up with fresh ideas and new suggestions. I was used to calling my English companies for every hour of every day – the ensemble approach. This company worked the year round together, they had a poker school that they ran in the Green Room *during* shows. They also had a shrine to Elvis Presley that they could touch as they approached a stage entrance from the wings. If they were called for rehearsal, they wanted to use the time to work on their own role and go home again. My 'ensemble' approach (and perhaps the reason I had been invited to work there) felt like a proposal so naïve, I never brought it up.

Washington is the most political culture in America. There was no problem with audience attendance. A visit to the Shakespeare Theatre was a prestigious night out and tickets were bought far in advance because it provided an excellent way to invite, and get to know, important colleagues and visitors to the capital. Season tickets were sold out before rehearsals begun. The theatre was full whatever the reviews – though negative word of mouth could lead to unused tickets and empty seats. The effect of this was to make the whole theatre experience the opposite of the 'rough magic' that I loved. The elite audiences, most of whom were in some form of political posting in the capital, were on the dull side. A night at the Shakespeare Theatre was part corporate event, part social duty. Floyd and Philip, who knew how tough this audience was, were expert in their wit and timing. In the main, the audience enjoyed the performances of *Comedy of Errors*.

It was my naïveté to have expected the company to think like I did about Shakespeare. The result was that my production was a conventional one, with solid panelling and a stately pace. I didn't recognise my own hand in it. I was lucky to have a brilliant designer (Russell Metheny) and gifted composer (George Shakar). In 1995, Michael Kahn, the director of the Shakespeare Theatre, revived the show for a long summer run in the Carter Barron, a very large outdoor theatre in a Washington park. The performances were "FREE FOR ALL" and so this was a much more relaxed ambience for the play and for the company; families and young audiences replaced the suits.

The Shakespeare Theatre is just off Pennsylvania Avenue and my apartment was in a condominium just around the corner. I walked to the rehearsal room behind the food market every day. During my time in Washington, Bill Clinton was inaugurated as President and I danced to Chuck Berry (live) at one of the inaugural balls. My family came out to spend Christmas and New Year together in a new wonderland.

PERICLES AND *THE COMEDY OF ERRORS*, OXFORD, 1993

I came back in time to start the OSC rehearsals for *Comedy of Errors* and *Pericles*. Grant Parsons (Antipholus) and Tony Howes (Dromio) greeted me on the first morning; they didn't know each other and none of us had worked together before. But they were fooling around, trying out physical gags, laughing at and with each other – they were already playing before I said, 'Sit down – let's read the play'. Everyone was so excited to work because most of the cast were unemployed the week before rehearsals. The difference, above all, from the American company, was their irrepressible physicality. They seemed to think with their bodies as much as their heads. This is the English way in classical theatre. I felt at home again.

Comedy and *Pericles*, so different in character and genre, are both set on the Eastern Mediterranean coast in the merchant city of Ephesus; Pericles ends his journey there and it is the setting throughout for *Comedy*. What

Philip Bowen as Pericles journeying to Ephesus

interested me most was the romantic affinity in these plays: each one ends with a powerful scene of family reunion. Both have the infrastructure of a romance, one in the form of a farce, the other shaped by a quest.

The two plays happened to pair well in terms of casting – every member of the eleven-strong ensemble had rich characters to play. Karl James, who had played Trinculo in *The Tempest*, now turned composer and created the score. Music is central to *Pericles* not only because the recognition of Marina by her (now aged) father comes through her song, but also to convey the ceaseless journeys that constitute so much of the narrative. Julian McGowan, doing his third Shakespeare production for OSC, designed the set and costumes.

The 'magical realism' of *Pericles* had attracted me the moment that I read it on a stony beach in Northern France, holidaying after the opening of *The Tempest*. I love Shakespeare's wilder plots and finding the narrative that lies beneath apparently disconnected episodes. *Comedy of Errors* is entirely clear as a narrative – the trick is to make all the mistaken identities as credible and as authentic as possible. *Pericles*, like all four of Shakespeare's late plays, requires concentrated reading and discussion with the performers to find the emotional narrative. In the late plays, of which *The Tempest* is the greatest and the clearest, the poet is in evidence as much in the *plot* as in the language.

We opened *Pericles* in Oxford in July 1991 and *Comedy of Errors* in Gdańsk, Poland, in the first week of August: a contemporary account of this event follows.

THE COMEDY OF ERRORS, GDAŃSK, POLAND, 1993

Saturday 31 July, 1993

It is almost 350 years since English companies, fed up with the plague, puritanism and slow business at home came across Europe, or sailed to Danzig (as it was until 1945) to play. We are here to reconstruct the journey of the English companies into Gdańsk and to make our application to perform to the Mayor (and to Neptune), as our forebears did. This ancient negotiation is recorded in Dr Jerzy Limon's book *Gentlemen of a Company*. Dr Limon is our host. He is a charismatic academic and a native of Gdańsk.

Dr Limon is responsible not only for books on this early period of English touring theatre; he has also made a sensational discovery. The only Elizabethan theatre in Europe, based upon the plans of the Fortune Theatre and identical to it, existed here in Gdańsk from about 1610 to the early nineteenth century. It is now a car-park next to the main Warsaw by-pass. Within ten years The Gdańsk Theatre Foundation hopes to have raised sufficient money to create yet another miracle of Polish reconstruction and to see the theatre once again standing on its original site, abutting the city walls of Gdańsk. The whole plan is romantic and irresistible, and under Dr Limon's impassioned leadership, looks likely to succeed. He is also a close friend of Prince Charles, who has expressed his full support to Dr Limon's project.

Oxford Stage Company is thus the first English company to revive the past in Gdańsk, and by lunchtime the actors are up on a large cart running through the silent ten-minute version of *The Comedy of Errors* that we have prepared in the rehearsal room at home. It is rumoured that the main square (the size of two football pitches) will be packed and that upwards of 5000 will be present. We have also prepared a series of tableaux to perform up on the cart whilst moving from the Golden Gate to our patrons waiting by the Town Hall before the Neptune Fountain.

This will be the first pageant through Gdańsk for 350 years. It's a scene of frantic collaboration amongst strangers and the adrenalin infects everyone present. Dr Limon passes through with a wild look of surprise.

Evening

Eventually, the cart, last of the procession, moves into the main arena. The crowd is so gigantic that we cannot go to the steps (as fixed with the coachman) and a burst of speed from the 4 horses maroons us 100 metres away from the city steps in an ocean of people and umbrellas. Leader Hawkins (Gower), in front of considerably more than 5000, reads out the intensively learned script, 350 years old, imploring the Mayor to permit us to play. His lovely voice rolls out around the square and, amidst many bravos and applause he completes the four pages. He does so with great grace and precision. The company sent waves of support from the distant cart.

Night

A reconstructed pageant in a reconstructed square. What a cycle of birth, death and rebirth has led to this ephemeral moment. And how much the passing parade can occasionally catch something even more enduring than bricks and mortar; the need for the peaceful and prosperous conditions that allow us to perform and for a whole city to gasp later at the fireworks that lit up the night sky above the Green Gate at 10.00pm.

Thursday 5 August, 1993

The actors are extra-nervous on the first night. As Sue Colverd puts it, they are on a "long promise" to their hosts, having enjoyed such hospitality. And it's a new show. It is a solid (rather than an inspired) performance, as the actors find their rhythm again to a different audience reaction. At the end the response is ecstatic, the longest curtain call I've ever known, multiple bouquets of roses. Ritualistic? Official? Unreal? As the director, perhaps I don't know, but the joy in the performance and the particularity and warmth of the unceasing congratulations that follow – alongside the surprise on the face of Iain Seaton of the British Council at seeing a Polish audience respond in this way – all help me to believe that we got more of it right than I thought. At the official reception, long speeches, vodka and no food.

Back now in 2023, I am happy to report that the Gdańsk Shakespeare Theatre was built and opened in 2014. It thrives as both a cultural centre and a classical theatre.

Leader Hawkins as John Gower in *Pericles*, 1993

Grant Parsons and Ginny Holder in *A Comedy of Errors*

Dr Limon, who died of Covid, aged 70, on March 3rd, 2021, achieved a great deal for the port city of Gdańsk.

THE INDEPENDENT, Tuesday 17 August 1993/Paul Taylor

Height of profile and depth of quality are by no means necessarily connected in the arts world … Meanwhile, a smaller-scale touring outfit like the Oxford Stage Company under the direction of John Retallack goes largely unsung in the media despite treating its audiences each summer to a level of Shakespeare production that, for theatrical vitality, warmth of spirit and interpretative penetration, has precious little to learn from the big shot Bardic organisations, and that includes the RSC.

ROMEO AND JULIET, 1994

Romeo and Juliet is a different kind of play. It is one of the clearest of Shakespeare's plays to read. It has less subtext, a strong linear story and more physical action. He wrote it in 1595 (a year after *Comedy of Errors*) and he is showing himself to be a virtuoso in all he writes – *Comedy* is a mistaken identity farce for *two* sets of twins; *Romeo and Juliet* uses an unprecedented range of poetic and prose registers. The play switches between tragedy and

Tybalt (John Higgins), Benvolio (Sam Bond), Juliet (Tara Woodward) Stephen Moyer (Romeo), Mercutio (Michael Higgs), 1994

comedy when you least expect it (ie the Nurse when she believes Juliet to have died), it has thrilling physical conflict and Romeo increasingly speaks in sonnets. The language and the action are glorious. Youth teaches crabbed age how to live before the tragedy of their own violent deaths. It is the most popular story of all his works and it has been adapted into every possible genre, multiple times. So why do yet another version?

There were three reasons: the express-train pace of the text; the sword-fights; and the tragic ending of the story. These were the elements that I felt missing in my experience of seeing the play. In the event, I think that I got the first two right but that I failed to capture the terrible poignancy when Juliet awakes and finds Romeo dead beside her – and then takes her own life. I'm not sure I know why that scene is so difficult to realise – is it because everyone knows the ending? Or is it because a self-stabbing is so hard to believe on stage? Up to that point, the verse-speaking was well-paced (after a very slow start in rehearsals). It had clarity, intensity, versatility between registers; it was all there after the first few weeks of playing. By December, when I saw it again in Tokyo after a gap of six weeks, it was electrifying to hear them speak the verse. And that worked alongside the physical confrontations in the play. I had long found sword-fights dull and unconvincing in respectable high-end productions. I wanted the cast to excel in them and brought in a

Tony Tarrats, Michael Higgs and Sam Bond in rehearsal, summer 1994

brilliant fight director, John Waller, to direct them. With the enthusiastic support of the young cast, they became breathtakingly intense combats in which the audience could believe that death was the outcome.

If my production was not as moving as I had intended, I found it pulsating. I really battled with Stephen Moyer (Romeo) over his verse-speaking. He said that he just wanted it 'to be different every night'. I said I wanted it to be 'better every night'. I wasn't prepared to leave it to chance. This battle of wills led to so many extra rehearsals with him that the older actors playing the Montague and Capulet parents came to me and demanded my attention – I was spending so long with the young ones that they were losing out badly in rehearsal time. They were right, of course. Directing *Romeo and Juliet* is a bit like running a football team full of very talented, self-centred young men – apart from Romeo, there is Mercutio, Tybalt, Paris and Benvolio to deal with. They must be hot-blooded and my casting had ensured they were. Once we had opened, they became a brilliant ensemble who delivered a powerful account of the play – and their elders matched them in cruelty. Tara Woodward played Juliet. The only other women in the cast are the actresses playing her mother and her nurse – it is otherwise an isolated role for a young woman amidst a lot of competitive young males. Tara took them on and her performance grew alongside theirs.

ROMEO AND JULIET IN TOKYO

In late October, Karl James, the assistant director, and I went to Tokyo to direct a second *Romeo and Juliet,* in Japanese this time, for the Tokyo Globe company. The Japanese production was scheduled to open at the same time as the OSC production when it arrived in Tokyo from its UK tour. (My younger brother Guy, also a theatre director, took over the English tour of the play and was partly responsible for the excellent shape the production was in when it arrived in Japan.) We had a good translator in the rehearsal room and the play was very fresh in our minds, so we knew what line the actor was speaking for most of the time. The Japanese company were very sound – they had all worked together before. Romeo and Juliet were both well over twice the age of the characters that they played but both were uncannily youthful in appearance – and well-known to television audiences.

The group itself prized teamwork very highly. We introduced them to a popular game called *Zip Zap Boing* and they loved it in a way we never imagined possible. After a week they came in *an hour early* to play it together. It is a game about keeping an imaginary ball in motion – if you 'drop the ball' then the game stops and the culprit must stand down from the game. They began to keep account of times – their record was eleven minutes without anyone dropping the ball. Yet as it went on, they began to mock and penalise anyone who did drop the imaginary ball. It became obsessive, until all the actors lived in dread of failure. We introduced the game to foster

Romeo (Stephen Moyer) and Juliet (Tara Woodward)

teamwork and, instead, fostered conflict. In the end, we started rehearsals earlier to prevent them playing – but they went on playing after we left for the day.

Our Japanese production was well received and it was shown on Japanese television, as well as running at the Globe for a fortnight. It was fascinating to bring the English and Japanese companies together and the Globe laid on a great buffet to celebrate this meeting of cultures. Karl and I enjoyed living in the city and seeing Japanese life on the ground. We stayed in a hotel 40 minutes from the theatre and found a back route to work that ran alongside gardens and railway lines. Tokyo is a grey blur from the air, but beautifully maintained at ground level.

At that time, artistic directors of companies were entitled to a sabbatical period of three months. After six years in post, Renata and I went out to Tokyo in the autumn of 1996 as guests of Keio University for whom we ran workshops on Shakespeare. Our children came too (Hanna, 11 and Jack, 9) and they went to a Japanese school where none of the pupils spoke English. They wore the school uniform and took the bus (unaccompanied) every day for the 45-minute trip to Jiyu Gakuen, the strikingly progressive school that they attended. We were free to be tourists in the capital. We walked and cycled all over the city and attended performances of Kabuki and Noh theatre. It was a completely different world for each one of us.

A MIDSUMMER NIGHT'S DREAM, 1998

In *A Midsummer Night's Dream*, there is no natural lead part. It is the nearest thing to an equal opportunities play.

Karl James was composer and he had a lot to do. The dream-like nature of the play was to be conveyed by a musical ensemble who played both the fairies and the mechanicals. Karl is especially good at bringing groups to life, facilitating a positive and up-beat mood. He got great musical results but this company was hard to 'lift' as a group. Maybe it was us who made the mood hard to lift, so intent were we on not producing another cliché-ridden version of this over-performed play. We had both seen versions of the play that had no depth and little meaning. We were determined to make a *Dream* that was a transforming and profound experience. It was the reason for doing it.

I cut the play substantially. I got the running time to exactly two hours and we performed the play without an interval. This greatly helped flow and the creation of an uninterrupted dream. It was possible by editing the beginning and the end of the play to focus on all that is inexplicable and wondrous. We were barely out of the dream itself and the play was over.

Feste (David Brett) and Bottom (Nicholas Beveney)

Anna Francolini as Helena

The company played it better and better as the tour went on. Their final week was in Glasgow at the Theatre Royal and their penultimate performance was abruptly stopped, not by a storm this time, but by a bomb scare. Fortunately, there was a final performance in the Oxford Playhouse on October 11th, 1998 for an invited audience.

THE GUARDIAN
Arts Review / Monday 2 November 1998 / Lyn Gardner

This is as fleeting a Dream as you're ever likely to experience: it's almost over in a blink. It is also one of the best. What we witness are the most magical of transformations – those of the heart. The fallings in and out of love of the four lovers, their words of reproach and rapprochement are played out in a fierce, physical ballet, a kind of poetry in motion. In the heat of feeling they grab and pull at each other, roll away, pummel and punch in a bruising, athletic display that constantly underlines how much love can really hurt. It is also a triumphant reminder that Shakespeare and physical theatre create a highly successful marriage. Just as he mixes old ideas with new, Retallack has assembled a cast that represents experience and young blood, whose members are capable of playing together quite beautifully in every sense of the word.

5
YOUNG PEOPLE
Directing new plays for young audiences,
1991-1999

INTRODUCTION

At the age of 40, with two children aged three and five, I went through something of a re-set in terms of what I wanted to create in the theatre, much aided and abetted by Renata who has always had a specific interest in this field. Shakespeare was an essential ingredient in every working theatre year but we had begun to take our own children to the theatre from time to time and found that they were not very excited by what they saw. They didn't talk about it very much and they were not as absorbed as we expected them to be. Work for children appeared to be a sub-set of theatre, not taken seriously by most actors and directors. Performers seemed to shout at each other or the audience, and there was little emotional life in the characters; it became clear from the actors' bodies that they were not invested in what they were performing. Even the curtain calls were bored.

    I wanted to concentrate on what was happening in new work for young people in Europe. Rumour had it – and watching the work of visiting companies from Germany and Italy confirmed it – that work for children and young people was very well funded in continental Europe and that the work was taken seriously by artists, funders and audiences alike.

    I went through a pattern of change in my work comparable to my visiting Europe to see theatres and to meet directors in the 70s. Once again, it seemed that it was essential to leave England for a time and to see how they were making theatre over there.

    But first of all, I commissioned Renata to write some fresh work for children at Christmas, based upon classic folk stories – even stories that were usually turned into pantomimes. I directed all three, *The Witch and The Magic Mountain*, *The Magic Storybook* and *Tom Fool*. They were performed on the stage at Oxford Playhouse and they drew very good audiences. They were different from other Christmas shows at the time because they told the original folk stories in unsparing detail. Each show had four or five stories, some famous, others much less well-known. The productions found different forms for each story. For instance, Cinderella was performed as a silent film, using a great deal of mime. (We received some complaints on the opening night from parents who found the sisters cutting off of their toes too upsetting and gory. Of course, there was no blood or gore involved – everything was mimed.) Jack and the Beanstalk was in rhyming couplets with a chorus. It covered the same source material as a pantomime – but in a completely different way. *The Magic Storybook* also contained an Anansi story, an African tale called *The Girl and the Snake* that was sung through, and the fifth of the tales, *The Good Clown and the Bad Clown*, adapted from a Native American story about two slave owners.

Our new approach to the conventional Christmas slot paid off immediately. In 1991, *The Witch and The Magic Mountain* was nominated for the Martini/TMA award for Best Show for Children and Young People. In 1992, *The Magic Storybook* actually won the Martini/TMA award for Best Show for Children and Young People.

Howard Goodall was the composer on all three of these shows and his music was integral to their success.

The Good Clown and The Bad Clown in *The Magic Storybook*

THE MAGIC STORYBOOK/THE GUARDIAN, 1991/ Mick Martin

Renata Allen returns you to the original folktale, and the director, John Retallack, combines colour, sound, light, and movement to immerse you in a near-surrealistic nightmare … A variety of styles are used to stimulate, rather than to direct or manipulate, the imagination and emotion of both young and old. Narrative clarity, energy, and vivid visual power, meanwhile, are the constant factors in a distinctive and slickly performed show that … successfully marries the simplicity and animation of storytelling with the spectacle of theatre.

THEATRE FOR CHILDREN IN HOLLAND, 1992

In 1992, on the strength of these shows, I received a small bursary from the Arts Council to visit the Kunst Junior Festival in Den Bosch, Holland, where it was said a golden age in new work for children and young people had arrived. At this time, work for children in England was still in a strong tradition of fairy tale and folk stories. In Holland, Germany, France and Italy work for young people was better funded, more searching and original. Avant-garde work for *children*, was something hard for me to imagine, coming from a market-driven theatre culture. Box office and fees were core to the survival of all theatre in the UK. It was also said that in Holland rehearsals were *eight* weeks long for shows that lasted only 60 minutes. Below is an extract from my first visit to Holland to see this work. I saw a lot of striking and original plays. Here I focus on one outstanding production by the Wederzijds company.

CHILDREN'S THEATRE FESTIVAL, HERTGENBOSCH, THE NETHERLANDS, 13 -16 May 1992

Extract from festival journal

> I got to 'The Casino', the festival centre, slightly apprehensive at meeting loads of English festival and theatre people, but I'm the only foreigner as far as I know, despite extensive notes provided in English. This means that I have no one to talk to, let alone fend off. It's

all Dutch. There's a bright guy called Dennis Meyer from the ITI who is very charming and helpful, and he has sorted out my tickets. One production is truly remarkable:

HITLER'S CHILDHOOD
Wederzijds

This was the outstanding production of the festival, the most talked-about piece by the most admired group in Holland. It is the favourite to win the festival prize, and it was a scoop to get a ticket.

Hitler's Childhood is playing in a large gymnasium. A deep and wide black cloth is laid on the ground, far wider than a normal stage. Behind it is a black cloth of equal size that forms the backdrop. Both blacks are stretched and look very good. You first see five actors, standing at each corner of a 6-inch wooden platform at the centre. They are terrifyingly made up; one looks like Hitler, though much older than Hitler ever lived to be. Then three mad-looking women, two scrawny and angular and one big and blonde. All are in exquisitely made, thick woollen costumes. In the centre of the wooden platform is a beautiful boy with long hair gelled straight back, in a leather apron and grey stockings; he is holding a puppet's head in a bucket and is motionless. They are all motionless. As people are still filing in, they change positions and stand immobile again. At either extreme of the stage floor is a crazily tilted armchair that looks as if it is made of very weathered steel. There are also two equally tilted windows with curtains and a hideous rusted metal pram with prison bars on it, very truncated and box-like, but deep. It's a striking theatrical image, all this, even before the play has begun.

I had read some material on it in advance; about the Polish psychoanalyst Alice Miller and the Swedish author of the 1983 play, Nicolas Radstrom. I was very intrigued to see if the thesis worked and how it could be effective as drama for a teenage audience. Here below is a short extract from an interview with Alice Miller:

'My desire to learn more about Adolf Hitler's childhood did not emerge until I began to write this book, and it took me quite by surprise. The immediate occasion was the realisation that my belief, based upon my experience as an analyst, that human destructiveness is a reactive (and not an innate) phenomenon either would be confirmed by the case of Adolf Hitler or would have to be completely revised. This question was important enough for me to try to answer, although I was very sceptical at first that I would be able to summon up empathy for this human being, whom I consider the worst criminal I have ever known of. Empathy, ie, the attempt to identify with the perspective of the child himself and not to judge him through adult eyes, is my sole heuristic tool, and without it, the whole investigation would be pointless. I was relieved to discover that for the purposes of my study I was successful in keeping this tool intact and was able to regard Hitler as a human being. Hitler grew up in a time where systematic beatings and physical punishment were believed to be good for the child – it developed discipline, drove out wickedness and allowed 'goodness to grow'.

Hitler's own words are in the programme:

"My pedagogy is hard.

What is weak must be hammered away.

I want the young to be violent, domineering, undismayed, cruel.

They must be able to bear pain.

There must be nothing weak or gentle about them.

The free, splendid beast of prey must once again flash from their eyes.

I want my young people strong and beautiful.

That way I can create something new."

The style of the piece has all the precision and attack of, say, Berkoff's *Greek*, although its moods are more diverse. We watch the upbringing of the young Hitlers, for there are two – out of the bucket emerges a blonde Fanny and Alexander-like sister, dressed identically. The aunts in this house are as neurotic and violence-hungry as Bergmann's film. The two children grow up in this hysteria-laden environment and are brutalised terribly by the father. He says what a happy childhood he had and how he was beaten and is all the better for it. A terrible beating is portrayed. The father, his back to us, thrashes the steel pram with loud regular strokes of a leather belt carrying a thick leather buckle on the end. The noise is sickening. Young Hitler reveals his back at one point which is 'still' covered in angry red stripes.

It's clear – if you brutalise this child, he will, in turn, brutalise his own. Violence begets violence. Was Hitler born a monster? Or was he made one? Many of the large schools' audience here know little about Hitler – and there is far-right political activity in this region, significantly with the Vlaams Blok at this moment and its Jongeren (Youth) wing.

I am told later that this group, Wederzijds, come to a school at 9.30 am. They participate in lessons, both in character and out of character. The company does not perform till 2.00pm. They always perform in daylight; it is key to them that the actors and the audience share the same light. After the show, they do a follow-up discussion with the children and teachers and leave about 4.30pm.

In this area of North Holland, 120 children per day, over a 6-week touring season, partake of these days. The shows do not happen without the integrated lessons, discussions and workshops. Yet this performance is of such a high standard, it could be put on at the Cottesloe tomorrow.

The music is taken from Dutch fascist songs; the music has been very well recorded and the cast sing exceedingly well, direct to the audience.

It turns out that the 'bad' Hitler is not a beautiful boy but a girl. He goes on an ecstasy of violent declamation to the most rousing of all the songs. It is a terrible sight and the entire audience sat transfixed. I could see two women crying. The children were open-mouthed. Yet the control of staging and playing was awesome.

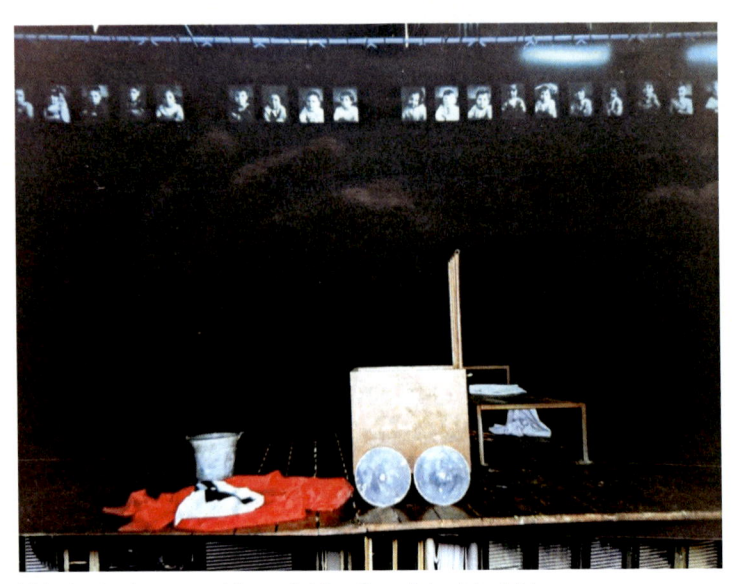

Hitler's steel pram and the unfolding line of Jewish children

At the top of the black back curtain were hidden a row of fifty photographs of young Jewish children who were killed in concentration camps: a twitch upon a black thread and they were revealed, at first one, then four, then nine and on until the full 50 were revealed, a great gallery from end to end.

The young Hitler's building bricks (which emerged suddenly when the bucket was overturned) were built up into a neat city. At the end, the four adults became a tight crowd of citizens, moving towards us in a precise funeral-slow dead-march. The group approached the bricks and trampled them down; then kept on moving and only stopped when they were inches short of the audience, physically implying that this phenomenon could march on through us, the audience.

There was tremendously strong applause, no cheering or standing, it was too awful a parable for that. As the players left the stage, an utter silence fell upon everyone present. I was alone but I saw friend turn away from friend. There was a collective staring at the floor or into space, as the audience got up to leave. Some chose not to wait for the coach to the town centre but preferred to walk back. This was good theatre on an issue that refuses to be buried. And for the adults, everyone knows about the end of Hitler, but who has thought about the beginning of his life? And the children know little of either; hence the carefully designed programme that fences in this dangerous piece.

Never once was there a moment of indulgence or gloating or piety in this performance. It was acutely judged and conceived with real imagination and intelligence. It makes theatre for young people an exciting prospect and makes me speculate if that might be an exciting step to take, personally. Writing and performing for young people adds political thrust to the activity of theatre.

I met Winnie in the evening, she is one of the three aunts in the play. She tells me that she has been with the company for six years. Wederzijds was founded ten years ago by a brilliant writer/director called Ad de Bont. The company has four shows on at the festival, including one called *My Mother Can't Remember* about senile dementia – real plays about contemporary issues immensely helped by being addressed to a target teenage audience. And all their pieces last about an hour.

Later, at the Festival Club, I meet the director of *Hitler's Childhood*, Matthieu Guthschmidt, and he says something so important to me that I had to write it down verbatim:

> *Children's Theatre has little – in my view – to do with the audience as a group, but much more with regaining an original feeling for life – a return to the childlike, spritely aspect of man. A playground, in short, in which societal norms are de-regulated and re-evaluated; the adult audience will always wish to safeguard its norms as it strives towards its own comfort. A place in which harmless but naughty pleasures originate. A place of shivers, delight and excitement.*
>
> *I feel that adults have to see this work too. They need it as much as children do. This is the theatre I would like to put before adults as well as children.*

WEDERZIJDS THEATRE COMPANY, AMSTERDAM

The festival at Den Bosch changed my outlook on theatre for the rest of my directing life. I now wanted, above all, to meet Ad de Bont, the Artistic Director of Wederzijds and find out more about the company and its work. After this trip in 1992, I conceived *Making the Future*, the purpose of which was for OSC to bring new European plays for children and young people over to the UK in home-grown translated productions.

I met Ad in person in Spring 1993. Their base was close to a canal in a former primary school. This gave them a lot of studio and rehearsal space on the ground floor and pleasant, light and spacious offices on the top floor of the building. The floors in-between were occupied by other arts organisations. Ad was tall, slender, with strong pointed features – and a direct gaze. He wore up-to-date casual clothes, usually quite new looking. He was a life-long teetotaller and non-smoker. He drank fruit teas all the time. He spoke good relaxed English (that is, making mistakes didn't bother him at all, he was always articulate and clear and switched from German to English and back to Dutch without blinking. And he was so frank, I was always trying to cover up the fact that I was a little shocked by his openness.

Ad is a natural and flowing talker, both about his work and life. He is also full of interest in what you have to say. He had run Wederzijds for the last decade. He is clearly intelligent in his choice of work partners, creative teams and actors. Above all, he is a prolific playwright and his work is regularly staged in Germany and other European countries. He does everything with intuitive efficiency and clarity but never seems to be rushed. I have never met anyone like Ad before – both principled and focused but also a natural comrade with whom one has the best time. We remain in good contact.

During the next two years, I got to know everyone connected to *Hitler's Childhood* – Matthieu the director, all the actors and Ruth the dramaturg and Lin the woman responsible for taking the educational programme into schools. They were all committed to the company and its many projects, plays and the revivals that toured well beyond North Holland. It was a privilege to be an insider to this group, to imbibe the way that the company functioned on every level. There was a confidence and an openness that I greatly admired.

What led to me working with the company (which was to shape all the consequent moves that I made in my theatre career) arose out of one play that I happened to be on hand to hear for the first time. It was autumn 1993 and the play was *Mirad, Boy from Bosnia* by Ad de Bont. At that time, the Bosnian war was on our television screens every night of the week – the sensational news was that these accounts (and images) of concentration camps and of genocide were happening in a country that was within driving distance of Holland and only two hours flight from Heathrow. Not only did nobody know how to stop it, nobody really knew what was going on in Bosnia, Croatia and Serbia. The history, the geography and the names defeated educated people and few adults could have given you a clear description of the mainsprings of this conflict; no child could have done so, unless, like Mirad, they were a refugee of this war.

There were a lot of refugees arriving in Holland at the time that Ad wrote the play. His protagonist is Mirad, who we never actually meet.

Dirk and Marika perform *Mirad, Boy from Bosnia*

The story is told through his aunt and uncle, Fazila and Djuka and the letters that Mirad writes to them. They have been searching for Mirad for months and when they arrive in Holland, he has already left. In the play, which lasts only 50 minutes, and is told out of chronological order, the complexity and barbarism of the war is illuminated in clear, precise, poetic language. When I saw it performed one autumn afternoon in an Amsterdam school, as the light was fading, I was amazed that the audience were only 8 and 9 years old. It was performed by two actors that I knew and it was told at a scorching pace. They were dressed in everyday clothes and had only a cymbal that they struck in between scenes. It was essentially a recital.

I felt that even in Holland there was some nervousness about the subject. It felt to me as if it could be slower. Yet an animated discussion followed in the classroom between the two actors and the children. Afterwards when we sat in a room and discussed this first try-out, I asked Ad if he would send me an English translation as soon as there was one.

I was moved by this bringing together of a school environment and an experimental attempt to find a language for, at that time, a seemingly impossible subject. This was a play about a war that was *still going on*. Yet, as I was to discover when I read it in translation, the subject inspired Ad to write a breakthrough play in terms of storytelling. Here is the opening scene, most of it direct address to the audience:

PROLOGUE

FAZILA: Sorry.
Sorry that we are here.
That we take your time.
DJUKA: Sorry.
FAZILA: Sorry that we breathe in your air.
DJUKA: That we walk on your ground.
FAZILA: That we stand in your view.
DJUKA: Sorry.
FAZILA: Sorry.
DJUKA: Sorry that we look like we do.
FAZILA:. So ugly.
DJUKA: No, not ugly.
Different.
FAZILA: Ugly.
We are ugly people.
DJULA: Maybe I am but you are not.

FAZILA: *Ugly people in ugly clothes.*
DJUKA: *You are not ugly.*
FAZILA: *Yes I am.*
For them I am.
DJUKA: *For me you are as beautiful as …*
FAZILA: *Djuka please.*
DJUKA: *Sorry.*
FAZILA: *Sorry that we disturb your rest.*
DJUKA: *As if you don't do enough for us already.*
FAZILA: *Sorry that we are not grateful and happy.*
DJUKA: *Not grateful enough.*
FAZILA: *And that our name is not David or Catherine or Peter or Mary.*
DJUKA: *But Djuka.*
FAZILA: *And Fazila.*
DJUKA: *Sorry that we live in a normal house, one of your houses.*
FAZILA: *That we didn't say no.*
DJUKA: *That we sit in your trains and buses.*
FAZILA: *And on your benches in the sun.*
DJUKA: *And sorry that we brought nothing.*
FAZILA: *No filled vine-leaves or other delicacies.*
DJUKA: *Or a series of slides.*
FAZILA: *Or hand-painted puppets.*
DJUKA: *The only thing we have is a story.*
FAZILA: *Not even a happy story.*
DJUKA: *But it is ours.*
We don't have another.
Ours and our nephew's, Mirad.

There are many ways to interpret this prologue, a direct address to the audience, whoever and wherever they may be. It can be read in a subdued way, in an ironic sarcastic vein, it can be flippant or it can be profound – or it can be without any subtext and simply be the heartfelt apology of two bourgeois people who are suddenly refugees in a new country.

The play was picked up by many other theatre companies, almost overnight. It was soon translated into a dozen languages; this was before there were books or television documentaries about the Bosnian war. Every leading theatre for young people presented it, even if it meant a complete re-arrangement of existing schedules. The most well-known and respected young people's theatre in Europe at that time was the Swedish company, Unga Klara. Its director, the legendary Suzanne Osten, distributed 24 copies to her permanent company of 12 men and 12 women; she asked all the women to learn the principal female character, Fazila and all the men, the principal male character, Djuka. The company then received a playing schedule for a schools' tour of the area in and around Stockholm. No two actors ever played with the same Djuka or Fazila – each combination was unique. Every child in a vast urban and rural area saw *Mirad* and talked about it with the actors. Ad is always clear that plays can't change the world; yet I feel that those multiple *Mirads* in Stockholm might have had a lasting effect on one generation of teenagers and their compassion for the refugee.

The English translation of *Mirad* dropped through my door in Oxford a couple of months after I had seen it in Amsterdam. I opened the envelope and took it out. At that moment, the phone rang. A conversation started. As it did so, Renata wandered into the room and picked up the play. She started reading it, waiting for me to finish on the phone. The call went on for some 40 minutes. When I finally put the phone down, she held the play up and looked at me.

'Have you read it already?' I said.

'Yes – it's so good. You must put it on and get as many people to see it as possible.'

'That won't be easy.'

'Get someone famous to do it. In the Playhouse.'

'Just like that!'

'Read it.'

So I sat there and read it, this play I had only seen – but not heard. Renata was right.

The next morning I had to go to London and to my surprise, Sinead Cusack was standing in the queue for a train ticket. I ran to the phone box and called Renata.

'Is Sinead Cusack married to Jeremy Irons?'

'Yes. Think so. Why?'

'Can't explain now. Call you later.'

I had the script with me to read again on the train. I got on the same packed carriage as Sinead Cusack but felt too nervous to do anything then and there. Instead, I sat further along, where I could see when a seat near her might become vacant. As it happened the train got seriously delayed after Reading because of an incident near Paddington. There was a space and I went over and introduced myself:

"I really hope that you don't mind me interrupting you but I have a play that I would very much like you to read …"

I saw her face stretch with irritation, I realised that I sounded like an author who was being a pest; it must, I suddenly thought, happen to her all the time …

'This is a very special script that I've just brought back from Amsterdam, it's about Bosnia now and I think that you and your husband might be really really interested in reading it because I know that you're both involved a lot politically…'

She gives me a look, a sceptical look, and puts down her paper and says, 'What is it?'

I take out the envelope with foreign stamps on it and slip out the thin A4 script and pass it over to her …

'It's called *Mirad, Boy from Bosnia…*', I start. And we're off and we're talking together about the play. She then starts reading it and the train still doesn't move. By the time, the train does roll slowly into Paddington, she's finished it. She doesn't say much about it but she does say,

'I'll show it to Jeremy.'

And she's off down the platform.

A week later I get a call from Jeremy Irons.

His first words are, 'I've just come in from hunting.'

I'm nonplussed by this. Jeremy forges ahead.

'I've read your script. It's good. Needs some work. But Sinead and I are interested.

Perhaps we could meet at the Playhouse and read it through.'

'That's great! I'll fix a room.'

'If we do it, it will just be a reading. You understand that?'

'Of course, of course.'

We got started and worked on the play together for three full days. What took time was Jeremy's detailed suggestions and amendments to the text. He has a perfect ear for rhythm and idiom. The script improved so much; this was to become the standard English version of *Mirad* under the translator's name Marian Buijs, a Dutch journalist who simply wanted this story to be heard and seen beyond Holland. The phrasing of the English version is largely the work of Jeremy Irons. It was Sinead who agreed to perform it in January on the Playhouse stage and said to her husband, 'We'll have to learn it – I can't just read this in front of 600 people.'

Jeremy and Sinead performed it twice in the Oxford Playhouse before two packed houses. I put movement into it. Sinead and Jeremy filled the stage – it was not a recital at all, it was a fully realised play. It had come a

Jeremy Irons and Sinead Cusack in *Mirad*, Oxford Playhouse, January 30th, 1994

Brochure for Channel 4 production of *Mirad, A Boy from Bosnia*

long way from the pair with the cymbal in the classroom. Ad de Bont came over to see it. He was surprised to see it as a play in a large, full auditorium.

Two things came out of these two performances of *Mirad*: Ad de Bont wrote *Mirad Part 2* in which Mirad and his mother are the principal characters; and Jeremy Irons decided to take his first foray into directing a film. The film opened on January 9th 1997 and was subsequently shown on Channel 4.

Longman published Mirad Parts 1 & 2 in 1995. Soon after, the play became a set text for GCSE. The book has run into several impressions and been widely performed in the UK.

Extract from interview with Ad de Bont

YOUNG PEOPLE

INTERVIEWER:
Do you think that Mirad is suitable for a young audience?
AD DE BONT:
I was trained as a teacher. I believe education has to prepare children for life that is real, and too often I believe over the past fifty years in Western Europe we have just prepared children for a "youthland" that adults think is real. And it isn't. Terrible things happen in this world. I mean as a girl you can be raped, even if you are just 11 and live in a village. If there is war, you know almost for sure you might be raped – you are very glad when you are not. Nobody says in war "I won't shoot your father because you are too young". What I can say is that children who have seen Mirad say to me that now they understand how people at war can be so terrible to each other.

In May 1994. OSC invited teachers from all over London to two free performances of *Mirad* at the Young Vic, performed by Sinead and Jeremy. Turnout was very good indeed and an intense discussion followed the afternoon performance. One teacher questioned the right of the author to place blame upon the Serbians for the atrocities depicted in the play. After

Ad de Bont, JR, Jeremy Irons during filming of Mirad, Autumn, 1996

THEATREMAKER

all, the evidence at that time was not yet conclusive. Sinead, clearly familiar with public debate, retorted crisply to the questioner who was becoming persistent, "To borrow Stefano's words in *The Tempest*: 'Thought is free'."

Several of the Wederzijds acting company came over from Amsterdam to see the evening performance. They were startled by the naturalism and warmth that Sinead and Jeremy brought to such a compressed and stylised text. They had been performing in schools and this version was a revelation to them. They wanted to talk to the couple and Jeremy invited the eight of them out for a pizza. It was a touching event for me to see the ten of them gathered around, analysing passages. Jeremy and Sinead asked, in turn, about their acting lives and the whole meal flowed on, genial and engaged throughout.

By late 1993, I wanted very much to bring *Mirad* and *Hitler's Childhood* to our own audiences. I am not a producer but a director, so I wanted us to create our own English versions of these plays, to reinvent these texts for our own place and time.

Oxford Stage Company launched *Making the Future* in September 1994.

MAKING THE FUTURE 1, 1994

This was an effective project because nothing else like these plays existed for children and young people at the time. We successfully created a different version of *Hitler's Childhood* (translated by Frank Perry), though I don't think I have ever been so self-conscious about *not* copying a show that I had already seen and been very influenced by.

Karl James shared the direction of *Mirad 1 & 2* and the plays toured to schools all over the UK.

Leaflet for OSC's *Making the Future*

HITLER'S CHILDHOOD
TIME OUT Review
Oct 25, Young Vic

Niklas Radstrom's *Hitler's Childhood* is based on the writing of psychologist Alice Miller; this is a haunting vision of the birth of brutality. Abused, ignored and resented, the young Addy (Michael Matus) has no choice but to learn not to feel. The Freudian 'child within', played by a separate actor (Vicky Licorish) is initially his playmate and comfort, but as Adolf's humanity is beaten out of him, so the child is rejected and extinguished. Scenes, fragments, phrases or gestures litter the stage as they might an adult subconscious: the eerie debris of a demolished childhood. Led by the growing boy and his ailing inner humanity, we tiptoe through these shards of innocence in appalled disbelief. It is a work of arresting originality performed with exquisite stagecraft. Utter folly to miss.

Michael Matus and Vicky Licorish share the role of young Adolf

MIRAD, A BOY FROM BOSNIA/
THE GUARDIAN/September 20 1995

De Bont's prime objective is to confront us with the human realities that underlie the crisis – and that is achieved by simple means. Largely shorn of movement, action and overt emotion, the circumstances are harrowingly presented through direct personalised narration in John Retallack and Karl James's wonderfully controlled production.

PERFORMING ARTS LABS, 1995-99

At the time that *Making the Future* was running at the Young Vic, the producer Susan Benn and the poet Maura Dooley approached me and asked if I would direct a series of 10-day workshops for Performing Arts Labs (PAL). PAL was an organisation founded in 1987 by Susan Benn to make active research into aspects of dramatic writing and performance.

In my case, I was asked to centre it on playwrights who wanted to write for children and young people, an area still under-served by new plays. The location for Performing Arts Labs took place on a beautiful farm in Kent with a Jacobean manor house on the estate and many barns and outbuildings that had been converted for rehearsals, accommodation and communal dining. Writers could apply for a *free* place to attend the ten-day workshop; accommodation and meals provided. The first one was in 1995 and I ran four between then and 2000. Maura Dooley raised around £50k from different trusts and foundations for each one of these workshops. It seems astonishing to me now that such monies were available; there were ten writers, four actors, two directors including myself, two eminent playwrights; Bryony Lavery, April de Angelis, Suzanne van Lohuizen and Pauline Mol all participated in one or more labs. There was also a range of eminent visiting speakers who were met at Tunbridge Wells station and driven out to the idyllic setting of Bore Place Farm, deep in the countryside near Edenbridge. The visitors included Aidan Chambers, Philip Pullman, Jackie Kay, Melvyn Burgess. Directors were interesting too – Antony Clark, Ben Harrison and Tony Graham.

The way it worked was the writers brought no more with them than typewriter or laptop and an idea that they wanted to write (but, as yet, had never dared). No re-writing of an existing play allowed. Apart from morning group sessions with the senior writers, they wrote all day long. These sessions were life-changing for several writers; they had never had such close and scrupulous attention paid to their work before. By the end of the working day, if they had two or three pages that they felt confident with, they handed them to me and I would work on these with the actors. After supper, everyone would come to the barn and we would act out these just-written pages to the group – and a discussion would follow. By the third day, there was a queue of script extracts waiting to be enacted and shown. Some writers wrote an entire play within the ten days – the poet and dramatist Glyn Maxwell was one, and the Scottish writer Douglas Maxwell was another.

In an indirect way, in these pressured conditions, I also found a new type of acting. There was simply no time for the actor to reflect or do more than follow the lines and the instructions on the (sometimes hand-written) page before them. We rehearsed, but always swiftly. The result was it brought out the very best in each actor. Each one brought invention and light to the written word. As a result, I have always loved the alertness and self-effacement of good play-readings.

During the PAL workshops, when the evening readings were over, everyone went over to the Jacobean living room with its great log fire and drank wine till it was very late. Bryony Lavery had the most robust constitution. I can't remember her ever saying, 'I'm tired now, I'm off'. But she was always at breakfast, as bright as she was the night before. For the writers the retreats were a chance to mix with other writers and lose the sense (that many had) of isolation in their writing lives.

For me, over four PAL retreats, it dawned on me (repeatedly) that I had never written a play, I only adapted the works of other writers. That's as far as I got at this stage but that feeling was to surface again – actively – a year after my last PAL lab.

MAKING THE FUTURE 2, 1998

By this time, especially after running three PAL workshops, over a period of three years, I felt that OSC should be able to commission British dramatists to write new plays for children and young people and not have to rely exclusively on European playwrights for inspiration. Accordingly, I commissioned Jane Buckler, who I had met through PAL, to write a play for children called *Johnny Blue, Where Are You?*, a moving play about a little boy whose father dies when he is very young. Karl James directed the play and it drew primary school groups and families to the theatres that we toured. My part in this programme was to adapt Melvyn Burgess' novel *Junk* for the stage; this production was intended for a young teenage audience.

Junk

At this time, the biggest issue around young people was the abuse of drugs, especially by young teenagers. Melvyn Burgess had just published *Junk,* a novel that not only won the Carnegie Medal in 1997 but was also fast turning into a best-seller. Karl James walked into the office one morning waving the hardback, saying, 'You have to do this book, you have to!' I sat down and read the first chapters and by lunchtime we were onto the agent, asking if the stage rights were available. What I loved about the novel was that each chapter was in the voice of either Gemma or Tar (the two protagonists), Lily or Rob (the two antagonists); single chapters were carried by other key characters. The sequence of the book was linear but it was possible to use both direct address and naturalistic dialogue in a stage version. And every chapter was headed by reference to a punk song; Melvyn had to invent pop lyrics of his own because of expensive rights issues when it came to quoting real pop songs. At that time, a theatre company could play an entire track by the Buzzcocks or The Cure or The Stranglers and pay only a set price to PRS (Performing Rights Society) for every month the play was on tour. Add to the music, a powerful story, well plotted, and believable young characters with a great turn of phrase; it was a natural for the stage. Karl James seized the music and created the soundtrack. Ben Harrison helped the cast to 'chase the dragon'. As ever, as a director, I was in debt to the talents of other specialists.

When we opened, after much discussion, nervous about audience reaction, we classified the play as 14+. On the first preview at the Oxford Playhouse, I walked out of the building one hour before curtain up (probably to smoke a hypocritical cigarette) to see a long queue of children from different schools, aged between 11 and 13, all excited to see their favourite book on stage. I went up to the first teacher and I said to her,

'They are a bit younger than I expected …'

She replied, 'They've all read it – they brought the book to school, not us …'

Emma Rydal as Gemma in *Junk*

YOUNG PEOPLE

Niki Turner (designer), Patrick Martin (Executive Director), Katrina Gilroy (Production Manager), Ben Harrison (Assistant Director), JR, Emma Rydal (Gemma), Dan Rosewarne (Tar), Renata Allen on JUNK winning the Martini/TMA Award for Best Show for Young People, 1998

I sat in the fifth row in between two 12-year-olds; at the climax of the first half, when Gemma and Tar are both seduced into taking their first hit of heroin, the girl next to me whispered, 'I couldn't resist that, I know I couldn't.' The book, and our adaptation, were a cautionary tale that showed why a young person might, to up-end the cliché, say yes to drugs.

Melvin Burgess on Junk
There was a period in July 1997 when Junk became one of those books that everyone had an opinion about, whether they'd read it or not. By and large the most sensible remark, and the one truest to the spirit in which I originally wrote it, was said by a fourteen-year-old girl.

'Well, the pop stars are all saying how great drugs are,' she pointed out, 'And the press is always saying how awful they are. This is a book that tells the story and lets me decide for myself.'

I write this having just come back from Oxford, where I went to have a look at rehearsals. One of the first things that struck me was the way so many members of the cast resembled the people I had in mind when I wrote the book ... it was like watching their brothers and sisters get up and go through the same stuff. We talked about punk, about how people talked, dressed and behaved ... there's a lot of fun to be had making it look and feel right. We watched the run-through ... and it's a pleasure to be able to say in all honesty, that I was enthralled as well as flattered. I was very much taken by how much John has truly tried to adapt the book, rather than interpret it. He's used the characters so much in the way I did.

Melvyn Burgess 1997

6
DIRECTING IN ANOTHER CULTURE
Reaching for new horizons, 1988-2000

INTRODUCTION

The following section is about the gaps and breaks in my career, when I sought refreshment and change from the English theatre scene. Most of the freelance work took me to another country, or culture, as was the case with both *The Comedy of Errors* in Washington and *Romeo and Juliet* in Tokyo. Sometimes I worked in English and at other times, in Holland, Japan, Norway and India, I worked with a translator.

Of course, everything is different when you direct in a foreign language. It's not something a director should do too much or too often. To be honest, it is boring to sit and hear an English text that you know almost by heart spoken in Japanese or Dutch all day long for six weeks. It doesn't necessarily sharpen you as a director. Steven Berkoff writes about this hilariously in *Coriolanus in Deutschland* (1992) where he can only get through the day's rehearsal by thinking exactly of what he will eat that evening. It is an honest and funny account of what it feels like to direct a play you love in a language you do not understand. Yet from time to time, to work like this is inspiring as I was to find later on in my career, especially in Holland and Japan.

There is of course the whole question of what is an English theatre director doing directing *Hamlet* in Hindi, a language that he doesn't speak or read? This was common practice for English directors all over the world, greatly helped by the British Council in its desire to disseminate English culture. The notion was that the director comes from the same culture and language as Shakespeare or Wilde or whoever. He or she will bring something of that culture to the theatre or drama school. It is hoped that the essence of that author will remain with the actors, and the theatre, after the director has departed. Hard to say if that was true in every case. From the director's side, it is a fantastic opportunity to live for a sustained period in another culture and to soak up the way they make theatre.

Though I doubt that the British Council is as supportive as it was, if you are lucky enough to be invited to direct anywhere else in the world, accept the offer if you are free to do so. It is mind-expanding and horizon-widening for the director – if he or she can benefit so much, surely this meeting of cultures can still apply positively to the host company and its actors and directors?

1 1988 (September – October)

WARRENPOINT, NORTHERN IRELAND

We moved to Warrenpoint in Northern Ireland for September and October, 1988. I directed a huge community play called *The Fair Day* written by an Irish actor and good friend called Patch Connolly (Stephano in my 1991 *Tempest*). Again, we were all there together and there was plenty for Renata and me to do, as well as look after our two babies. We had a nice house to stay in by Carlingford Lough. Every morning I checked under the car for bombs. But this is also a very friendly part of the world as well as a sometimes dangerous one. After three years in one place, it was an adventure.

Here is the article I wrote about this experience for an Irish Theatre magazine:

> **'FAIR WARRENPOINT'**
>
> **John Retallack recalls his recent stint as director in Warrenpoint of a community epic, *The Fair Day*.**
>
> In September I arrived in Warrenpoint with Renata, my wife, and our two children, Hanna and Jack, aged three and one. We rented a house with an apple orchard and a large kitchen with an Aga. Six came to supper on our very first night, to meet us and to discuss the poster, the props, the sheep and the drop-outs and new recruits to the original cast-list, made up on an earlier visit in May. The fact that we had no telephone meant that all messages came in person.
>
> *The Fair Day* is about the historic annual fair that used to take place in the town. We had decided to stage it in the town hall. Its vastness allowed us to build long stage platforms down both sides of the hall, and a special thrust out from the existing stage. This left a sort of basin where the audience would sit or stand and watch the action going on around, through or across them. On the floor was a huge ex-opera floor-cloth, covered in a form of shredded black rubber that

happily resembled a vast number of sheep droppings. Along both walls – some twenty yards each – there were to be scale paintings of the Warrenpoint coast. The end-on thrust was surrounded by coloured bulbs and represented Johnson's Concert Hall – a former music hall in Warrenpoint – now, improbably, a girls' convent school.

The basic structure was up on the day we arrived. This kept my spirits up as I waited with Jim, the caretaker, for anyone to arrive for the grand read-through on the first day of rehearsals. After about fifteen minutes some half-dozen did turn up. "The other fifty should be here soon!"

There is no connection between commitment and punctuality in Warrenpoint. I am a martinet about punctuality in professional rehearsals, I'll stamp my foot and lock the door to latecomers. But this clearly isn't the way to behave to people giving up their free time to a community event. I did feel, however, a rising sense of panic in the first week – it seemed so hard just to get everyone there. There were still key parts to be cast, sixty yards of wall to be painted, script still to be re-written. Equally disconcerting, other things were ahead of events; Gerry Kelly had the sheep for me to inspect, and a museum of ancient implements that I couldn't imagine how to use. And the music – Colm Sands had written ten lovely songs – but who was going to accompany them? More to the point, who was going to sing them? The first week made me as tense as the production week of a West End show. Why was everyone so happy? Why were the people who did come along to rehearsals so obviously reassured by how

Meeting some of the cast, Warrenpoint, September 1988

organised everything was? I went through daily disorientation, always to finish in Bennett's Bar with Liz Boyle – the organiser of everything, and the warmest teetotaller I've ever known – mocking my anxiety, and saying we were ahead.

Well, I was a tired professional director used to running a rep, suddenly face to face with the roots of drama. Here was a community motivated to tell its story. Of course, nothing was sure or fixed – but everyone had agreed that they wanted it to happen – so it would happen! I suspect the tension I generated in the first ten days was invaluable. It got everything started. But by the third week it couldn't have been stopped. Liz knew her cast and her technical team and had full confidence.

The evening rehearsals grew from 7-9.30 pm to full five-hour affairs starting at 6 pm. Everyone was cast – 'could we squeeze in a few more enthusiasts?' Weekends, we worked flat out: all Saturday, and on Sundays, after a production meeting, we'd have our weekly run-through. Our first Sunday was the turning point for me. It was a sort of first read-through/blocking-cum-run-through all rolled into one epic afternoon-long social event. Eileen Kelly made hundreds of cups of tea, and dished out as many slabs of cake. The kitchen and bottom end of the rehearsal room became a spontaneous green room and a place of sometimes noisy reunion. During some of the songs, the rehearsal and the tea-party converged, and at one point everyone applauded Patricia Reilly singing 'Little Boy'. Just keeping on top of the afternoon's events was an exhilarating experience, and led to bringing the cast together for the show's final fifteen minutes.

It was the long first Sunday tea party that convinced me that we had got that spirit of the town on stage. A courtroom scene, the wake, and a final wedding were rethought to express Warrenpoint's most indisputable asset – that of being a town that enjoys itself.

Warrenpoint, uniquely for a town of its size, has staged its own annual panto for years. It even has a Panto Club. André Quinn and his father Jim build the sets; Liz Boyle produces it; and Christie McGuigan, the postman, writes it. Who could possibly be better placed than he to know all that goes on, but also skilled enough to incorporate all that happens in the Warrenpoint year, into the story of Aladdin? We had a number of local panto stars in *The Fair Day*, and also local legends from Newry, who (unprecedently) came to perform in a Warrenpoint show.

Sean Hollywood (and Mairead Murphy painting) in rehearsal for The Fair Day

And what performers! Sean Hollywood and Charlie Smith were as good as any actors I've worked with, while the young ones who played the lovers were natural forces on stage. I felt strongly that this corner of County Down is a cradle of theatrical talent. I mused that were this Spain or France there might be a long-established school and theatre that trained its gifted sons and daughters, creating its own particular brand of performer. Warrenpoint, so conveniently placed between Dublin and Belfast is a natural place for a theatre movement able to draw on influences from both North and South. If Galway can do it, why not Newry and Mourne?

For me, my working days were upside-down. Free till five, busy till midnight. Weekends frantic. 'Thank God it's Monday morning', we'd say. (Not so Liz Boyle, a full-time buyer at Reid International.) Of course, there was plenty to be done in the day, not least placating the ever-rising panic in the author, Patch Connolly. Patch was adopted when he was three by the Kelly family, so has an almost mystic love for Warrenpoint because it always seemed to him a matter of good chance that he turned up there at all, and found a family he loved so much. He was phobic about not letting anyone down. But his long and shaggy presence was always inspirational, benefitting now from the daily attentions of his hairdresser niece, Elizabeth, who was determined to make Patch the Writer an even more striking presence than Patch the Actor. Looking always somewhere between a comedian and a prophet, he hovered with just the right balance of intensity and levity, letting us know that this play was the most important thing in the whole world.

The final week of rehearsals was very creative and immensely enjoyable (this combination is rare). I was relaxed and confident the nearer the opening came. Very odd, but in Warrenpoint, I didn't have to worry about the performance having sufficient energy or adrenalin. Those usual professional worries were out. And the set and the costumes were being assembled around me as I worked. André Quinn really is a gifted builder and has a natural sense of design. I trusted him completely. And Mairead Murphy's massive wall painting of Carlingford Lough was a Sistine Chapel of a thing – staggeringly bold in its size and delicate in its execution. Cahill McAnulty's playing on the accordion was so assured that the music had an irresistible drive to it. The cast were now excited at the thought of a 'sensurround' production, and tickets were suddenly selling fast. In a community production the set and music and costumes coming together act upon the performers in an explicitly sensual way – an undisguised enthusiasm is shown that's quite opposite to the professional actor or director who gets tenser as everything comes together, because he knows that the first night and the critics are alarmingly near. All this heightened further my sense of normal theatrical life turned on its head.

On the eve of the first night, I remember Liz Boyle's sister Marie coming in with two bottles of champagne, full of praise for our afternoon preview. Patch and I were so touched by her words, we ended up painting the entire stage floor ourselves. They know how to get what they want, these County Down teetotallers.

The first night, and the hall was a picture to walk into. I just watched the faces of the public as they came through the door. Sixty or more people in '30s costumes, children and animals, the now five-piece band playing, signs evoking the old Warrenpoint hanging the length of the hall. A thoroughly relaxed cast mixed with everyone, and the audience looked full of delight and wonder. The one thing we couldn't estimate accurately was the optimum audience size. Over the first three nights the cast and audience found a natural 'rhythm', and an environmental production occurred, if not strictly a 'promenade'.

DIRECTING IN ANOTHER CULTURE

The space wasn't big enough for the latter – and by the third night there were too many people to permit much more than an elemental ebb and flow according to the staging. That said, I don't think anyone had seen anything quite like it before.

After the Civic Night on Tuesday, as many queued outside every night as actually got into the hall. They were there from 5.30pm. It was poor Liz Boyle, she who had steered the project from idea to reality, who was left to politely but firmly apologise. We were completely sold out. And no-one really believed this after so much 'come one, come all' publicity; despite an extra performance, there were still hundreds of local people being turned away. It's a shame it had to happen like that, but it would have been an even bigger shame if it hadn't.

I left after the Civic Night to go to India to direct *Hamlet*. It wrenched my soul to leave, so fond had I become of this exquisitely pretty town and its vivacious community. I think that Newry and Mourne has some of the loveliest countryside in Europe and I dearly wanted to stay. My daughter sobbed as we drove away crying 'go back, go back, Warr'npoint!' We all felt the same.

I'd love to return after doing Patch's excellent play (he was a happy man, I must add), and devise a piece of true 'story-telling theatre' with music. No town could do it better.

JR, Autumn 1988

Patch Connolly (author) and Liz Boyle (producer)

2 1988 (October – December)

NEW DELHI, INDIA

I flew to Delhi ahead of Renata and the children. Renata was directing a Barry Heath comedy at Oldham Coliseum for the new Artistic Director, Paul Kerryson, and I went out first to prepare *Hamlet*. My purpose was also to ensure that the accommodation would work for Hanna and Jack, and that we could locate a reliable source for food and the kind of medicine that we might need as a result of arriving somewhere so completely unfamiliar. My employer was the National School of Drama situated at the Sri Ram Centre in College Road, a leafy part of Delhi. I was there under the aegis of the British Council.

Here is a letter I wrote to Renata after my first days there:

> I'm just in from a long first day at the NSD (National School of Drama) and feeling lonely already, especially sitting here alone in the flat, with the old ceiling fan blowing the rice-paper pages on which I'm writing, but keeping me cool. I seem to have adapted to so many changes in such a short time. Everything is different – all my habits and customs seem to evaporate in the heat. I drink tea and lime soda all the time and I take everything gently.
>
> I have a young man called Ravinder who will cook for us. He studied our photos with deep fascination. He sees things in them one would not consider; the darkness of the Irish sky on the Spelga Dam, our car parked by the family tent; things like my driving licence intrigue him profoundly. We went shopping together and he watched the prices for every half-rupee I'm cheated and he reads out the name of the manufacturer and the address on the side of a bottle of chutney before he agrees to buy it.
>
> On Sunday night, I was taken to a beautiful open-air theatre across the road from the National School of Drama (NSD). The stage has an enormous tree in the centre that spreads over most of the acting area. It's just an earthen clearing with seating for 200. I was put in the front row between Sunita and Krishna, editors of a theatre magazine called ENACT. The play was Molière's *Le Bourgeoise Gentilhomme* and a couple of senior staff at the NSD had told me it was 'really awful' and only agreed to me seeing it because it was performed by the students who were to be in my *Hamlet*. It was in Hindi and it was 'Indianised'. It turned out to be a slice of high-energy rough theatre;

music was electric guitar, accordion and a very loud drum kit. The performance was wild and uninhibited in sections, yet always clear as a narrative and as a satire. Despite being hot and uncomfortable, I enjoyed it all. The actors are talented and all funny in their roles. They played those extended short-line Molière dialogues at express rate, always moving. Energy just poured out. And, it turns out, they rehearsed the whole show in twelve afternoons. A writer/director called Ranjit Kapoor adapted and directed it and I met him and his three-year-old son afterwards. I heard two comments about the show; Sunita, my front-row neighbour said, 'It's the first time I've really laughed in the theatre for fourteen years!' A young lecturer at the NSD (who had worked for Leeds TIE company) said, 'It's terrible. This is easy for the students. They are just having a good time. There is no aesthetic.' I'm not used to student theatre being as divisive as this. I sense they fear the anarchy of Molière. The audience laughed constantly through the show.

I went to the student 'mess' for dinner. A large bare room and a TV with Rajiv Ghandi speaking on it. I was issued an aluminium tray with recesses in it, veg curry in one part, curds in another, a little sauce in a third and a chapati in the fourth. And a glass of water. The students came in and I congratulated them on their electrifying performance. They looked sheepish. 'How did you feel it went?' I asked. In short, they didn't like it. They thought it was too crude and broad – too 'easy'. It seems this much sought-after 'rough theatre' is not much esteemed where it comes easily.

Then they asked about me. I talked. Then the only Christian Indian in the group, Kenneth, who has been brought up in English, told me that half the group could not understand English, especially my English. They could only understand 'Indian-English'. He said there is an interpreter at the NSD and it would not be a problem. With the help of Kenneth, I then talked about staging and costume and my way of working. This was approved, especially the bit about not sitting around talking, but talking as we worked. They said that they would need voice training if they were to perform outside again. (Their voices were powerful and crystal-clear in the Molière.) They are very interesting, quite the strongest group of young people I've met, both in opinion and expression. They want to be really stretched and they will have their say. Kenneth said that they'd had such a rough ride in the last two years because of staff changes at the NSD, that they were now very clear on what they wanted. The girls are as confident and outspoken as the boys. They debate with seeming ferocity. I'm very intrigued.

> The next day, we meet for our first rehearsal morning – it turns out that they do want to talk about *Hamlet* before we start. They have twice seen the wonderful 1964 Russian film of *Hamlet*, directed by Grigoriy Kozintsev. This will be hard to follow because I think it is the best account of the play ever made, in any medium. They bring in an ancient record of Gielgud doing it and are stupefied by how it sounds. We also listen to Olivier, text in hand, which they like more. The thing is – I am a lot more nervous than I look, not because of them but because of the play itself. I have studied it and read a lot about it, but directing it in another language is another matter. If I had already done the play before it would be daunting enough – but I have to grasp the life of this play in Hindi..."
>
> Letter home from 25 Defence Colony, New Delhi, 17.10.88

Grey linen – John and Renata at the NSD, November 1988

Rehearsals went ahead and Renata and the children arrived three weeks after me. I have a picture of Hanna and Jack having a 'bath' in two plastic buckets, a red one and a blue one.

Renata worked on vocal exercises with the cast every morning. The only dispute that I had with the company was the way that the actors spoke to stage management, shouting at them to move a chair or bring a prop. This was a shock, coming from a more democratic system (so democratic, on the fringe, that actors sometimes would shout at *directors* to get a clear instruction, instead of yet another question). The caste system produced a powerfully opinionated company who were not afraid to disagree amongst themselves or to slag off each other's performance. Of course, this breaks a fundamental protocol of ensemble work. And I could only follow the tone, not the content, of these shouted orders to the stage management and the endless bickering between the actors.

These shows had big casts, 30 in *The Fair Day* and 20 in *Hamlet*. I've always thought of myself as facilitator-director rather than a demon-headmaster-director. I'd never thought that a voice of power and depth was a necessary attribute in creating successful productions.

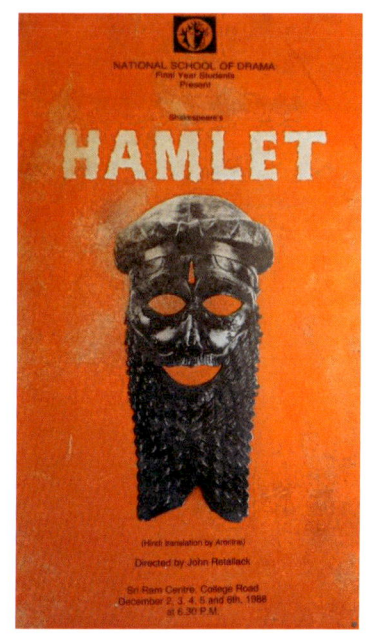

Delhi was a much tougher call than Warrenpoint. The actors were united in their desire to act but divided in almost everything else. I have never seen a group argue so much with each other. To prevail in the room and to just move the rehearsal on, you had to 'command attention'. However much I wanted to do it quietly or discreetly, no one would have heard me. By the time we got to the technical for *Hamlet*, the cast became stressed and even more argumentative. And since the technical took place outdoors, audibility became a vital factor in the final days before we opened. I maintained control and delivered a robust production but I can't say that I liked my new 'commanding' style very much. I seldom took on large-scale projects after that and I avoided opera. If you have those responsible for lighting, costume, set design, movement, voice and production sitting *behind* you, and 25 actors in front of you, directing becomes a true test of personal confidence, especially when a scene is going badly and repeatedly not working. Some directors thrive in this kind of pressure and they (deservedly) make a lot of money for doing so. I like to think *with* the actors, not for them, and so I like a peaceful and collaborative rehearsal room.

Loath to return immediately to our house in Oldham, I looked around to see if there was somewhere we could stay on in India for the rest of December. At the invitation of the Kala Academy in Panjim, Goa, I did a workshop production of *Macbeth* over a two-week period. This provided accommodation for the four of us and, because the workshops took place

Hamlet, December 1988

in the evenings, plenty of time on the beautiful black sand beaches of hippy Goa. This was a holiday break for all of us and we arrived back in Oldham on Christmas Eve, 1988, with just enough time to get to the butchers in Springhead and buy a turkey.

3 1997/1999

AMSTERDAM, HOLLAND

I became a freelance theatre director in January 1999 and I had no idea what I was going to do next. I had left Oxford Stage Company of my own accord; I hadn't fallen out with the board or the team. In fact, 1998 was a good year – *Junk* won the TMA Best Show for Young People's award and *A Midsummer Night's Dream* and Arnold Wesker's *Roots* both had a great critical reception.

Ruth Jones, Sally Mates, Samantha Spiro, Jack Chissick, Gerard Fletcher, Angela Ridgeon in *Roots* at Watford Palace Theatre and on tour

But my interest had turned decisively towards new work for young audiences. I was deeply influenced by what Wederzijds did, year in, year out. Ad de Bont and this company were the key influence behind my decision to leave Oxford Stage Company after ten years.

Here is the key extract from their Artistic Policy:

Bringing theatre to the place where children and adults live and work together, day in, day out, expresses our thoughts and

feelings that theatre should be a feature of everyday life and our belief that art and culture are not sacred terms to be expressed in special buildings (theatres/museums/concert halls, etc), but which should be made available everywhere where there are people. In fact, we would go one step further in our belief, in that we consider the role of theatre to be strengthened if, during a performance in a sports hall or a classroom, the "miracle" occurs: gradually, bit by bit, this everyday room is transformed into a world in which wonderful extraordinary events take place. Events which throw an unexpected light on something that before was difficult to see or even completely invisible.

I was brought up in a school, had been trained as a teacher and taught in schools – schools were my habitat. These subversive words struck a deep chord in me.

I also had begun to do freelance work for Wederzijds. In April 1997, they had invited me to do a staged reading of Helen Edmundson's play *The Clearing* (1993), a very modern play about Cromwell's 'clearances' in Ireland. 'Clearances' is a euphemism for genocide, just as 'ethnic cleansing' was being used at the time in the Balkan wars. Later, in 1999, I returned to Holland and directed a full-length version of the play for a 10-week tour of North Holland schools. But it was the 1997 reading, two years before I left Oxford Stage Company, that directly influenced my decision to resign and to set off on an entirely new journey in theatre.

We had two weeks to rehearse the reading in 1997. Although it was meant to be a 'reading', all the Dutch cast learnt their lines in English. With Helen Edmundson's permission, I cut the play to 90 minutes, no interval. It was bare boards – just a couple of chairs when they were needed. No costume design, just clothes the actors owned that suited the 'line' and status of the character. There was alertness and urgency in the rehearsals because we all knew that a new Wederzijds event at the annual Kunst Junior festival would be packed out. Especially this one, as there was only one performance.

Dutch actors are used to eight weeks rehearsal for their major shows. Their pace is more relaxed. They bring their own lunch box to rehearsal and all sit round and chat during their breaks. English actors, at that time, might need to call their agent and prefer a breather from each other – they are more likely to buy a sandwich and a coffee from Pret. In Amsterdam, there is a calmer atmosphere to that I was used to. All of them had worked together before. Yet the very emotional nature of the play pushed them hard. Dutch theatre is very intelligent, inventive and original. It is also quite controlled.

Ilya and Bente in rehearsal for *The Clearing*

They were new to the big life-and-death emotions that build over a full-length play. (Few plays in their repertoire exceed an hour in length.) They wanted the challenge that *The Clearing* offered and I was impressed by the seriousness with which they went about it.

After two weeks, the acting company de-camped to Den Bosch, an old and beautiful city, 50 miles from Amsterdam, in the Catholic part of Holland, where at that time the Kunst Junior festival always took place. The festival is timed to coincide with the café terraces opening after the long winter. For many, this is the first open-air coffee or beer of the year. In April 1997, it was sunny and warm and there were shows on all day long. *The Clearing* was to take place in a gym, familiar territory for this company of actors. I arranged the 150 chairs as best I could, to create a thrust stage – that is, the playing area was surrounded on three sides, enabling most of the audience to see the action clearly. Then Ad de Bont came in.

'Why don't you make a clearing?' he said.

I paused, seeing what he meant and being alarmed by it – the performance was to take place in three hours' time.

'This is how the actors know it', I said, 'it's a bit late to put it in the round. Isn't it?'

'Let's try', he said, and I knew that I'd already lost the argument.

He, I and the actors re-configured the 150 chairs in 10 minutes. I put in four entrances. Ilya, who played the main role of Maddie, said very calmly,

'We need to work quite fast.'

We re-blocked the entire show in an hour – and then we ran it quickly, right up to the moment the audience arrived to grab their seats.

Of course, it worked brilliantly. Ad had seen it all as he walked into the gym and everyone knew it wasn't worth arguing. He would be right.

There is nothing better to make an ensemble alert in their minds and quick on their feet than *change*. The circle of chairs brought out the meaning of the play twice over – and the aesthetic of the staging perfectly suited this event. There is a law (written in the sky) that all performances that are done only once, work beautifully. At the end of the 90 minutes, there was an explosion of applause and the company was – as so often with Wederzijds – the hit of the festival. Suzanne Osten, artistic director of Unga Klara in Stockholm, went straight to Ad and told him that he had to tour this production as a matter of urgency. Helen Edmundson was also present.

For the first time, I felt an actual part of what I had admired so intensely on my visits to Dutch theatre for young people since 1992. Directing *Mirad* with Jeremy and Sinead had shown that English acting could bring real illumination to a Dutch text. This event gave me confidence that English directing had something to offer Dutch actors too. If you asked me what that something is, I would say it is our deep familiarity with Shakespeare and the profound emotional and intellectual challenges that his plays make on the actor and director.

I returned in the summer of 1999, now a freelancer, to direct *The Clearing* in a full-scale production – that is, we rehearsed for eight weeks, not two, there was a full touring set and costumes, a specially composed sound track and an education programme. There was even real grass in the clearing. Ad decided the play would be in English – after all, teenagers were used to TV and cinema in English, why not a play? There was a long tour ahead and I saw only the opening performances and then returned for the final two. Yet I already felt that the production was nothing like as good as the version done in a circle with no props, no costumes, no soundtrack and no grass.

The staging was more cumbersome, the experience more conventional and the actors were nothing like as free to tell Edmundson's brilliantly dramatised story as they had been two years earlier. What we had done in ten days in 1997 was immaculate. This 1999 production exposed how the trappings of orthodox theatre can suffocate flow, communication, pace, immediacy – and the imagination of the audience. The fact that it was in English was tough on Dutch adolescents; there is so much *talking* in theatre!

In hindsight, we ought to have toured the original festival version – in Dutch.

4 1999

BERGEN, NORWAY

Bergen is on a smaller scale to Amsterdam. It is set dramatically in a natural port surrounded by seven mountains. Like Gdańsk, it has been a sea-trading port for a thousand years. It is the second city of Norway and it rains as much as Glasgow, perhaps even more. I had never been there until I received a call from Neil Wallace in Amsterdam asking me if I would be interested in directing two Beckett plays (*Footfalls* and *Rockabye*) for the Bergen Festival the following May. I said yes. As it was now mid-December, he told me that I needed to fly out to Bergen in the next few days and meet Bergliot Jonsdottir, the Icelandic director of the Bergen Festival.

A brief digression: I had got to know Neil Wallace in Glasgow. He, with Bob Palmer, was one of the prime movers behind Glasgow becoming the first City of Culture in 1988. At the time, everyone was sceptical about this city being able to bring off such a prestigious challenge. The festival was an outstanding success. Neil created the biggest scoop – he got Peter Brook over from France for the only British performances of the great director's masterpiece, *The Mahabharata*. Like many other theatre people, I made the pilgrimage to Glasgow's former bus depot, the Tramshed, to sit for three interval-free hours and absorb this exotic and beautiful work. Everything about it was on a scale that British audiences hadn't seen before and Neil was the mastermind behind bringing it to the UK. Glasgow earned the respect it

Neil Wallace, Amsterdam, 1995

deserved from that day on. Subsequently, Neil moved to Amsterdam, learned to speak Dutch and ran his own operation, Offshore, a production company for international theatre projects. I thought of him as 'a performing arts dealer' and that is what he was – passionate about theatre and even more passionate about classical music.

So, of course, he was, amongst many other roles, an advisor to the Bergen Festival, famed as much for its music as its theatre. In 1999 Bergliot had put together a programme that mixed a lot of Beckett and Bach with the work of contemporary composers. The major theatre visit was Fiona Shaw performing in Deborah Warner's adaptation of TS Eliot's *The Wasteland*. The feel of this *fin-de-siecle* festival year was existential, questioning and severe. I felt honoured to be invited to contribute to it.

I flew out to Bergen just before Christmas, 1998. There was thick snow on the ground and every window had a candle in it. I was greeted by Bergliot and taken to the Neptune Hotel in the centre of the city. I was introduced to Bentein Baardson, (Director of the National Theatre in Bergen – Den Scene Nationale) who I would get to know very well over the next couple of years. Bergliot was intense, nervous and dressed always in black. Since she employed artists from all over the world, she took calls on a 24/7 basis. Bentein smoked incessantly, even as he ate. I had only just given up cigarettes and my resolve didn't last long in his company. Bergliot was clearly the genius

Leprosy Museum, Bergen (Lepramuseet)

behind the extensive music programme but she looked to Bentein to oversee the festival's own theatre productions.

During the meal, Bentein explained that the two Beckett plays were to be staged in the city's former Leprosy Hospital. The building is an 18th century wooden structure, kept exactly as it was in the latter part of the 19th century, when lepers lived together at close quarters, shielded from the general public. It is a dark building, without heating, full of ghosts and a fit setting for Beckett's *Rockaby* and *Footfalls*, two plays that each hover between life and death.

The leprosy hospital is the coldest place I have ever worked and the most depressing. It was a good choice for a visitor to watch a play by Beckett but a tough ambience to work in for a month. The rooms were scrubbed and hard but the agony of those who had been incarcerated there remained ever-present.

I had never directed Beckett before. These two plays are as sealed in to themselves as the hospital was to its patients. There is no historical research to do, no 'interpretation' to make, no improvising 'around the text'. The stage directions are precise, exacting and admit no deviation of any kind. I have never felt in such a servile relationship to a dramatist. With enough concentration for short periods, I and the actress could reproduce in three dimensions what Beckett demanded on the page. He leaves nothing to chance. He is utterly insistent about what he wants.

Here is a sample from *Footfalls*:

Strip: downstage, parallel with front, length nine steps, width one metre, a little off-centre audience right.
Pacing: starting with right foot (r), from right (R) to left (L), with left foot (l) from L to R.
Turn: rightabout at L, left about at R.
Steps: clearly audible rhythmic tread.
Lighting: dim, strongest at floor level, less on body, least on head.
Voices: both low and slow throughout.

My preparation was done mostly on my frequent flights to and from Bergen. I would open the two short texts (neither play is longer than 20 minutes) and read them again and again. I felt like a dog going around and around a steel fence, seeking somewhere to break in. I came close to knowing the plays by heart myself but that brought me no nearer their meaning. Norwegian is a beautiful soft language to listen to and naturally captures Beckett's insistent rhythms. The most appropriate audience for these plays would have been the former patients who lived here. So profound is Beckett's feeling for those who exist in a twilight state that they would have understood his words (from *Rockabye*) immediately:

> *so in the end*
> *close of a long day*
> *went down*
> *let down the blind and down*
> *right down*
> *into the old rocker*
> *and rocked*
> *rocked*
> *saying to herself*
> *no*
> *done with that*
> *the rocker*
> *those arms at last*
> *saying to the rocker*
> *rock her off*
> *stop her eyes*
> *fuck life*
> *stop her eyes*
> *rock her off*
> *rock her off*
>
> *slow fade out*

Ruth Tellefsen in *Rockabye*

BERGEN FESTIVAL

In the festival evenings, I had a season ticket to a wonderful range of musical and dramatic work. I worked on and off for Bergliot for three years – I organised several concerts, installations and a banquet. I directed two opening ceremonies for the King and Queen of Norway. Everything was a high-stakes one-off event and I enjoyed the tension and drama of these occasions.

Benthein read my adaptation of *Junk* and decided that he wanted to produce a Norwegian version at Den Nationale Scene – and he wanted me to direct it. I asked him how much was the fee. He said, '£12,000', which was a lot at that time, 'plus full expenses, accommodation and per diems.' 'Very good,' I said, happy to accept, but he interrupted to say, 'but if you are English … you get twice as much.' My heart beat a little faster. 'You mean …?' 'Yes, £24,000 – will you do it?' 'Let me have a think,' I said. But l couldn't hold a straight face any longer. 'Of course, I'll do it, Bentein.'

It was far more than I had ever been paid before for a single show. £24k was a year's salary and it took away the worry about the freelance year – and I would have enough to bring my family over for ten days. The rehearsals were nine weeks.

This was my first job in the new century; rehearsals began on January 2nd 2000. The rehearsal day was 11am to 4pm, coinciding with daylight hours in mid-winter. At this time of the year there were no tourists in Bergen. It was dark, wet and lonely. I can't pretend it had the same buzz to direct the show for a second time – in Norwegian. The company were quieter and nervous of getting it wrong. But this was my first-ever year when I was dependant on freelance work and I wanted to do it well.

Working in these countries gets lonely at times, no longer surrounded by a company, by actors or by family. I communicated with Renata via daily rambling faxes, most of which have now faded to illegibility, like ancient documents. The aloneness was a challenge and it intensified a sense that all this travel had better be worth it – Renata was looking after our family single-handed while I was away. I don't think I ever missed them so much as during this period.

Renata came out with Hanna and Jack for the promised ten days in 2000. I'd saved my ludicrously high expenses for their visit and we went on various extravagant events and trips that were intended to make up for my prolonged absence from home. I told Renata that I had been invited to apply to be artistic director of the Bergen National Theatre. She was horrified at the thought of us moving to Norway. 'Do you think you'll manage here on your own?' she said.

I spent enough time alone in Bergen directing *Junk* to know I *wouldn't* manage there on my own. I filled the time left over from my very short rehearsal days learning to operate a computer for the first time. Benthein Baardson's secretary taught me the rudiments of MS Word and I increased the little knowledge that I had by adapting Camus' novel *The Plague* into a stage script for production at Dundee Rep later in the year. Sometimes bright days were so rare that I would run out during the lunch break and walk up the hillside near the theatre just to enjoy a few precious minutes of sunlight.

On March 5th, the opening night, the theatre was packed with civic dignitaries. I think they were bemused by *Junk* and wondered why they were invited to see it. Bentein went through all the 'national premiere' rituals of flowers and champagne on stage for the benefit of the audience. Given that *Junk* is the story is of two children whose lives are destroyed through heroin addiction, pouring champagne over them seemed an odd celebration of their performances – at least it was to Melvyn Burgess who had flown out to see the opening night. The champagne moment was all over the front page of the news-starved Bergen paper the next day; Bentein knew what he was doing.

I was more than happy to go home. I was finding it increasingly difficult to sleep in this day/night world.

Black on black; Bentein and Bergliot, May 1999

After I left, I missed Bentein's company – I enjoyed how much he talked and his fluency on every aspect of Norwegian history. I think running the theatre in Bergen tormented him with the endless round of meetings and speeches. Like his famous father, he was a gifted actor. I think directing plays engaged him and vexed him in equal measure. He was detached in some way from all he did. As I lack this quality, I admired it in him. I was very touched on one occasion when he said to me, 'I am so happy I learned to know you.' Those exact words. He had a most beautiful office, all parquet floor, leather seats and brass handles, with a view over the town and the water. The whole building was beautiful, exquisitely preserved and polished. Essentially, Bentein was a freelance soul in a very traditional organisation.

If Wederzijds gave me an overall sense of direction, it was in Bergen I found the time to conceive what a new company in England might look like. When I got back to London, I started work on forming a company that promoted new European writing for young people. I recall Bergen as a peaceful state of mind, where the combination of water, sky and music encouraged me to reflect more on life than I had done before. It was a mid-life retreat, much stimulated by conversations with Bentein.

From a letter to Renata, May 9th, 1999

'... Norway is a much less complicated place culturally and historically than home ... it must be the only country I know without some kind of subtext ... at least I don't know what it is if there is one at all. It's such a practical and challenging landscape, there's no need to let things fester, it's just so exhilarating to be outdoors here. Everyone skis and sails. Being out in this very fresh and cold air – in hot sun – makes you feel marvellous ... at the end of my run this morning I felt I'd live to be a 100! Everything seems so visible to me. I can see that Ibsen and Munch could put things more nakedly and more brightly, just because there is no complicating subtext. Men and women, people and nature, this world and the legendary world ... it's all so absolutely vivid here that people expect strong clear plays or vivid striking pictures ... how would you do them any other way? And yet this country has been the operating table on which extreme emotions were analysed and explored. It is strangely different to Scotland which has its problems with being clear and direct. Norway is a plain-speaking place, noble, vast and peaceful ...'

Den Nationale Scene, Bergen, January 2000, (signed by Bentein) with its statue of Ibsen

5 2000

SCOTLAND

Before I could focus on forming a new company, I had two shows to produce in Scotland: my adaptation of Camus' *The Plague* for Dundee Rep and, immediately after, Renata's play *Santa and Nicolas* for the Macrobert in Stirling. *The Plague* was a good adaptation – I have a letter from Catherine Camus, the late author's daughter to say that she felt it was the best dramatisation that she had read of her father's novel. Sad to say, the production wasn't as good as I had dreamt it to be when writing it through the Bergen winter.

The ensemble at Dundee took against me from the first reading – they were mostly 'senior' actors and the main male role of the young Dr Rieux went to a newcomer. The older members of the company all played smaller roles or were in the chorus that I created to represent the city of Oran. It was good to have 15 actors on stage but it was a grim and near-humiliating experience for me. Right from the start, the actors would play to the letter the non-smoking rule in rehearsals by standing in the corridor and saying the words from the open door while they smoked a cigarette. Some 'worked to rule' (if they had a choric role) while those with more substantial parts worked with more energy. It was uphill work all the way. I was a visiting artist; the Artistic Director of the theatre made the house rules.

By the time the technical arrived, the production manager and his team took the same approach. I had to endure blanks and sulks all around me. This had never happened to me before and it never happened again. I cringe to recall how much it hurt my pride at the time.

I felt like the John Mills character in *Tunes of Glory* in which an English officer is blanked by a Scottish regimental mess, led by Alec Guinness. Like Mills, I preserved a stiff upper lip. I kept my head up and I didn't acknowledge how it made me feel. Maybe I should have done but I was a guest for a month in their theatre. If this was their response to me, then so be it. I'd be gone in a few days. I did as professional a job as I could, fulfilled my obligation to do newspaper interviews and beat it after the first night, the last day of my contract.

It's the first and last show that I never watched again after the opening night.

The production divided critics; after such a heavy experience, I quote *The Guardian*:

Elizabeth Mahoney
THE GUARDIAN
16 October 2000

John Retallack's adaptation of *La Peste* is a darkly gorgeous thing. Like a Hopper painting brought to choreographed life, pestilence never looked so lovely. In the novel, plague has gripped a city, which becomes a major character. The challenge for Retallack was to give a sense of this while making his drama an engaging story of individuals. This he has achieved through the use of music (Bach, Brel, Messiaen) and dance as a symbolic backdrop. The company, representing the city, moves in line, using jerky movements to suggest the monotony of life during the plague, the horror when it has a hold over them. They swoop to the city's gates as they close, shutting them in; they swarm through the streets, like the rats spreading disease underground ... Plague looks on, her lips twisted, the colour of blood.

Santa and Nicolas in Stirling was a much happier show. Working with a young dance troupe and four actors, this Christmas play was a show that told the story of a young boy in Scotland who set off on an adventure on the night of Christmas Eve to meet Babushka in Russia to discover what Christmas is really all about. The dancers created a beautiful, tempting but dangerous experience taking Nicholas into the deepest frost to meet Babushka. This alternative Christmas story was commissioned by the ever-innovative Liz Moran, then director of the Macrobert Arts Centre.

Renata, author of the play, came up and joined me on weekends. We've always enjoyed working together and it was a blessed relief after the misery of *The Plague*. Hanna and Jack came up for the opening and I remember a walk on a deserted winter beach and seeing how much (never mind the theatre) they loved these jaunts to distant places.

It took two years of living as a freelance director to convince me that it was better to have full control of production rather than be at the mercy of another director's play choice and casting. I'd now worked in Norway, Holland and Scotland and I was becoming an absentee father and partner. But to gain control of production I would have to found a new company; and that takes a lot of energy and time. To live at home and achieve this goal, I would have to earn very little money for a spell; perhaps eighteen months or two years. This is what Renata and I discussed next – in fresh surroundings.

6 2000

PARIS: TO FREELANCE OR NOT TO FREELANCE?

After so many separations, Renata and I took a long weekend in Paris. We had had precious little time together. We knew what we were doing that year but 2001 onwards was a complete blank. Later, we referred to this spring visit as the 'Paris summit'.

We discovered the newly renovated Canal St Martin and walked along past settings evocative of French movies like *Hôtel du Nord*, stopping at cafes and bistros en route. We had lovely spring weather and we ended up at Place de la Republique, after much strolling and meandering conversation around the topic. We agreed that I would not go down the conventional route of applying for another straight rep or touring job. Rather I would set up a new company which would have its own mission and programme, dedicated to new work for children and young people.

I knew the name for the company from a 'moment' crossing London Bridge a few months before: Company of Angels. Given that we had no money to invest in this company, only our time, it expressed a hope that we would find support; the name also referred to a vision of a group of artists, inspired too by this area of work, who would form a loose, but nevertheless committed, alliance to do great work in this field. At the time, there were very few good companies that we felt could produce a show that might excite or interest a modern teenager.

When the name Company of Angels came to me on London Bridge, I had a real palpitation of excitement. I felt that I must live up to this 'instruction' to found a company with this name. Renata said that she was prepared to share this risk too.

I felt that we could go ahead and apply for some funding from the Arts Council and London Arts.

Over the ten years that I led Company of Angels, the situation changed; my company became one of several taking a fresh approach to theatre for young people. I also wanted to do something first-hand. Directors express themselves through other people. Ad de Bont had shown me that there is a true artistic freedom in writing for young audiences. A play for young people did not have to be a 'lesson' in anything, it could simply be a play.

Here is a diary entry about a recurring feeling that I had experienced on the journey home from Holland, having spent time with Ad and the Wederzijds company.

> **Note to self**
>
> **16 May 2000**
>
> Sometimes I feel that I become caught between the fact that I set out to be a teacher, quite happy with that expectation; and then I became a theatre director. And that created new expectations and possibilities I was even happier with.
>
> But something's gone missing on the way, and it's my own self, me, my inner flame whatever that was and is and will be – it's not as bright as it was. I find myself so dissatisfied inside despite doing such conspicuously interesting work on the outside. I find I am often working in a rush with insufficient independence or individuality.
>
> And theatre goes past with so much energy and not a ripple is left on the water. I feel low and I want to hibernate. I want to take two or three years to come up with one profound idea and have something to show for it. I want more relaxation, more travel, exercise, more time with Renata and Hanna & Jack – then I will not think, at 60, of all my 'wasted time working'.
>
> I would so like to concentrate on one or two things – not 99 different ones. I feel there is not enough to show for the years running OSC. I'll leave it one day and someone will dig it up and re-plant it. There will be no trace left. I'd like to make time pass more slowly.
>
> I want to write a play myself.

7
WRITING PLAYS
Company of Angels, 2000-2011

INTRODUCTION

It was early 1999. I'd left Oxford Stage Company. I was at home on a weekday, thumbing through a huge stash of A4 black and white photos of former OSC productions. Some of them were nearly ten years old. There were so many on my lap that their weight caused them to slip and they fell all around me on the floor. I looked down on them, irritated that I would have to put them in order again. I thought, as I looked at them, spread out before me in no order at all that this was the trouble with directing. All of this work is past and forgotten now; look at how these beautiful pictures flow around me like so many leaves on a stream. Theatre is ephemeral by nature and you have to BE THERE to experience it – no recording captures the full impact of the live experience. It's so immediately over. And a really great ensemble performance is always so hard to recapture, night after night. Why else would all those great directors, mentioned earlier, repeatedly watch their companies perform the same show? Because we are all trying to pin down the incredibly ephemeral nature of live performance.

I wanted to do something with theatre that was more hands-on, more lasting, somehow less ephemeral.

This was all caught up with the early death of my mother, some fifteen years earlier. She had died suddenly at the age of 62 and I wanted to create something lasting for her. I think I wanted to give her a book of my unwritten plays. I didn't feel that these wonderful black and whites were enough to show what I had been doing since her passing. I could do better. I could go deeper. It was time to open up. Never mind my father's discouragement when I was 25 – this time it would be for my mum.

I was also married to a powerful dramaturg. Renata taught A level Drama at nearby St Dunstan's and she knew John Truby's *22 Steps* by heart. Truby is one of the best American theorists of dramatic structure, a subject that I intuitively avoided and had shown no interest in whatsoever. Yet, as I came up with my first idea for a play, she responded with a key question about what happened next – and further questions followed – what is the obstacle, what does your character want, who is actually your protagonist – all specific questions that I begrudgingly went away to consider further.

By the time I had completed the first draft of my first play (aged 50) it was her rightful boast that it contained every one of Truby's 22 steps – including the dark tunnel.

I needed money if I was to make this first play happen and I pitched it some time before I had worked through Truby's steps.

Pitching a play and writing it are very different states of mind.

HANNAH AND HANNA, 2000
Channel Theatre Company

I took my pitch to Judith Hibberd at South-East Arts. (She was a colleague who had helped a lot with the PAL labs in Kent and been a supporter of my productions at Oxford Stage Company.) I told her briefly my idea for a play, about two girls, one a refugee from Kosovo, one who lives in Margate. The two enter a bitter conflict which has a surprising resolution. Margate was key because it was in the region for which Judith was responsible. She said that she would nominate it for a project grant on the condition that I directed it. She put me in touch with Channel Theatre Company in Margate who later agreed on the collaboration.

At the time, I agonised about the pitch. I'd driven to Tunbridge Wells (where the South-East Arts office was) and got out of the car still not knowing what to call this play or what the action of the play really was. At the time, my daughter Hanna's best friend's name was Hannah and they were both around the house a lot. *Hannah and Hanna*…the title arrived in my head as I put coins in the slot of the parking meter. The pitch came in a rush as I climbed the steps to the offices. I waited in the foyer and jotted down the headlines. Judith came in after a few minutes and I was ready.

We needed the commission and we needed the money – the Norwegian money was going fast because we had just bought a house in south-east London. We kept going for a time on Renata's salary and a year of record-low earnings from me. When the time came to pay the tax that year, I remember using my credit card for the entire payment. The whole period was high-risk, especially after the relative wealth of the year before.

I spent the spring of 2000 writing *Hannah and Hanna*, mostly at home – and testing it out on occasional trips to Margate with Leisa Rea, a friend and a brilliant workshop leader. We would go into local secondary schools and set up improvisations with 14- and 15-year-olds. They enacted numerous scenarios and all came back to one essential conflict – us versus the Kosovans. Kosovans were thieves, whores, they ripped off the NHS and stole from supermarkets, they had numerous children and all the men wore Rolex. They all had mobile phones too, a major status symbol to Margate teenagers at this time.

The demonisation of Kosovans came from the racism they heard at home – yet these children were as innocent as the refugees they cursed. They knew about Margate and that was all they knew. When we got back to London from those workshops, I realised I wanted to write a play about the Margate teenager as much as I wanted to write about the Kosovan refugee. The Kosovans had been on the front pages of the papers the previous year, thousands in exodus from their country, burnt to the ground by the Serbians. Thanks to the military intervention instructed by Tony Blair, they were now here in Britain and being housed in a variety of towns and cities, including defunct hotels on the South Coast and tower blocks in Glasgow. Their presence excited compassion and loathing in equal measure. In Margate I saw National Front demonstrations and in Glasgow I marched with many residents who welcomed the Kosovans to their city.

When I wrote the play, teenagers in schools in Britain were told very little about why large groups of people from other countries arrived overnight. All they knew is that they were 'asylums', people from nowhere. National and local community leaders showed little interest in 'introducing' these strangers to the local community. In school classrooms, pupils sometimes did not know what country the boy or girl in the next desk was actually from.

How could a local Margate teenager – in that climate – ever meet, let alone befriend, a Kosovan teenager who'd survived the invasion of her country and ended up in Margate? And at what point, supposing that a friendship did develop, would two girls open up to each other? Were there any circumstances that could bring about a real and unprompted exchange between them?

I wanted to acknowledge the role of us, the British audience, in the drama of the refugee. 'We' are the hosts who determine the fate of such people; they are our guests. 'We' are central characters, not onlookers and outsiders. To the asylum seekers, 'we' are the main players. That's why I started with two teenagers; they mimic the attitudes of their parents and guardians, yet, unlike their parents, they still have time to change their minds.

We went to Margate to make the show; Channel Theatre provided a beautiful rehearsal space and organised a tour of the region. There was an enforced break in the middle of rehearsals because I had to go to Bergen for a week. I was deeply grateful because it gave me time to catch up with all the re-writes the script needed. Writing the dialogue of teenagers worked when I was at home but Alyson Coote (Hannah), a working-class South London girl herself, kept saying it *better* every time she made a mistake on the rehearsal floor – and Celia Meiras (Hanna), a part-Spanish Londoner, kept reminding me how a young girl might actually feel about what had happened to her as she escaped Kosovo. In Bergen, I re-wrote the last section of the play.

The key quality of *Hannah and Hanna* is that the two girls share a love of, and a talent for, karaoke. Both actresses sang exceptionally well, especially together. Nathalie Imbruglia's *Torn* was a highlight. The songs are what bring them together and why the Margate Hannah is rejected by her gang – they cannot tolerate her making friends with an asylum-seeker. They treat and punish her as if she was an asylum-seeker herself. Towards the end of the play, the Margate Hannah jumps aboard a lorry going to Pristina with the Kosovan Hanna in the front seat, innocent of Hannah's presence. They reunite, and separate, on Kosovan soil. Margate Hannah is 16 and without a passport. She can't stay and Kosovan Hanna can't return to Margate. Their last song together is their final parting.

The play opened to controversy in the local paper – the town council had given some money to asylum-seekers for them to see the show. The first night at Margate Theatre Royal saw a tiny touring set on the big stage of one of the country's oldest theatres. In the stalls were most of the local police force who formed the backbone of the amateur dramatic society at that time. In the dress circle sat a range of asylum seekers and refugees from all over the area. The representatives of the National Front and BNP who'd turned

Hannah and Hanna, Celia Meiras and Alyson Coote, July 2001

up to object to the play, and the presence of the asylum-seekers, kept their distance outside the theatre. The show went ahead without interruption and was given an exceptionally warm-hearted reception.

Hannah and Hanna also helped to keep me going financially. I directed a French version in Brussels; a Swedish company performed it 200 times; it was translated into Hebrew, Portuguese, German, Swedish, Japanese and Dutch; it won a Herald Angel at Edinburgh, a Race in the Media award and was nominated for TMA best show for young people; it was broadcast on the World Service and published by Oberon; the British Council sent it out on three separate tours of India and the Far East; most importantly, it kept touring the UK and bringing a steady income to my new company.

The success of the play also allowed me to form what I had been planning since I left Oxford Stage Company – a company that would promote new and experimental work for young audiences. By the end of the year, I registered *Company of Angels* as a charity and took on a board of trustees.

THE SCOTSMAN /Joyce McMillan

Hannah and Hanna emerges as one of the most timely and significant shows on this year's fringe. Its simple staging is beautifully assured and well crafted, particularly in its seamless knitting-together of music and action. It offers a notably sharp, thoughtful pen-portrait of new wave British fascism. Alyson Coote and Celia Meiras give absolutely luminous performances...and finally the sheer human ordinariness of their teen friendship, set against so much hatred, is tremendously moving.

THE HERALD/ Mary Brennan

John Retallack's play could just as easily have been set in Glasgow's Sighthill, any place where asylum seekers find themselves in conflict with local residents. It's in yer face, abrasive, yet genuinely fresh and irresistibly funny. Everything conspires to prise the friends apart. Coote and Meiras make the heartbreak transparent ... lots of us cry, because we know it's happening somewhere for real. It's an outstanding piece of honest, inspiring theatre.

COMPANY OF ANGELS, 2000-2011

In Ad de Bont's work for Wederzijds I found a depth of thought and a stylistic flair that I was familiar with from growing up and competing in a theatre world whose standards in England were set – for me – by Mike Alfred's Shared Experience, Theatre de Complicite, Cheek by Jowl, Deborah Warner's Kick Theatre Company and in France and Germany by Ariane Mnouchkine, Peter Brook and Peter Stein. These were my lasting formative influences. ATC (1978–1985) and Oxford Stage Company (1989-1999) were shaped by watching the work of these companies and through meeting and knowing some of the directors in question. They were my 'gold standard'.

But none of these great directors and companies made work for children. If the books I read to my children were so good, written and published in England, why were they not matched by a similar achievement in the performing arts? Why was funding so low and why was there such limited respect for this genre of theatre work? All the brilliant companies that I mention above played overseas and were known in Europe – but an English company at a young people's theatre festival in Europe was a rare sight.

My surprise in discovering the very high quality of work for children and young people in Holland, Germany, Italy, Belgium and France was that these companies were clearly working to their own 'gold standard'. In visiting theatre festivals in these countries, it was, for me, like finding an undiscovered theatre world as exacting and inspiring as the one that shaped me. I am a trained teacher and an untrained theatre director. The discovery of work of such originality and engagement in the domain of theatre for young people linked worlds that I thought had no connection.

In Den Bosch, for example, I discovered that I could see a lot of shows in one day because they seldom exceeded one hour in length. The pieces – I can't always say plays, because few had a conventional narrative structure – were diverse and performed with skill and grace. Language was used sparingly. Much of the work I saw had the very qualities of curiosity and seriousness that I felt to be missing in English theatre.

During this time of career change, Neil Wallace advised me (on a leisurely boat trip on the Amstel), 'Don't try and do what you want to do in your name alone; create a company and a mission, give it a name – and then produce your plays.'

Company of Angels was partly a shop-window that allowed me to write plays and to find co-producers who would agree to part-fund and stage them. In this I used my reputation as a director to persuade other companies to collaborate with Company of Angels. As a 'new writer' I would not have staged my plays if I had not founded a company to produce them.

But Company of Angels became a lot more than that. Amongst other activities, we originated Theatre Café, a project that brought previously untranslated European plays over to the UK; we created a scheme to support and train young theatre directors who became interested in work for young audiences; we instituted The Gap Project that worked on creating big participatory theatre events for children leaving primary school and about to start in secondary school; and we toured a number of plays for children and young people by English and European writers into schools, arts centres and theatres.

Though I was the artistic director of Company of Angels, I never became part of the company's monthly pay-roll. I worked as a freelance and took my income from commissions and fees on the specific work I produced for the company. This meant that all the new work that we staged was in co-production with another theatre or touring company – from *Hannah and Hanna* in 2001 with Channel Theatre Company to *Truant* in 2011 with National Theatre of Scotland.

Company of Angels was founded on the following manifesto:

1. Theatre 'for young people' is sometimes depicted as if it were itself a 'junior' art form.

2. The political and emotional centre of social change revolves around young people.

3. Cinema and television seek unanimity and passivity from this sector.

4. Theatre has a counter-cultural identity when it is prepared to leave its familiar audiences and buildings behind.

5. Theatre to young 'non-theatre' audiences in 'non-theatre' spaces can stimulate avant-garde work of originality and beauty.

THEATRE CAFÉ

In order to bring the kind of outstanding plays that I had seen in the festival at Den Bosch, the company created Theatre Café. Teresa Ariosto, who was the executive director of Company of Angels throughout my ten years with the company, was Italian and a natural linguist. Teresa was also highly effective at raising significant additional funds from the European Union. Her ease in several European languages made her a versatile ambassador for this project and, through her and others, we discovered many exciting and original European texts. All were performed at Theatre Café, our annual week-long festival of plays new to young people's theatre in Britain.

We designed a special stage for readings, one on which the actors could create their own groupings and blockings, so multiple and suggestive were the angles afforded by this original set-up, designed by Liz Cooke.

Delegates bought tickets for a day or more and there were discussions facilitated by, amongst others, Purni Morell (then Director of the NT Studio) and Chris Campbell (then Literary Manager at the Royal Court.) Company of Angels produced some of these plays and some found producers in other theatres. The best plays were published by Oberon in two volumes, *Theatre Café Plays One* and *Theatre Café Plays Two*.

We presented Theatre Cafe six times in various forms, including one in Amsterdam.

It was an original way to disseminate new European drama – and the readings produced some of the best spontaneous acting that I saw during my time running the company.

Theatre Café play anthology published by Oberon

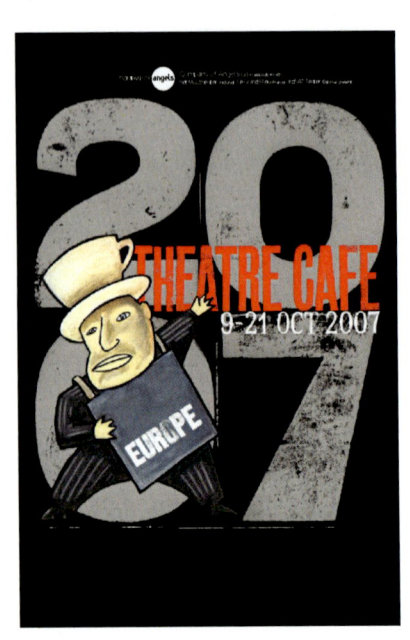

> *I didn't know what to expect from a staged reading but I must say that the Theatre Café performance went far beyond what I dared to hope for. The setting itself made a very good connection between audience and actors, and the play worked perfectly in this atmosphere even though it is written for smoke, flying characters and a revolving stage. I kind of forgot it was a staged reading; the papers in their hands became something like a concept rather than a reminder of words or text.*
>
> *Author Andri Snær Magnason (Iceland)*

Theatre Café poster

'The GAP Project': 5-day workshop at The Junction, Cambridge for young directors

2001-2011, WRITING PLAYS

I wrote ten plays in my ten years at Company of Angels.

Apart from *Hannah and Hanna*, there are four more that, for different reasons, are worth commenting on further; *Wild Girl*, *Club Asylum*, *Virgins* and *Truant*.

1. WILD GIRL, 2002 Company of Angels and Quicksilver Theatre

Extract from copy sent to schools about *Wild Girl*:

> *When the Count and Countess first meet Memmie, she has a unique closeness to nature; she can run at an amazing speed, at night she can see a black cat sleeping one hundred metres away, she can even smell the difference between an apple tree and a pear tree. She is a fish in the water, a deer on the earth, a flying squirrel in the treetops where she eats and she sleeps.*
>
> *She can imitate birdsong so well that you might think that there was a nightingale in the bedroom – but she cannot say the words 'cat' or 'dog'.*

The Count and the Countess want to 'save' Memmie and make her a citizen who can play, study, make friends, work and even marry.

Why should she not have the same rights as everyone else of her age?

They have much to teach her.

And she has a lot to teach them.

Wild Girl approached childhood from a very different perspective to *Hannah and Hanna*. It was originally a monologue based on the story of 'Memmie Le Blanc', a feral girl of ten years old who was discovered on the country estate of a Count and Countess in mid-18th century France. I wrote the whole play outdoors, on a bench in a park in Biarritz, while on a family holiday. I'd go off for a couple of hours each afternoon and write in pencil on an A4 pad, then go back to the beach and forget about it to the next day. At this stage in

Dutch brochure for *Wild Girl*

my new writing career, I couldn't stop writing and I loved the novelty of imagining a different world and time. This is something anyone can do, I reflected; 'thought is free'. It felt liberating after so many years of organising, directing and administrating.

The story was liberating too because, in the end, Memmie decides that she doesn't want to stay with the Count and Countess. She runs away into the forest and never returns and this devastates her would-be adopters – who are childless. This story had a strong impact on the children who watched it (mostly aged 9 to 12 years old). The debate as to whether Memmie was right or wrong to make this choice divided children.

One thing was clear: in this story the decision-maker was the child and not the adult.

The play was inspired by Michael Newton's recently published book *Savage Girls and Wild Boys*.

I directed a distinguished and well-known actress in the role, Anna Calder-Marshall. She became intensely involved with the character of Memmie and, in addition to performing the role in South London classrooms

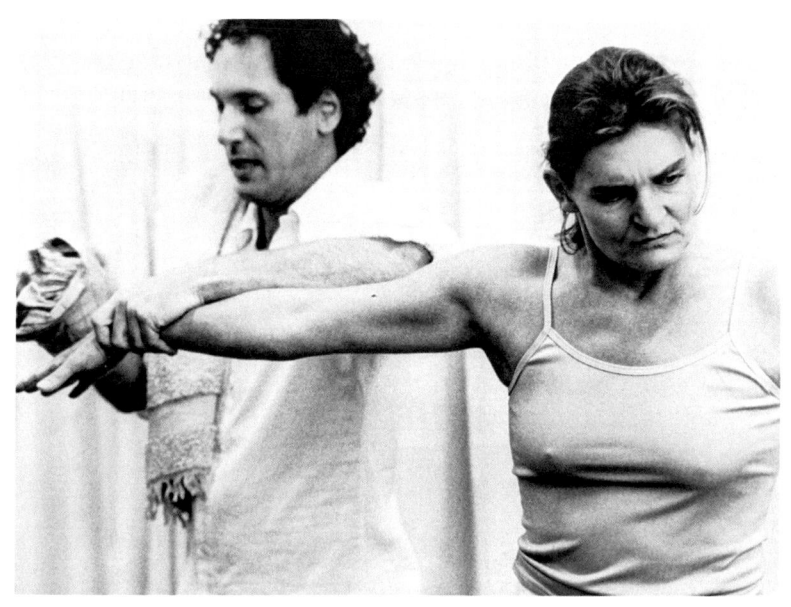

Wild Girl performed by Oscar Siegelaar and Ilja Tammen, Brussels, 2004

in full 18th-century costume, she created many paintings of Memmie. The surprise on the faces of children when she knocked on the door of their classroom was striking. They were never warned of her arrival and their astonishment was authentic.

I was happy with this result and, at the end of the tour, thought the play was over. But I received a call from Ad de Bont about the play, which he had read. He asked if Wederzijds could produce it and tour it in the autumn of 2004. I was delighted. Then he asked if he could adapt it for two actors, instead of one. I was excited by this proposal. The lines could be split between the Count and Countess and perhaps they could even find a way to personate the wild girl herself?

Here is my diary entry for November 7th, 2004, having just come away from seeing the play performed by two very good actors:

> Just returned from seeing *The Wild Girl* done by Wederzijds at the Bronks Festival in Brussels – twice, at 2 + 6 – a brilliant performance by Ilja Tammin (who I know well from her performance in The Clearing) and Oscar Siegelaar . It was haunting, even spell-binding, the audience of children from as young as five with their parents – a combination of story-telling with the most delicate physical theatre,

suspense created by a striking combination of stealth and silence – an object lesson in 'drawing the audience in'.

They have changed my play (written for one actress) to being the Countess and her husband who explain that they have no children of their own – the text (to its great benefit) is split between two voices.

The breakthrough is that they both act the wild girl herself – the first time that they do this, they semi-strip to a strange Arvo Part air, each suggesting the savage person they each might be below the surface, and they move and dig and growl in a haunting and terrifying way. Being Dutch, the show picks out the gruesome details and the gripped silence in the audience is because this girl is there before us, tantalising, utterly strange.

Ad de Bont, who directs, creates a startling sense of space using a table and a tiny thumb-sized doll on it that the actors manipulate. There is a life-size bench for Ilja to sit on as the Countess – then Oscar plays the savage girl. At other times the roles are reversed and Ilja drops her hair over her face and becomes a true alien as the Count dresses her at the end of the play in an exquisite blue ball gown.

The Count and the Countess are in elegant white cotton summer clothes, simple and beautifully made, allowing them great freedom of movement. The pictures that the Countess paints (and that form such a vital part of the play) are created by a wonderful artist called Cees Landsaat with great vigour and clarity. They inform and they illuminate, allowing, for one whole minute, the narrative to be told from a 'picture book' with no words. I saw (for that whole minute) the play that I had imagined when I wrote it in the summer of 2002.

This performance is a confirmation for me that the creation of new work for children and young people can lead to levels of theatre experience as original, luminous and poetic as in any other area of drama.

2. *CLUB ASYLUM*, 2002, Company of Angels and Macrobert, Stirling.

After *Hannah and Hanna*, I wrote *Club Asylum*. It was much more Dutch in style – that is, more thematic and less based on narrative. It was also a second collaboration with Andy Howitt, the most rough and tough choreographer I have ever met, always surprising, always on the ball. He created startlingly good moves for the company of five. He spent his working

The cast of *Club Asylum*
Left to right: Jane Howie, Umar Ahmed, Martin Docherty, Lee Hart, Cathleen McCarron

life running YDance, a company that worked all the year round in Scottish schools. He really knew the outlook of adolescents to each other and to outsiders. He was both grounded and unorthodox, always in a cap, always dancing with the classes he took. He'd watched everything and everybody in contemporary dance and had a very wide field of reference. He could 'read' an actor's body and knew how to challenge them to go further. He worked very fast and achieved results in a short period of time. We worked together several times after *Club Asylum*. Then he left for Australia and has done very well over there. He is a loss to Scotland; there is no other choreographer like Andy Howitt.

Asylum seekers were relatively new to Scotland at the beginning of 2002, and the manner in which they had been tenanted overnight in schemes like Sighthill was a very sore point for a lot of residents.

But the teenagers that we dealt with, from many countries, were animated by Glasgow and liked their new home. Their fear was not of staying in the city but of leaving it. Most of them were deeply impressed by the schools – fourteen-year-old Somalians and Kosovans would gravely tell you how good the education was. The special units in the schools for asylum seekers were superbly run and very welcoming; in some schools, like St Roch's, they were managed by men and women who were once refugees to

Glasgow themselves. The teenage asylum seekers responded with incredible energy to these new opportunities and they brought a new intellectual standard – a new level of aspiration – into the city. Studies have shown that young asylum seekers under this sort of pressure out-perform teenagers from indigenous families.

There is a growing awareness now – thanks to organisations like the Glasgow Campaign to Welcome Refugees and Positive Action for Housing. The most affecting story is that of the 'Girls' and the influence that they brought to bear on Jack McConnell, then First Minister for Scotland. This is a singular development – it's clear that young asylum seekers and local teenagers (or 'old and new Glaswegians') are now standing up for each other. Is this happening anywhere else in Britain? So openly and effectively? It was one of the first indications of a new and radical intelligence emerging from the big asylum intake of 2000/1.

The exchanges and poems that make up the text of *Club Asylum* can be explored in any order and there is no set way that dance and text should be performed. In our version, all of the poetic passages were spoken chorally – the 'I' was always plural.

The patron saint of Glasgow is St Mungo; he is also the saint of the homeless. This is how *Club Asylum* begins:

ST MUNGO

My mother was raped at fifteen by a Welsh crazy
My grandfather was so mad at her for getting pregnant
He threw her off a cliff one hundred metres high
In a cart.
That didn't kill her.
They towed the cart with her on it out to sea
And cast her adrift for days.
That didn't drown her.
After two days floating in the sea
The tide changed
She was hurled by the waves onto a beach.
She dragged her body across the sand
Dropped down half dead by an old campfire.
Then the birth pangs began.
There in the wilderness in a storm.
Alone and fifteen
She gave birth to me.

A man found us and took us to a priest.
The priest gave shelter to my mother
And me, he lifted up in his arms,
'Dear One' he said
Or, in the language of the day,
'Mungo'
I was a spiritual person from the day I was born.
I loved the man who saved our life
I loved the place he found us.
'Dear green place' I said
Or, in the language of the day,
'Glescu'
The founder of your city was an orphan
Or, in the language of our day
'Refugee'

The rousing acclaim that the show received from the press and audiences alike suggests that the company had a sound, and a style, that worked for young audiences.

Joyce Macmillan/THE SCOTSMAN

In some ways, Club Asylum is one of the most important theatrical shows created in Scotland in the past year; not big, not flashy, but nonetheless one of great significance in Scotland's struggle to come to terms with the latest wave of migration into our cities – particularly Glasgow – caused by the global refugee and asylum crisis … Its strength lies in Retallack's thoughtful, well-muscled script, which leaves no aspect of the experiences untouched, from the dangerously hostile initial reaction of the damaged communities into which asylum-seekers were sent, to the final mood of tentative progress supervised by a St Mungo figure in a baseball cap who knows all Glaswegians were newcomers once; and in Andy Howitt's choreography, which takes the basic group movements of crowds of teenagers everywhere and turns them into a brisk clear-sighted meditation on aggression and harmony, fun and danger, conflict and belonging, that perfectly matches the searching quality of Retallack's text.

3. *VIRGINS*, 2006 Company of Angels and The Junction, Cambridge

Virgins is about a white middle-class family who live in Brighton in a three-bedroom terraced house. The children are aged 17 and 16, both parents work. Because it is about a world to which I was so close, it proved much harder to write. Essentially it was about that period in a family's life when simultaneous sexual relationships are going on, in different bedrooms, under one roof – how does a family negotiate and grow through this sometimes fraught rite of passage?

At the time, I read an academic paper that says English and American families tend to *dramatise* adolescent sexuality (highlight negative risks and speak ominously about the consequences – pregnancy, infection, effect of drugs, etc) whereas Dutch and Scandinavian families *normalise* it: that is, they talk openly about their sexual lives, accommodate the changes and see no cause for over-reaction. It's clear that the same adolescent would behave quite differently if he or she is subject to one or other of these two approaches.

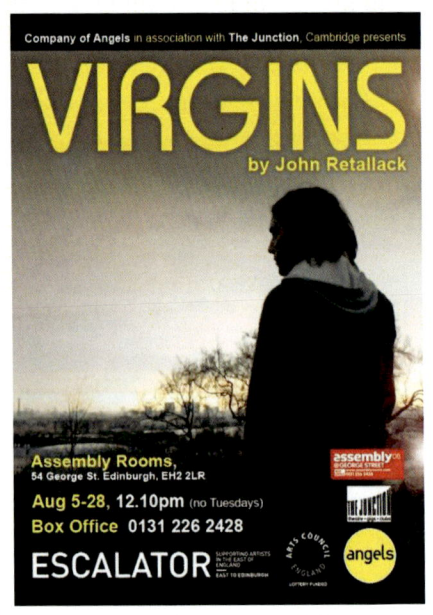

Poster for *Virgins*

The play deals with the fall-out after the son, Jack, goes to a party, gets wasted and is then accused of having had unprotected sex with a girl he hardly knows. The story of the play comes out of a culture that dramatises sexuality rather than normalising it – Jack's wild night at the party is a response to this climate. A 'Dutch' family would have talked through the pointlessness of a night like that long ago. Jack's family are reactive but unable to open the subject until it has become a source of conflict.

I wanted the audience (whether adults or teenagers) to place themselves into the family and into this situation. A key aspect is the sexuality of the parents themselves. If the family is a happy one, there will be a sexual narrative going on with the parents as well. At certain points in a family's life there is a lot of sexual energy under one roof. English houses are quite small and all the bedrooms are usually on the same floor.

The play was written over an 18-month period and I was always nervous that people would just say, 'So what?' Yet it spoke to adults as well as to teenagers. *Virgins* was translated into French and German – and Swedish! It toured Austria twice and the Swedish production played over 150 times and was seen all over the country. The French turned it into a comedy and it was the very best of all the versions that I saw. The play toured England but it was much more successful in Europe. The reviews here were good but theatre managers seemed wary of the subject matter.

I worked with a very fine choreographer, Fleur Darkin, on creating movement for this play. The ten minutes of dance in the production took up 70% of the rehearsal time. The music was from John Adams *Book of Alleged Dances*. But that was a hard collaboration – the language of a playwright and a choreographer are very different.

THE SCOTSMAN/Joyce MacMillan

John Retallack's latest Company of Angels show is a fine little piece of modern British family drama.

[...] Its subject – the complex sexual politics of the modern family with teenage kids – touches the lives of millions, and is desperately under-explored in British theatre.

[...] it's unusual to see it handled with the level of quiet eloquence, emotional sophistication, and sharp, down-to-earth realism achieved by Retallack's fine script. The play is punctuated by some strong, precise dance sequences by Fleur Darkin, and features an unobtrusively clever set by Liz Cooke, built around the miniature doll's house image of the ideal home. All four actors give performances of terrific conviction and humanity ...

4. *TRUANT*, 2011, National Theatre of Scotland and Company of Angels

How do you find your limits without breaking the rules? Teenagers need to play truant from their parents to establish their own identity, their own personal values. But what happens when parents play truant from their children, when they avoid their parental duties? Everyone has family, but who is making and who is breaking the rules?

Adam Philips, the psychoanalyst, wrote an essay called *In Praise of Difficult Children*. It struck me as original and worth exploring dramatically. I went to meet him

Leaflet for *Truant*

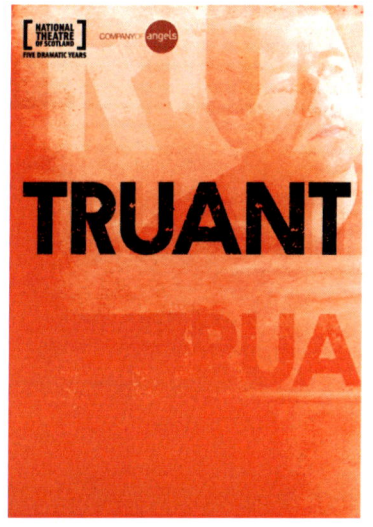

in his clinic in Notting Hill and he talked to me for an hour. He inspired me, not least because his interest in children was so clearly authentic – it is the area of practice in which he had started.

I provide a synopsis of his argument here:

When you play truant you have a better time.
But how do you learn what a better time is?

You see that there are many good times to be had.
Often they are in conflict with each other.

When you betray yourself
When you let yourself down
You have mis-recognised what your idea of a good time is;
Or, by implication,
You have more fully realised what your idea of a good time might really be.

You thought that doing this –
Taking drugs,
Lying to your best friend –
Would give you the life you wanted;
And then it doesn't.

You have, in other words, discovered something essential about yourself;
Something you couldn't discover without having betrayed yourself.

You have to be bad to discover what kind of good you want to be.

Adults who look after adolescents have both to want them to behave badly,
And to try and stop them;
To be able to do this
Adults have to have truant minds themselves.

They have to believe that truancy is good
And that the rules are good.

Someone with a truant mind believes that conflict is the point
Not the problem.

The job of the truant mind is to keep conflict as alive as possible.
This means that adolescents are free to be adolescents
Only if adults are free to be adults.

The real problems turn up when one or other side is determined to resolve the conflict;
When adolescents are allowed to live in a world of pure impulse
Or adults need them to live in a world of incontestable law.

In this sense therapy for adolescents should be about creating problems –
or clarifying what they really are –
and not about solving them.

I wanted to make a 'mosaic' play – that is, a series of scenes that are connected through theme – but not through narrative. My inspiration was *Cet Enfant* (*This Child*) by a French author called Joel Pommerat. He has a knack of ending scenes with a character in a dilemma – a dilemma that he leaves the audience to figure out. My aim was to achieve a similar effect to Pommerat.

I made this show through a great deal of improvisation with the cast. I presented a series of situations to them and asked them to freewheel into being a mother, a son, a father or a daughter. The cast never failed to come up with a strong scene that reflected what Adam Philips is saying in the above passage. The production toured all over Glasgow to community centres, youth clubs and theatres. It was an hour long with its series of scenes around domestic conflict, followed by a discussion with the audience. My direction was sound and the actors were outstandingly accurate and resourceful – but I always felt that my writing owed too much to the cast and not enough to original thinking of my own.

This was a time of change for me – *Truant* was my last show for Company of Angels, and its rehearsals took place during my move across to Bristol Old Vic. I had uprooted and unsettled myself with my decision. I found my focus adrift and I suffered an uncharacteristic loss of confidence. This was not like the nightmare of doing *The Plague* in Dundee, where I kept going despite a demoralising environment. This was an interior sense of not being on top of material that I had prepared and understood well. It was

Cast of Truant, from l to r, Gavin Kean, Daniel Cahill, Clare McCracken, Fiona Wood, Hannah Donaldson, Ross Allan, Chris McCann, Michele Gallagher

another reminder of how tough it can be to work as a freelancer on new material, where everybody is new to you and you are new to everybody. By the end of rehearsals, you feel ready to start…

I had to face an uncomfortable fact or two:

> **From my own diary, November 2011**
>
> In 2000 when I wrote *Hannah and Hanna*, I felt that I could write a play about young people by sitting at home and working out a story. It was called *Hannah and Hanna* because that was the name of Hanna's best friend and she was round at our house all the time.
>
> *Virgins* also reflected life with my son Jack at a certain time – I lived very close up to a boy going through all the pleasure and pain of being 17. It was not so difficult to invent a fictional family for him.
>
> Now Jack and Hanna are adults – Hanna is applying for her first job in September '09 and Jack, who left home two years ago, will be 21 in June.

> I'm now aware of how detached, in my daily life, I am from young people. It just never occurred to me as an issue before now.
>
> Renata and I live together without the daily drama of two teenagers to react to and to deal with and to discuss.
>
> I know no more about young people than the average 60-year-old does – except that they are, through Company of Angels, my 'professional interest'.
>
> I have to ask myself, at this stage in my life, whether they are a *real* interest – or perhaps a professional one.
>
> Have I grown out of 'youth' – time to move on?

It was ten years since I founded Company of Angels. Was it time, once more, to re-appraise what I was going to do next? When Tom Morris, artistic director of Bristol Old Vic, offered me the chance to be his associate director at Bristol Old Vic, it looked like the kind of fresh start that I sought. I accepted his offer and disrupted our domestic life again by moving to Bristol in the weekdays and coming home every weekend.

8
LATE PRODUCTIONS
2010-2018 Bristol Old Vic, 2011-2013

After ten years as artistic director of Company of Angels, I was employed as Associate Director at the Bristol Old Vic in late 2010 and I remained in post until summer 2013. I was responsible for all aspects of outreach and community engagement. I greatly enjoyed the experience of being a part of such a large operation – and not being the boss. I saw Tom Morris, artistic director, and Emma Stenning, executive director, at work at close quarters – this was new and it was stimulating.

For the first time since the beginning of my theatre career, I was not the number one in an organisation. This is what I enjoyed most about the job – I could talk to everyone in a far more relaxed way than I was used to. I was only boss of a department, not the whole building. My lack of top status seemed to make everyone much friendlier to me than I was used to – or perhaps I just had time to notice. And there were so many people in the building to know. This was a novelty too. I was used to a company that was made up of only five or six individuals. What with the long meetings, the coffee-breaks, the acting companies, pre- and post-show drinks, the long suppers out with Emma or Tom to talk through new moves, I seemed to spend most of my time talking. When I wasn't talking, I wrote e-mails. Occasionally, I directed a show which was a relatively silent activity in comparison to the normal non-stop noise of an admin day. What did you do today, Renata would ask me on the telephone in the evening; 'Admin,' I said and I could remember little about it, except how fast the time had passed.

I was, as it turned out, a producer of schemes, programmes and projects for the widening Bristol Old Vic community. Over the two and a half years that I worked at Bristol Old Vic, there was a transformation in terms of engagement and participation and Lucy Hunt, my successor, has continued this work with great success to this day. Renata, who joined me in Bristol after the first year, worked in the same field as me for The Egg in Bath.

Tom and Emma's triumph was to renovate the building throughout; between 2009 and 2018, they transformed the Bristol Old Vic from a grand but dilapidated building – gaffer tape on threadbare carpets, grim breezeblock corridors painted black and a canteen-like space for audiences

Bristol Old Vic re-opens after £26 million refurbishment, September 2018

to gather at the interval. To get the building to the beautiful state it is now in, everyone worked through years of office turmoil and improvised working space; I had three different offices in my short time at the theatre.

The show that I cherished most was my production of Tim Crouch's beautiful trilogy, *fairymonsterghost*, which we toured all over the region to schools and fringe venues.

This trilogy is made up of three one-man shows, one featuring Peaseblossom in *The Dream*, another Caliban in *The Tempest* and the last Banquo in *Macbeth*. Each play looks at the world through the eyes of a character who has little control of events in their respective play. The plays mix contemporary speech with elements of Shakespeare's language. All three produced a compelling hour of dramatic story-telling and Tim has gone on to write a very successful one-man play based on Twelfth Night, *I, Malvolio* and another on Julius Caesar, *I, Cinna*. What I especially like is the 'daylight' nature of these texts – they can be performed anywhere, inside or outside, with only natural light.

The mash of modern English and Shakespearian quotation is evident in the opening address to the audience in *I, Caliban*:

> *I know what you're thinking. I know. You're thinking what an ugly man. What a bald ugly man. Why have we come in here to see such an ugly ugly man. What an ugly tortoise of a man. You're thinking, he's not a man. He's more fish than man.*

A strange fish. Legged like a man and his fins like arms, but a fish all the same. Aren't you? You're not? You should be. I'm ugly. I'm disgusting. Here, look. See.

(Rubber bands to totally distort the face.)

Ugly enough for you? Could I make myself any plainer? Am I ugly now? Am I?

Well, YOU'D BE UGLY IF YOU'D HAD A LIFE LIKE MINE.

(He takes off the rubber bands, picks up a book and throws it out over the audience.)

This is my island.

Or, rather, this island's mine.

In one of these shows, the lonely actor had the longest 'dry' I have ever experienced. The actor simply stopped talking and stayed silent for what felt like an eternity for us and, of course, for him. What made it especially tough – and this may have been the cause – was that the author, Tim Crouch, *and* his family, were sitting in the front row opposite the actor in question. The actor changed colour, stopped breathing, he smiled and he grimaced but no sound, no *word*, came from his lips…and so it went on…until, when I thought that he'd not only dried, but died, on his feet, the words returned.

Tim Crouch's I, *Peaseblossom* performed by Kate Mayne in Ashton Court, Bristol 2012

The relief was so great that the actor laughed – and so did everyone present. The spell was broken and he continued to the end of the play without a hitch.

After I left in the summer of 2013, Tom Morris invited me to direct two shows: Purcell's *Dido and Aeneas* in the summers of 2014 and 2015 – and then a play called *Pink Mist* by Owen Sheers in the summer of 2015.

I did more directing for Bristol Old Vic after I left than when I worked in the building.

Pink Mist was a play I had championed before I left but utterly failed to get off the ground. To my delight, two years later, Tom Morris had second thoughts.

PINK MIST: BRISTOL OLD VIC, THE BUSH AND NATIONAL TOUR, 2015-17

Owen Sheers' play is based on 30 hours of interviews with ex-soldiers. It has been dramatised for radio, stage and the film rights have been bought. Sheers has not been a soldier or served in the armed forces, but he is an exceptionally good writer and known for the accuracy of his 'lyrical reportage'.

I had read it as a dramatic poem and heard it on Radio 4 in a series of five readings. When I left the theatre in 2013, I told Tom that it would make a fantastic theatre piece, not least because it was about three teenage lads from Bristol who decide to enrol with the Marines because their own jobs are so rubbish. They go together to Afghanistan and all three eventually return to Bristol – one has lost both his legs, another has lost part of his

The cast of *Pink Mist*

Phil Dunster as Arthur in *Pink Mist*. Phil received an Olivier nomination for his performance.

mind and the third, the one who inspired them to go in the first place, returns in a coffin. The dead man is called Arthur and he retains his voice beyond his death. Despite the play's tragic nature, Sheers has a light touch and the play inspires and saddens in equal measure. The text is written in

THE GUARDIAN; PINK MIST REVIEW
Bristol Old Vic, 5 Jul 2015
Lyn Gardner

Owen Sheers' dramatic poem takes its name from a military term for the spray of blood that mists the air after a sniper or roadside bomb attack. Inspired by interviews with returning soldiers, it never shirks uncomfortable truths about the realities of war, including blue-on-blue incidents and what happens when a six-foot-two man loses his legs and is reduced to four-foot-three, but is still determined to stand tall. It confronts the cycle of love and grief and revenge that fuels war, the urge of boys to try to be men in whatever ways they can, and the mental scars that never fade. It also heart-rendingly articulates the experience of the mothers, wives and girlfriends who pick up the pieces…Beautifully performed by its young cast, John Retallack and George Mann's production finds a physical language – a mix of Frantic Assembly and Gecko style movement– to match the brawny verve of Sheers' poetry.

blank verse and it allows great freedom of movement. I co-directed it with a brilliant movement director called George Mann. Directors and movement directors don't always see eye to eye – not so with George. We liked working together and he produced stunning tableaux as well as highly energised action sequences. Our cast were all, bar one, graduates from Bristol Old Vic Theatre School and they had a zest I'll never forget. They were as fearless as the men and women that they portrayed.

Pink Mist was exciting to stage because Bristol Old Vic stripped its main auditorium right back, so that the stage came out over the first dozen rows. This highly physical and poetic play was happening in the very centre of the auditorium. The sound by Jon Nicholls and lighting by Peter Harrison intensified the visceral impact. It only ran at the Old Vic for three weeks but the response from audiences was so strong that Tom Morris endorsed a London run for it in the future. This happened in January 2016 at the Bush where it ran for a month; in 2017, it went on a national tour. That was my final engagement with Bristol Old Vic, some four years after I thought I had left for good.

My collaboration with Owen Sheers' writing has continued; the two of us since have worked together on *Unicorns, Almost*, a one-man show about Keith Douglas, the best known of the World War 2 poets. The producer Emma Balch presented it at the Hay-on-Wye Festival in 2017 and 2018 to outstanding reviews. The performance was recorded for Radio 3 who broadcast it in 2020.

***HANNAH AND HANNA IN DREAMLAND* 2016/18**
UK Arts International/HOUSE
Turner Gallery, Margate 2016
Marlowe Theatre, Canterbury and tour, 2018

Since writing *Hannah and Hanna* in 2001 and having seen it performed in different parts of the world, I thought that the play, and that chapter of my life, was over.

The summer of 2015, and the news of borders going up all over Europe to refugees, changed that. Jan Ryan, the tour producer of *Hannah and Hanna* in 2001-2004, suggested a second part. I agreed very quickly.

Hannah and Hanna in Dreamland takes place in 2015. The girls are now women of thirty-two. They have, for various reasons, had almost no contact since they parted company on the road to Kosovo, near the burnt-out bus where Hanna was raped by Serbian soldiers before she came to England.

Migration had become the biggest challenge facing Europe. The largest group by nationality to take the perilous sea routes from North Africa or Turkey were Syrians. The war in Syria has caused a massive exodus of people from that country.

The Syrians joined people fleeing from Iraq, Pakistan, Somalia, Eritrea, Sudan, Nigeria, Afghanistan and elsewhere. In 2000 (when Hannah and Hanna met) less than 100,000 people a year were claiming asylum in continental Europe. By 2015, the number had grown to one million.

The increase in numbers had led to a hardening of attitudes towards the sheer chaos and distress that people witnessed in those who have lost everything. Yet there are many citizens who express themselves through individual and collective acts of kindness to migrants. I spent three weeks in and around Calais in the spring of 2015 and I was astonished by the energy and purpose shown by a number of retired middle-class French people who committed all their time to helping people stuck in 'The Jungle' and unable to smuggle themselves into England. These pensioners were outdoors all day in the incredibly high winds that swept over the dunes, ferrying wood and plastic sheeting, generators for phone chargers, supplying hundreds of meals, doing whatever they could to make life bearable for the thousands trying to stow away to Dover.

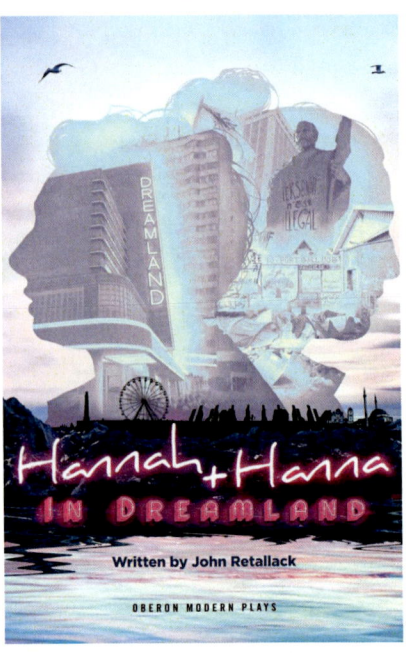

Cover to the Oberon edition of *Hannah and Hanna in Dreamland*

It's much harder for adults than it is for teenagers to change their ways, their habits and their views; to really put themselves out. I found these French people inspiring. They changed my view of retirement completely because they felt that they had to act on behalf of the migrants.

It's this extraordinary change in the attitude of the over-sixties that made me ask if someone – like Margate Hannah – could have a change of heart. She gains so much inspiration and life from Hanna that she surrenders to her own better feelings and lets her world be turned upside down.

The French organisation, Odyssey, provided accommodation and transport for me to visit Calais over a three-week period and talk to the some of the thousands of people who camped out there in atrocious conditions.

Lisa Payne as Hannah, Celia Meiras as Hanna

I felt that though I would never do what these French pensioners did, day in, day out, at least I could write a play about this place at this time and the vast amount of suffering contained within it.

Extract from Hannah and Hanna in Dreamland
Hannah and Hanna are now fifteen years older.
Hannah is an estate agent, dressed stylishly in suit and heels.
Hanna is in jeans with bright beret.

HANNAH: *This is Margate from my window.*
Margate from the window of my car.
My new Phelps and Phelps branded Mini Cooper two-door hardtop.
I see two towns – both called Margate.
One is the dump I should have left long ago.
The other is the one I sell to people…
Do I see a grey shitty house in a street with an abandoned sofa on the pavement
Overflowing dustbins and loose cables flapping in the wind,
Dog shit and slime and broken bottles on the steps?
Is that what I see?
Or do I see a Victorian six-bedroomed townhouse with commanding views over the North Sea?

A magnificent early nineteenth-century dwelling in the centre of Margate?
I see the Margate it pays to see.
I thought I'd never make any money in this dump. But now I sell Margate
Brick by golden brick.

HANNA: *This is Pristina from my window –*
The window of the City Hospital Emergency Unit. I work here.
It's where my mother was a doctor
Before she died.
I should have been a doctor like my mother,
Or at least a pharmacist.
But I didn't have the money for studying.
So I'm a driver.
I drive ambulances.
I'm the first woman ambulance driver in Kosovo.

HANNAH: *Couple of months ago, I sang 'My Heart Will Go On' at a Celine Dion tribute night at The Walpole.*
I still sing now and then.
This blazer walks in while I'm singing and when I've finished
He keeps on clapping,
Buys me a large one and suggests I might like to sing at his conference.
He says he's just the song for me,
Written for the occasion and it's in a calypso style –
I say, 'No problem for me, I'd love to do it!'
He roars, 'And we'll pay you, you know!'
I say, 'All the better! Who's the conference for?'
'UKIP', he says
'I've heard of them – what is UKIP exactly?'
We introduce ourselves.
Nigel explains that he's the leader of the party...

AUGUST 2022 – *THE HUMMINGBIRD*, by Sandro Veronesi

Edinburgh Book Festival 2022
Radio 3, 22 May 2022/1 January 2023

In April 2022, The Story of Books, run by Emma Balch, commissioned me to adapt a novel called *The Hummingbird* (winner of the Italian Strega Prize in 2021) for Radio 3. The novel is 80,000 words and I had 9000 words to dramatise it, the amount contained by a one-hour adaptation. The novel has an extraordinary mixed chronology and tells the story of Marco Carrera, an ophthalmologist, from his infancy to his death at the age of 71 – also my own age. I had to abandon his mixed time-scheme and tell the story in a linear form. This turned *The Hummingbird* into a moving novella, something different from the full-length text but also a minor work of art in itself, that worked according to its own form. The Edinburgh Book Festival picked it up and a group of 50 people sat in a specially designed room and listened to the Radio 3 recording. It was the first time that I had listened to it 'freely'; that is, I was listening as a punter, not as the adaptor/director, fussing over this and that. It is a very moving story and I was surprised to find myself welling up – and to see the same happening to the translator, Elena Pala, to my right, and to the commissioner from Radio 3, Mathew Dodds. Obviously, we all knew the novel inside out. But it caught us, just as it did the audience. All the satisfaction I should have felt on completing the adaptation several months ago, was compressed into this single experience of being both outside one's own work and inside. And my admiration for the sound composer, the actors and for the author came upon me in a rush.

The adaptation was nominated for Best Adaptation in the 2023 BBC Audio Drama Awards.

9
TEACHING PLAYWRITING
Ruskin College, Oxford, 2013–2017 and Oxford Playwriting from 2017

INTRODUCTION

Since I left Bristol Old Vic for Ruskin College, Oxford in 2013, Renata and I have stayed put in this city and become very much involved in its theatre scene. I worked at Ruskin College for four years and then began my own playwriting course Oxford Playwriting in 2017 and I continue to run that today – as I write, the sixth year begins with 22 writers next month. Along the way I have continued my writing and directing with smaller freelance projects. Most of all, I have read and seen many more contemporary plays than at any other time in my theatre career.

The real pleasure of these later days is that I no longer run a theatre company or organisation. I was extremely fortunate not to be running a public company throughout the pandemic; for a director to be denied his stage, his audience and his repertoire is the worst possible form of professional house arrest. And you are expected to communicate with, and even build your audience through online means. That would have been difficult for me. What I love most about theatre is the close-up contact with other human beings; the opportunity to work together creatively.

It is good that we have come out of the worst of the Covid experience but, as everyone knows, theatre has been scarred, most especially in the regions where it is so hard to make a functioning business model to stage original new work. My period at Oldham Coliseum and Oxford Stage Company now look unimaginably prosperous.

I am now a freelance theatre maker and so is Renata; she directs at Pegasus Theatre, writes plays for the Story Museum every year and has a long-running workshop programme in schools for Oxford Playhouse.

I wrote this memoir during the lockdown months. If I was asked what do I regret, looking back, it is the vast amount of time consumed by admin, meetings and e-mails. I have much less of that now and life is the better for it. I kept papers and schedules from all the companies that I ran – they were actually useless when it came to writing the story of the last forty years. It was good to shred the lot.

RUSKIN COLLEGE, OXFORD, 2013-17

In the spring of 2012, Renata and I visited Oxford for a night to see some old friends, Neil and Fusa McLynn, the couple who had masterminded our sabbatical to Tokyo in 1996. We stayed in Corpus Christi (Neil's college) for the night, woke early and walked to the High Street before breakfast. Both of us were struck – all over again – by the beauty of the city where we had lived for ten years from 1989. We'd been in London since 2000 and our current spell in Bristol was an attempt to adopt a new home outside of the capital. In fact, we were both Londoners who were finding it difficult to live (in our eyes) so far from London. I remember Emma Stenning giving me my train ticket on an early morning London trip from Bristol Temple Meads and it had cost the theatre £179 return. £179 is too far from London. Oxford is a great city and it's 48 miles from London Town – 48 miles from Jack and Hanna, 48 miles from the West End, 48 miles from everything the capital has to offer a couple who've moved out to 'the country'.

From then I was on the lookout for something in Oxford…

I saw the advertisement for a post at Ruskin College, Oxford during a short Easter break from rehearsals for *The Last Days of Mankind*, a co-production with Bristol Old Vic Theatre School. The post was for Head of Writing for Performance to start in September 2013. I applied and hoped very much, at 63, that I would get an interview. I did but the letter stated that I had to teach a 40-minute class to 'students and staff' as part of the interview…

I used every trick I knew to surprise and subvert expectation. 'Do you want the projector or the white board?' asked the technician, as I walked into the crowded interview room. 'Neither, thank you', I replied, knowing that I would fumble helplessly with any technical equipment if I was nervous. Which I was. I turned the session (with 24 individuals seated around a long table) into an impromptu theatre workshop. So far, so good. Then an interview with the principal and the other members of the department. There was a four-hour gap between the two events, so I walked around the brand-new building; the college had only just re-located from Walton Street to its Headington campus.

Ruskin is a college with a very proud century-old tradition of taking working class men and women who had missed out on education when they were of student age and wanted to begin their studies in mid-life. It had always been known as a home to radical thought. Rather than having links to the ruling class and the establishment, it was very close to the trade union movement – everything about this college as an institution was in opposition to the university. Because I had only begun to write plays at the age of 50, I felt an affinity with the students that I expected to meet. The profoundly left-wing bias of this college in the middle of Oxford felt abrasive and exciting. By the time that the four hours (waiting for my interview) had elapsed, I wanted the job.

The second interview happened in the canteen with the principal of the college and two staff members. She said that I would have to go on a 'steep learning curve' to understand the administrative demands of the job. It was clear that my expertise in 'writing for performance' was more advanced than the other candidates – during my long wait, various students who had been in my workshop-interview had told me as much. But, still, I knew far less about academic procedure than the other applicants. I had got my B.Ed. 40 years ago. Strangely enough, I think this ancient legitimacy got me across the line. As I drove home to Bristol, I got a call from the principal: 'the panel is unanimous – we would like you to lead the Writing for Performance programme. Please let me know your decision by the end of the week'.

The leaving of Bristol and the many people that I had got to know caused me much doubt and distress. Bristol Old Vic was surging forward and most of its senior staff did the work of two people. Not so at Ruskin. Staff there would tell me they were exhausted and that everything was 'a nightmare.' All I saw was that the staff had all left the college by 4pm on most days, that hardly any tutors came in on a Friday, that the vacations were long and there were other 'time bonuses' like 'Reading Week'; in addition, there were days when one had no lectures or tutorials at all. The first autumn day that I walked home at 4pm, I felt in a trance – what would I actually do between now and 8pm? I simply was not used to having so much time at my disposal.

Yet this was the main reason that I had left the theatre – to have time to pursue my own activities, to write for myself again. At Bristol Old Vic, I seemed to have meetings all day long, more and more 'admin' occupying all working hours. I felt that I'd slid from my normal creative working practice to becoming a manager who directed shows from time to time. At Ruskin, it wasn't long before I found a fresh opportunity for theatremaking.

Ruskin had a vast room at the centre of its new main building. It was as wide as the college itself and had six 20-foot-high windows that looked onto the rolling countryside beyond the ring road. All these had specially designed blinds and there was a simple lighting rack that could be adapted to any part of the room. The room itself could be adjusted to in-the-round seating, end-on or to a cabaret-style format with tables and chairs all across the space.

Leaflets for Ruskin Theatre Platforms

It was ideal for speakers or for readings. I invited Nick Kent, Mark Haddon, Maxine Peake, Owen Sheers and David Edgar to speak to the students in lectures that were open to the public. Tickets were free and the college had a rigid 'no-fees' policy that they never changed in my time there. It was based on Labour MPs coming from Westminster to talk to students: the principal said to me, 'Jeremy Corbyn doesn't charge!' After an excellent talk, it was David Edgar who ticked me off: 'don't you realise that is how writers earn a living?' After that we stuck to staged readings with local professional actors and these became very popular. Audiences of around 60 became the norm.

As I've written earlier, I believe that staged readings can be a highly effective encounter with a play; here is an extract from a blog I wrote for young directors who wanted to direct readings at Ruskin College.

ADVICE RE STAGED READINGS, May 2020

A 'STAGED READING' is performed by actors on their feet, in movement, within a defined space.

A 'PLAY READING' is the same thing except that the actors are seated throughout.

Actors will be wide awake from the moment you meet to discuss the reading. That is probably because they are already on a count-down to the event itself; it happens tomorrow, maybe it happens tonight.

The actor is in control, not the director.

The director is there to give certain indispensable – but minimal – directions re character, movement and timing.

Key Decisions for the Director in Advance

When the director visits the space in which the reading will happen, decide on how you will use the space – end-on, in the traverse, in the round?

The key is, more than ever, in the casting. A false note in an intimate staged reading is more detectable to the audience in a shared daylight space than it is in the darkened auditorium.

Do you take an interval or not? If the play is up to 75 minutes or a bit more, don't stop. If you are doing *The Tempest* or *The Seagull* or similar, the intervals can be magical as the audience and actors mingle – and there is still more of the play to come.

Ask actors to dress appropriately to the part in their own clothes. Ask them to bring some spare items too.

If you use music, keep it visible, whether it's you on an MP3 player or a live classical guitarist.

Avoid props entirely. The actors must be free to read and handle the turning of the pages. If the audience are to *forget* that they are reading (and they will) don't lumber them with any naturalistic props or manual activity that is restrictive. The actors need, first and foremost, to gesture freely and any prop will divert their energy from the text.

The only lighting that matters is the light by which the actors read their scripts – that said, try to create an ambience that does not impede the collective expression of the play.

Try to rehearse the play in a single day, if possible, but not for longer. The intention is to liberate the actor rather than to instruct him.

Print the scripts one-sided, not two.

Have a single sheet hand-out on every seat as the audience enters that identifies each actor, the length of the reading, the author of the play and the necessary thanks. Actors and writers might get work as a result of these events and it is important that the information is in the audience's hand when they leave.

Make sure the audience can all see and that there is also room for the actors to stand when they are not on-stage.

Staged readings are theatre at its most authentic and most elusive. It will never happen again – the way the actor said that line, the way the sun came through the window, the sound of the ambulance speeding past, even the dog that starts barking…it is all one for that unique reading.

Staged readings require very careful handling in their preparation. The results can be unforgettable.

JR

JR introducing a reading of *Two* by Jim Cartwright

At Ruskin, I took a greater interest in how plays are made; characterisation, structure and form. In the professional theatre, you are thinking of how best to stage, cast and market a play. How will you express this text, what are you saying with your interpretation? Above all, can you make it work at the box office?

In teaching students about plays, and how to write their own plays, that pressure is lifted. You are able to take an interest in the play for its own sake, to take it to pieces and to put it back together again. It's hard to express what a liberation this is – not to have to *sell* a play.

Audience at a reading of *Sweetpeter* by John Retallack and Usifu Jalloh

The readings satisfied my performance urge – for me, it was not enough to talk about plays theoretically. And, as always, it astonished me how much a cast and director can achieve in a day. We managed *Top Girls, A Raisin in the Sun, Posh, Rhinoceros, A Doll's House* and other diabolically difficult texts – the more the same actors returned and worked together, the more

Ollie Gomm in a reading of *Cock* by Mike Bartlett

confident they became. All credit to Paul Ansdell, Ollie Gomm, Abi Hood, Alex Stedman and the many others who made these events so thrilling to produce.

Teaching at Ruskin was linked closely to the readings – students took part and performed alongside professional actors and most of them stayed behind after a day at college to watch the evening reading. In the second and third year we recruited many more students. It was rewarding to have numbers and it took the recruitment monkey off my back for a few terms. That said, Ruskin took on an incredibly mixed group of students, mixed not only in terms of education, class and ethnicity but also in age – we had students aged twenty and seventy sitting side by side. Their enthusiasm was, in turns, electrifying, exhausting, enervating. A number of the students on our two-year course went on to become writers, or to work in related areas. The picture below captures their bond, their anarchic spirit …

Ruskin College, Writing for Performance, class of 2014

2014 and 2015 were busy years but Ruskin College was going through serious financial difficulties and changes of leadership. Recruitment was low overall because now every other Higher Education institution wanted our students – or students like ours, varied in age, qualification and ability. There was nothing in the collective Ruskin memory that had a grasp of commerce, of *selling* the college to new recruits. People had always beaten a path to the door of the college in the past – it was a unique place, welcoming serious men and women for whom Ruskin promised a fresh start, an opportunity they had never had when they were young. Now it was just another HE college that asked a lot of money for a place. The college had a serious identity crisis and in 2016 the numbers coming to our course dropped drastically. Many tutors were offered voluntary redundancy. I took that option in April 2017.

By the time that I left the college, it had affected me in a profound way, much as if I was a Ruskin student coming to my education late in life. I had trained as a teacher back in the early 70s and, to my surprise, I had started to enjoy teaching plays more fully than rehearsing them. The way that I explained this to myself was that a group of writers are less predictable than a cast of actors. The writers are meant to be expanding outwards in new and unpredictable ways; by contrast, actors are closing in on a text that has to be done in certain very precise and inter-dependent ways. The time at Ruskin also showed me how much I had been a hyper-active director, too busy to read enough of the repertoire. Though it was late in the day, I was beginning to catch up.

At 67, it was time for me to go fully freelance, to earn a living from the skills I had acquired from my career to date.

In 2014, Renata and I formed a partnership under the title of Oxford Playmaker (now Oxford Playwriting). Oxford Playhouse employed us to work on two different projects. I ran a workshop series for emergent professional writers. From more than one hundred applications, we chose seven writers who came to the Playhouse for a whole Saturday once a month over a period of four years (2014-2018). It continues to this day under the leadership of Clare Bayley.

In 2017, I decided to set up my own course, Oxford Playwriting.

I found a beautiful oak-lined room overlooking the High Street, almost opposite the Covered Market. It is rented from Vincent's, a century-old club for students who have played a sport for the University. The room is big enough to run staged readings of plays in the traverse for an audience of forty, yet intimate enough to run a course for six to eight writers around a table. It was the only venue that I found which was available in both vacation and term-time. As I write, I am entering the sixth year of my course and it still takes place at Vincent's.

Here is a typical list that a first-year group will read in the course of their 30 weekly sessions:

1   A RAISIN IN THE SUN Lorraine Hansberry
2   THIS CHILD Joel Pommerat
3   IPHIGENIA IN SPLOTT Gary Owen
4   TOP GIRLS Caryl Churchill
5   THE WRITER Ella Hickson

6   TWO Jim Cartwright
7   GUT Frances Poet
8   THE INHERITANCE Mathew Lopez
9   SNOWFLAKE Mike Bartlett
10 THE FATHER Florian Zeller
11 CLYBOURNE PARK Bruce Norris
12 CYPRUS AVENUE David Ireland
13 JOHN Annie Baker
14 HOME, I'M DARLING Laura Wade
15 PEOPLE, PLACES AND THINGS Duncan Macmillan
16 MIRAD, BOY FROM BOSNIA Ad de Bont
17 THAT FACE Polly Stenham
18 CONSTELLATIONS Nick Payne
19 THE AUTHOR by Tim Crouch
20 ALBION by Mike Bartlett

In 2017, I began with two groups of eight. I taught the identical session at 2pm and 6pm. By 2019, some writers requested a second year so I started a monthly all-day course on a Friday. By 2020, I had two groups, one in its second year and the other in its third. I now have four groups of six, at different levels. I find six writers the perfect number for a playwriting group.

The Friday sessions go like this: from 10.30 am to 1.30 pm the group discusses certain set plays that every member has read in the intervening month. The discussion revolves on what the playwright wants to say and the technique, style and genre through which he or she expresses it.

Vincent's Club

I use the reading of outstanding contemporary work to develop and enhance every writer's approach to the dramatic stories he or she wants to tell.

In the afternoon, from 2.30 to 5.30pm each writer gets 30 minutes individual attention from myself and the group on what they have written in the past month. All writers circulate their work 48 hours before the Friday sessions. Each writer reads every other writer's work.

This reading of each other's work is the core principle of the course. It means that every month a writer's play is absorbed and discussed by both the tutor and the five other writers.

I am as happy doing this as anything I have ever done – it has minimum admin and maximum creative focus. I hope to continue with it as long as I possibly can.

A recent poster for the course

10
AFTERWORD

It's taken the writing of this memoir to find its title, THEATREMAKER. I've called it by many names during its composition. Yet I believe this one is the right one. It is the umbrella word to cover all the activity described in the book. Devising plays, directing plays, producing plays, writing plays and now teaching plays. Each era has brought a new development and I love theatre because it is a house that contains many rooms.

There has been one unfolding shock to myself in looking back so thoroughly on decades of theatremaking. I knew nothing when I began and I took on the three of the greatest classic texts ever written – *Don Juan* of Byron, Cervantes *Don Quixote* and Shakespeare's last play, *The Tempest*. Yet only now, my 70th birthday past, am I learning how plays are constructed, or, more simply, how plays work. My playwriting course has taught me so much that I never knew until I taught it. I feel that my theatre education has happened in reverse – if only I had known then what I know now.

View of High Street, Oxford, from Vincent's window

Then I reflect that innocence, lack of fear and a willingness to learn can take us a long way. It also helped that I had a strong reaction against what the theatre establishment was doing at the time – and sufficient arrogance to believe that I could do better! In fact, the innocence and the ignorance begin to look essential criteria. The most exciting feature of the early years of directing plays was entering a world that was un-defined, a world in which you had to learn the rules for yourself because they did not exist in a book or a college or even in the English language. It felt an entirely original thing to do because no one knew what it was.

All people knew was that it was impossible to earn a living in theatre and it was definitely advisable not to get involved.

The only book that inspired us was Peter Brook's *The Empty Space* and even that was best at telling you what *not* to do.

So, if I had known all that I know now, would I have directed better productions, written better plays? No to the first question, yes to the second.

Directing is so much about facilitating a group of people and having a powerful desire to tell a story through that group. It requires a certain passion, this desire to drive your ideas *through other people*. I think youth and intuition *can* win over experience, especially to find joy in such intense and repetitive work.

Writing plays is a different matter – all the exciting playwrights in Britain and America, too many to name, have strong technique and a mature (or intuitive) grasp of form and structure. You can't finish a compelling full-length play without technique. I spent 18 months on a play called *Arlo*, because I didn't understand how a play was constructed – a bit of McKee or Truby or Jeffreys would have got me out of the holes I kept digging for myself.

It was lucky I was the director of my plays – that way, I saw their faults and re-wrote as I went. But this is a painful and sleepless way to create plays, even if they turn out right in the end.

I like adults who want to write plays. I enjoy teaching them. The writers on my course are often individuals who have done well in their life-careers and desire to express their ideas or their creativity through the craft of playwriting. Almost all their writing aims to reflect the world in which we live now.

This is why I love modern plays, why I pay the high box-office prices to keep up to date with what writers are saying and the form that they choose to say it in. Matt Lopez's *The Inheritance*, Lucy Prebble's *A Very Expensive Poison*, Lynn Nottage's *Sweat*, Mike Bartlett's *Albion*, Jeremy O Harris' *Slave Play*, Jez Butterworth's *Jerusalem*, Annie Baker's *John*, Sam Grabiner's *Boys on the Verge of Tears*, *et alia*, all spring to mind.

AFTERWORD

Over the last 40 years, I have moved from being a dedicated classicist (roughly 1978 to 2000) to an advocate of new writing. Of course, the classical plays don't evaporate, they are part of me now. I seldom watch them in the theatre. I'll always spend my money on a new play rather than an old one.

The willingness to learn remains. I enjoy that trait in my writers very much. I hope to continue running my course. In 2022, I opened a season of play-readings at the Old Fire Station in Oxford – there were a dozen plays that emerged from my course over its first five years that deserved to be seen. The dual impact of Covid and Netflix on theatres meant that new and original work became in danger of disappearing unless we could find do-it-yourself ways to launch these plays to a new public. I am glad to say that we have built a loyal following for Oxford Platforms (as they are called) and we average about 100 people at each performance. We have plans for further staged readings into 2027.

JR
February 2025

THEATREMAKER PART 2

CONTEMPORARY JOURNALS 1980-1981

What follows below are two long edited extracts from contemporary journals written in 1980 and 1981.

EUROPE JOURNAL, 1980

The first is a solo trip to Europe in which I learn a great deal about theatre on the continent and make close contact with amongst others, the great German theatre director, Peter Stein. The book I was reading at the time was *The Man Without Qualities* by Robert Musil and a number of coincidences on the trip inspired me to create a theatre piece based upon the book and called *Berlin/Berlin*.

PARIS, BERLIN, WARSAW, PRAGUE, VIENNA

October, 1980…

28 October 1980
Paris
***THE ORESTEIA* Aeschylus**
Directed by Peter Stein

A huge black wall, with a door and light from behind, makes Clytemnestra as super-real as necessary, in a dress that just touches the ground, so she appears like a statue because it is tapered – chorus very disciplined, a bit Kantor-like, moving around the auditorium; Agamemnon on a railway cart on tracks – rather absurd this – but one accepted the reality of it all completely – no quibbles. Perfectly realised and understated, it was all there. But afterwards Pierre Audi told me that the entire theatre had been converted – walls and ceiling brought from Germany – and the cost became evident and mind-blowing. Was it worth those hundreds of thousands of pounds? It basically enabled the chorus to whisper…

Of course, it's all in German and I am reading my English version to keep track. It relies on following intricately, and over a long period, the pattern and detail of what is being said and why Stein has chosen to have it said in this manner. The text is all, especially in a production of such undoubted integrity and purity as this. One certainly picks up the big picture – but these are expressed in slow crescendos and diminuendos that require appreciation of the complicated fretwork by which the whole thing is constructed.

The German character certainly worked well on the absolutism and ruthlessness of, say, Clytemnestra. One could believe in her completely.

Stein has the stature necessary to translate all sorts of different forms of expression into a quality of theatre that is as fine as any other art form. I am doing this trip for that reason really: to see if the theatre as a medium is an art form still capable of heights in both form and content. And, as there is no training available to me as a director in Britain, to try and glean how it's done. The intelligent engagement by the actors that I see in Europe is not something I've found in the big companies in England, not even in the RSC.

It is interesting that the larger the space and the bigger the audience, the more compelling the illusion of "real" conversation becomes. With Strehler's production of Goldoni's *La Trilogie de la Villégiature* and Stein's *Gross und Klein*, this intimacy of real conversation before thousands of people was thrilling, especially with direct address to the audience from characters who until that moment were absorbed in an intimate dialogue with another character.

The Stein/Strehler directorial method appears to focus very sharply on the actor as an individual – on the actor's capacity to see, in a directorial sense, the world of the play, and to perceive the people who they must embody. The actor has a mixture of instinct, of wide reading, of being modern – and a director who gives you your head.

This combination is not expected of actors very much in England. I'm sure they could do it, but the manager/worker split in England is as firmly deep-set in the theatre as in industry. The director is a sort of dashing freelance maker of gestures, letting others paint, design, light, act and manage his ideas, while the actor is a Schweik figure who'll pull down his trousers in front of 800 people if asked to do it in the right venue.

The dreamer in every actor is nurtured by the drama school and the business itself, until their natural energy is sapped, and they can't think anymore because they have become so fed up with waiting.

So, to come back to Stein, and Strehler, here are two directors who produce plays that seem genuinely adult, performed by individuals who are capable of what Jack Nicholson once called 'modern sexual acting'. I've seen a lot of it in Europe, not so much in England.

31 October 1980
PETER STEIN Speaking at Centre Pompidou, Paris

Peter Stein was unlike Brook, or Mnouchkine, because he patently resented any guru status. He wore black and grey, slightly dusty, and had the tension of one not lacking confidence, but intensely concentrating to be clear in all he said (in French, not much better than mine). Medium height, 43 years old, obviously goes to bed late, quite sharp features and wavy hair, non-smoker, given to expressing things – when not contortedly articulate – by various sorts of raspberries and kicks and stabs. He was straightforwardly likeable and clever, and very aware that to create great things in the theatre you need the combined intelligence of many diverse people, and a good text – and that getting that is only possible by listening to others, and never holding the idea of your own vision as a 'precious' thing, but rather recognising that it thrives through engaged discussion and questioning. A genuinely modern socialist figure he seemed to me, a combination of idealism from 1968 in the method of his work, and old-fashioned rigour in the work itself – all of this, of course, emanating from a man of considerable artistic talent and imagination. Perhaps that should be said first. My companion said he was like a "sharp vinaigrette". He was disarmingly direct and interested.

Gross und Klein by Botho Strauss, directed by Peter Stein, 1980

GROSS UND KLEIN
By Botho Strauss at Odeon De Paris
Directed by Peter Stein

I went on from the Pompidou to see *Gross und Klein*.

An opening scene, woman alone on stage talking to the audience, on a chair at a table with water and jug, and two empty chairs. She is sitting alone talking to a packed Odeon, about 2,000 people. Woman (Edith Clever) asleep in bed, man dressed, sitting next to it. Curtains drawn. She wakes, clocks him, screams. They talk, very natural. She goes to wash, off-stage, man goes to curtains, draws themn, blinding light of 10 am sun, real windows and street; he opens them, lights a fag in real wind, talks loudly to bathroom. Girl comes past in street, looks in, and gradually that begins a tour-de-force in which the woman in the bathroom brings all her clothes out, and the two women, one still at the window, carry on a lively debate, including a simulated fashion show. Girl at window eventually forced out (applause) and man and woman conclude. Strong, funny, silly. Sense of adults and real talk and time to let them become people. It's a movie in the theatre.

Good idea. Single saxophone. Then four rooms each lit individually; more surreal, expressionistic. Excellent sense of time, and of adults living in the city.

GERMANY
2 November 1980
BOCHUM REPERTORY THEATRE, West Germany

I catch a very different approach to theatre-making in this extremely well subsidised theatre in an industrial town. The neighbouring conurbation is Wuppertal where Pina Bausch has based her company since 1973.

Bochum is a good, dull, working city, very clean, with a magnificent theatre, very 50s and pristine, full of old ladies on doors, coat-checks, programmes. Of course, two-thirds empty for *Kurosawa City*, a new surreal play on the problems of Germany and terrorism. It is directed by Claus Peymann, the artistic director of the theatre and leading light of the avant-garde.

Extraordinary sets:

A great heap of rubber and coal and junk in centre of stage. Really enormous. People climb up and down it; the main character, now Manson-like, shoots his friend, shoots a policeman who crawls naked upon the stage, scalps them very graphically with a bread knife and then delivers a mammoth monologue to the audience, then turns around and shoots the sun. Some objection from audience happens, and people walk out; he stops and waits for them to leave, watching them! I admired his will.

Long scene-changes, no interval, no bar, nothing after the show, all trooped home boringly. Instead of programme, however, you get text and information, very impressively cheap, subsidy must be HUGE. Cost of sets is colossal.

Two beers in restaurant with two of the cast, two Swiss-German actresses. They were pleasant, open, very at ease, both young. What came out mostly was the complete job security they had there in Bochum; they were in what plays they were told to be in, they did what was required, they hated Bochum but liked the theatre, both had nice little flats.

I felt, after talking to them, that their contentment and ease with their theatre and its organisation focused the entire responsibility for the reputation of the Bochum ensemble on the director. Since the actors do not choose the play, or the reasons for its staging, or its methods of staging, they carry out the ideas of the director, quite literally embody the ideas in the head of the man at the helm. Hence good directors (Claus Peymann has been in charge since 1979) are attracted there because of an able and efficient, willing working-force, and a theatre which is tolerant of experimental image and text. But what this means with *Kurosawa City, Measure for Measure* (nude go-go Duke) is that nothing really changes, just that the subversive image becomes absorbed into the establishment; the actors comply through the obedient way they take direction. Anything can be done, as long as it is authorised by the director. There is far too little that comes from the actors.

At Bochum collective creativity is severely restricted but the director is entirely unrestricted. The actors are on a wage differential – more for each year that you work there – so that it carries always the incentive of staying. There is real security in keeping with the building, and the actor's status as employee is more as an actor-performer, not as a thinking stake-holder, with responsibility for its course. That is where the director comes in; crazy image-making, massively subsidised, an institutionalised anarchy on classics.

Bochum is an interesting variation on English repertory; I feel that the subsidy is so high that the director is spared having to worry too much about box-office percentages. In England, one cannot keep a theatre open – even with subsidy – without achieving a high cash capacity at the box office over the course of the producing year.

3 November 1980
WEST BERLIN

My friend Cosima welcomes me at the station. The shock was learning (to my shame) that West Berlin is a walled island in East Germany. Cosima's house is an early 20th-century apartment with six enormous rooms and a vast kitchen. Six young-ish people live here. Everything 'alternative' and friendly, and not at all informed about anything in Berlin, except the Rudolph Steiner school, which they all adore, and attend eurhythmy classes there. Cosima's boyfriend slightly hippy but very, very tidy. Germany has such an organised alternative society.

JR in Berlin, November 1980

Walk around, get lost, go to Checkpoint Charlie by train. I expected the wall to be 70 feet high; of course, it's two low walls, about ten feet tall, with about fifteen ways of dying between them. I go to the Checkpoint Charlie Museum, which fascinates me, although later I am to hear it run down scathingly by various people as a sensationalist shrine of the Springer publishing house.

Chilling to walk past the 1936 Olympic Stadium at night – everything so quiet and deserted. I went back to town and walked along Bismarckstrasse – all nearly deserted – a great central boulevard of restaurants, theatre, opera house, dance-halls and bars. Just hardly anyone around.

5 November 1980
CAFÉ EINSTEIN

11.00 am – meeting at International Theatre Institute – grim indifference from the President of West German ITI. The ITI partly exists to welcome and inform international theatre travellers. The President is scathing of the scene in West Berlin. Nothing to see, can't get near Stein or Schaubühne, level of plays rubbish, can't recommend anything, Berlin only alive when festivals are on, seeing Agamemnon enough of Oresteia to 'get the idea', try East Berlin, might be better there, nothing to interest you here, nice to meet you, can you find your own way out, goodbye.

Like Bismarckstrasse, Kurfurstendamm is a colossal boulevard with a vast number of cafes, restaurants, discos, bars, cinemas etc – the city needs another million inhabitants under 50 for the boulevards and their amenities to take on the appearance of being necessary. The only place I saw an outdoor crowd in Berlin was in the busiest intersection of the Kurfurstendamm and Budapesterstrasse. I was exhausted by traversing these street-fields after three hours, and collapsed into a large mixed-age café called Elsa's at 6pm, on a huge table with a low lamp over it. The relaxation of it was wonderful. I drank half a bottle of Beaujolais and had an enormous plate of Westphalian ham and Camembert.

Walked to the wall in Kreuzberg, and looked out over the river. The day was colourless, the weather bitingly cold, a little bit of snow everywhere. The wall runs on the West side of the river, and another "water wall" a line of hooked railings that also go deep underwater, covered with barbs. No movement anywhere, except the heads of two guards in the control tower. Climbed to the view-point, and looked over to more buildings in the East. Everything is so dull in its appearance, and so deserted. But it does feel better to be looking at it from this side in this mood, than from the other.

On this journey, I have been excited by reading the Picador version of Robert Musil's 1930 novel (in three parts) *A Man Without Qualities*. Walking around this city, I imagine setting it here, where East and West don't meet. It is a place where you can imagine extreme actions, whether political (the main character, Ulrich), or

The Man Without Qualities by Robert Musil

personal (the deranged ex-prisoner, Moosbrugger). I am excited by the thought of creating something modern for ATC. And tonight, at the Café Einstein there is a Robert Musil reading, by an Austrian actor/director called Nikolaus Haenel.

I meet Cosima at 7. Café Einstein is a great Viennese-style room with huge mirrors and a sofa going round the entire wall, marble tables, and newspapers and magazines on a stand. The reading takes place just off the back of the main Café. Haenel reads by candlelight to a packed room of 40. All in German. The young audience laugh a lot, and I am frustrated that I can't understand a word, but I am determined to be here because it is the 100th birthday celebration of Musil. I even discover he lived around the corner here in Berlin. It makes my re-location of the novel seem a natural move. And Haenel looks like Walter Benjamin, reading aloud from a stack of (untranslated) journals. At half time I go up to him, explain my particular interest in Musil, and ask if I could meet him the next day. He immediately agrees, and we fix 9.00 am at the Volksbühne theatre in West Berlin, where he is rehearsing a Hochhuth play. Afterwards, I press Cosima for

Café Einstein, Berlin

information, and what comes out, in the main, is that everything *she* has heard, I have read in a fictionalised form in *A Man Without Qualities*.

**7 November 1980
EAST BERLIN**

Met Haenel at 9.40 – he was late. We talk, he has to go to rehearsal, I go to cafe, write beginnings of plot idea, meet him at noon, go to his West Berlin flat nearby. It turns out he is in an unusual position. He is an Austrian actor who has worked in West Germany for years; last year he married an East German actress who performed with him in West Berlin. As such, he is allowed to live in both East and West Berlin, and to work in both sectors. Daily, he goes through Checkpoint Charlie, his passport a rash of DDR stamps, living in two systems, two cultures. I was fortunate in meeting one of a handful of "total Berliners" – there are fewer than 10 others. His West Berlin home is an enormous pre-war apartment; in his sitting-room is a bright parquet floor, and three chairs in the centre, in a circle, with a lamp by each one. The books are in two long lines along the floor of each wall. A stereo, and that's it. The bedroom has a double bed, a cupboard, and a cot. It is as big as the sitting-room. A dividing wall opens up, and gives you a room large enough to put on a play for 70 people. The only other thing is pictures along every wall, all modern, most abstract. He explains them in some detail, and then we go to East Berlin in his car. He helps me through the Checkpoint, and we drive into the Eastern sector.

There is an absence of colour, and an appearance of dust everywhere. The centre of East Berlin has roads even wider than in the West, and huge modern buildings set even further back off the streets. Of course, Berlin – East and West – was a single gigantic city complex – the scale really takes me aback. It's not only big in area, everything in it stresses size and space. Alexanderplatz is a vast, circular empty space with a cranky modern compass with the names of all the forbidden cities lit up all over it – Los Angeles, Honolulu, Paris, Caracas, Madrid, London, New York. There is scarcely any noise, only feet on pavement. I see dull faces, dull clothes, everyone looking straight ahead. There is almost no advertising. The extraordinary thing, as Nikolaus drives me around, is that here is a city so regulated that you can take it in at a glance. It's a relief after West Berlin, it is so uncomplicated, there is no light, no messages, no junk. We walked to Brecht's grave at twilight, and the city is ominously quiet.

When you drive in East Berlin, there is one thing I forgot to say: there are theatres everywhere. The Berliner Ensemble at the Volksbühne (E.), Komische Oper, Maxim Gorki Theatre are some of the big state theatres around the Friedrichstrasse. The theatres do have big advertisements on them, including dancing girls on the Komische Oper. It must have once been as fabulous as Paris. But all that Berlin was reduced to 75 million tonnes of rubble.

East Berlin, mid-1970s

It is a memorable introduction, and a cool one, and I thank Nikolaus at 5 on Alexanderplatz. Except that we never talked of Musil. He asks me to lunch on Sunday.

9 November 1980
NIKOLAUS HAENEL and JUTTA HOFFMANN

Met Nikolaus Haenel at Checkpoint at 1.00. Lunch on the very edge of East Berlin In his wife's exceptionally nice house. Apart from the unavoidable plainness of the food, one could be anywhere. Jutta Hoffmann, his very pretty, blonde wife, is famous for playing the leading role in Miss Julie in an erotic, defiant production at the Berliner Ensemble in 1975. It so scandalised audiences and critics that it was closed after 10 performances. Jutta speaks no French or English, neither does the elderly actress who is there too – so Nikolaus acts as interpreter, and it all goes very well. They are very interested to know what I make of their theatres. The older actress, Claudia, used to work with Brecht, and mourns the dull, obedient acting at the Berliner Ensemble now. Certainly I've seen a lot of obedience on stage in Germany – even in the Schaubühne, for all I know, perhaps the arch-obedient theatre of all time…

Jutta says she won't leave the DDR, where she is very popular, but recently she was put out of work for a year because she headed a petition against the refusal to issue a visa to a very talented East German musician to go on an international tour. She is gradually back in favour again. Nikolaus says that this time last year, they had a party for this artist; at 3 in the morning, 20 of them were sitting around, having a wonderful time. Now not one of that party is left in East Germany – they've all got out. I say (when asked) that the thing I notice most in East Berlin is the calm. Jutta nods vigorously – it is what they fear most, she says – no one will do anything. Every time Nikolaus says 'East Germany', she says 'DDR', correcting him. She is not a party member, yet she appears loyal. She gets many scripts from the West, but turns most of them down because 'they are shit.' Time and again she says, in one way or another, that the only thing that matters is the script, and what it has to say. 'It is the work itself that matters only'. Again and again she slips in this remark. Yet she is laughing, mimicking, joking most of the time.

Both are in a second marriage, with a baby one year old…but both are so privileged, both in freedom of movement and in relative wealth, that they are not typical. Between them they know both Germanies deeply – well, she more the East, he the West – and their consciousness of Germany, the particular place in European life that they have chosen, is interesting. If Jutta's life inside her house is agreeable, life outside can be extremely awkward…and she stays.

Nikolaus talks about the Schaubühne: he dislikes its perfectionism, its 'exquisite pessimism', its lack of spontaneity, its high-art place. He admits, though, that Stein is the only remaining German director for whom he'd like to work.

MOTHER COURAGE

I get the train to Friedrichstrasse and go into Brecht's *Mother Courage*, with text in hand. This production has been in their repertoire for over 30 years, was directed by the author and is their showpiece. This time, front row, free again, middle seat (thanks again to the East German ITI). First half is tedious and I am fighting sleep with the actors inches away from me. This is obedient acting of the most museum-like kind, and the direction feels dull. But the second half, when I change my seat for a box, is wonderful, because the play is so magnificent, and I am finally crying as Katrine bangs the drum again and again and again. I leave the theatre uplifted, and feeling wonderful. I note how the narrative of *Mother Courage* gains so enormously by the use of song and simple movement. I'm glad I saw it at the Berliner Ensemble. I get to the Checkpoint with a minute to spare, and straight home.

Nikolaus Haenel and Jutta Hoffmann, 40 years on

(Note: Jutta Hoffmann went on to play starring roles for all the leading directors in Germany after The Wall came down in 1991, including Peter Zadek, Luc Bondy, Thomas Langhoff and Robert Wilson. She also became very well-known for her film and television roles.)

11 November 1980
First Meeting with PETER STEIN

I go to the Schaubühne on Hallesches Ufer in Kreuzberg. No, impossible to see Herr Stein. I go into restaurant of the theatre. He's sitting there. I speak to him, assure him I'm not after getting a touring date at the Schaubühne, or working there, I just want to talk over a few points mentioned in my letter to him. He agrees to see me at 4.30. <u>AT LAST!</u> Write all afternoon on Musil, back at 4.30. Stein turns up at 5.00.

The first home of the Schaubühne in Kreuzberg

I tell Stein a little about ATC and why I've come to see him. He's got a sharp precise face, with very bright, small eyes, and a thin moustache over a thin mouth. He begins by saying that he doesn't know what play to do next – always he's not sure, but now he is particularly worried because of the point I begin on: the increasing age of audiences, the inertia and disaffection of young people. How can he make a play either for or about these people? He says he hates techno music so deeply; that when he visits these clubs for young people – not for the second or third time but for the fifteenth – they arrive full of fight and passion, but once the music has really begun, they go all limp – all the vitality drains from them. When they go home at two or three in the morning, they slouch off like old men leaving a factory, heads bowed. How can he get them into his theatre, how can he represent a phenomenon that he considers morbid and that he doesn't understand?

This concern is linked to another that I raise, that his productions tend towards a 'perfectionist aesthetic', the philosophical tilt of which is deeply pessimistic. He refutes this strongly, saying rather that the *Oresteia*, and all his work, has led to a theatre which always gives a 'vote for the survivors'.

So – as regards representing modern life in a spiritually positive, if not necessarily optimistic, way ... he said that a few years ago, when in effect the mood of '68 still carried over, he did not find it a problem to catch the young, and keep his theatre a place in which the theatre was representative of all that is strong and progressive; the churlishness of the critics also helped to set up a defiant ambience that made the Schaubühne fashionable in the way that a good theatre needs, both for its economic well-being and for the morale of its actors. But somehow, in the last two or three years, he has felt his age thrust upon him. He is now a prized possession of the West Berlin City Council; when he said he would leave Berlin if he didn't get a satisfactory new space, they realised that they would lose a vital cultural attraction as closely associated with West Berlin as the Philharmonic Orchestra. Consequently, they are building for Peter Stein a multi-millionmark new Schaubühne on the Kurfurstendamm, which will open in a year or so.

The Schaubühne has gradually come to occupy one of the highest places in cultural life in West Germany – but not the place where the young go. The Schaubühne has established a niche of such artistic excellence (somewhere between fringe and establishment), and is known to have received so much money, that its image in West Berlin has altered. Stein, at 43, has reached an age

Peter Stein 1980

when he can't go on being a maverick. His reputation is enormous; he can't go back. He is worried that he is just a little too well-educated, a few years too old, to have anything forceful to say to the student age-group – in short, where to go now? He wants the Schaubühne to be seen abroad, to show as he says, that "open political discussion" is what West Germany prizes most in its daily life. It is clearly what matters most to him.

Stein demands:

i) Long rehearsal for actors and for workshops (i.e. sets and costumes), so a whole beautifully-made little universe is produced annually.

ii) The play must allow scope, and be suggestive, at least, of more than can be found in its text. They usually work on a text for 12 months,

iii) Above all, the level of engagement by the actors must be of the highest order; they are expected to question every move.

iv) Note – 132 people work in the Schaubühne and only 27 are actors – the rest administrate, advise, make, publicise, assist, write, direct, and generally provide the kind of backup not usually found outside the Royal Family.

As You Like It, Schaubühne, 1977

MASTER OF THE REBELS www.theguardian.com
John O'Mahony

Stein returned to the Schaubühne in 1976 to take on his first Shakespeare, *As You Like It*. The research process was extensive, with lectures on Elizabethan stagecraft and a company field trip to Warwickshire. Instead of the usual practice of including research in a lavish programme, the company transformed it into Shakespeare's Memory (1976), four hours of masked processions, Morris dancing, mummers plays and extracts from the plays.

Perhaps unnerved by the complexity of Shakespeare's text, Stein was unusually tentative. "We approached Shakespeare as we would a great continent," he said at the time, "and perhaps our navigational means were not quite adequate, maybe the boats were too small and the sails too big." *As You Like It* premiered in September 1977. The action began in an unprepossessingly cool, ice-blue chamber, with the actors performing in a restrained manner throughout the first two acts. Then in Act 2, baffled audiences were led in single file through a tunnel filled with the sounds of the forest into the crepuscular labyrinth of Arden. Stein's distance even from the German Shakespearean tradition, his willingness to illustrate the text with daring settings and thematic choreography, gave the plays a vitality "unknown in British productions," wrote the Guardian's Michael Billington.

11 November 1980
On acting in England

Stein told me about his visit to the NT in London; he and his company visited the National Theatre in London in 1978. Over 6 nights in the bar after shows, English actors kept coming up, having a drink, and then saying ... "How exactly did you get that moment when... I mean... do you... how long did it take... and how...". And through all the fascinated questioning emerged a good conversation with many English actors, all deeply intrigued ... his company enjoyed their English trip for that reason ... the openness and curiosity of frustrated English actors.

He met Alan Howard years ago, and talked with him for a long time. He could never get Howard to see the significance of the questions Stein's actors ask themselves – 'why am I doing it?' and 'what is it for?'. The metaphysical, philosophical, political and other questions seemed so easily answered by Howard, so readily assumed. When his company watched his pyrotechnical performance of *Coriolanus*, they just sat there open-mouthed in bemusement, horror, wonder. How could he strut in leather, shouting this extraordinary, compressed and vital language, in a play that is the embodiment of civil friction and trouble? Stein was completely perplexed at Howard's divine ease of mind.

He felt that the performance was entirely unexamined and facile throughout.

Stein thinks that the danger in England is that we will 'laugh ourselves to death'. To the implication that he couldn't direct comedy, he said that their production of Labiche's *Das Sparschwein (The Piggy Bank)* was hilarious, and audiences loved it. The actors loved it too. He feels it is a far deeper problem not to be able to be serious.

He does have a blind spot about Shakespeare being funny. He made the point that in Germany there are not the regional differences to exploit, nor, really, the class differences either … that the German language has a democratic poetic charge, as in *Oresteia*, that English lacks. He is visibly bursting to make his points – as if he has not had a conversation like this for a long time.

'I can't get on with Mnouchkine, but I found your Peter Brook OK.'

12 November 1980
Second Meeting with Peter Stein

When I meet him the following night at the Schaubühne, he came up enthusiastically, teased and joked; quite a lot of banter between us about England and Germany being funny in different ways. He thinks our productions of Shakespeare are a 'pantomime horse'. At 7pm, I saw his production of *The Libation Bearers* and then at 10pm he took me off to his office in another building and showed me photographs of *Shakespeare's Memory, As You Like It* and *Gross und Klein*, until 2.00 am. And I felt I had not only met him but made friends with him, and he warmly accepted my suggestion that I write to him, sharing my Berlin story, and that he comment upon it. As luminous theatre directors seem to do, he smoked all my cigarettes. His last words after showing me these beautifully-filed photographs, all 10' x 8', was – 'never mind'. It sums up his acknowledgment that he carries with him an obsessive fascination with detail and structure. His English meant 'ah well', but it tilted into 'never mind'. We shook hands and said goodnight – and for the second night running I'd had a German talking at me unstoppably, showing me everything relentlessly, and I was so exhausted that I felt, too, in a way, 'never mind'. I had begun to feel sick with the photographs, that lacked the joy of Mnouchkine or Brook productions – the same intense, serious faces in each one. The photos were in a massive pile on the floor and someone would spend hours filing them back the next day.

But the concept of, say, *Shakespeare's Memory* is awesome – a gigantic De Mille history lesson in an old film studio, with numerous exotic, fabulous sets and decors and constructions for a 25-mark audience to pass through, lasting two nights, at three hours a shot. 100 performances in all (ie 200) in 9 months, at an outlay of one whole year of rehearsal and preparation – and, of course, millions of marks. What of that vast theatre set, now? The corridor cages, the great ark, the wheels of life, the Elizabethan theatre, the sculptures, the gorgeous costumes,

Antikenprojekt II 1980, director Peter Stein

the entire reconstruction of the Renaissance in plywood – all burnt? 'Please don't discuss this...'. He makes movies in the theatre, and the concept and structure is awe-inspiring. His feeling is architectural, his understanding deeply educated. He didn't feel he could take on the challenge of *As You Like It* until his company and his audience could understand the world from which the play sprang. To say Peter Stein presents me with a whole new way of thinking is an understatement.

He was a student of comparative literature for nine years. He would work for six months and then travel; so did Mnouchkine, so did Brook, all three great travellers. They are all good self-effacers when out in the world. All have a capacity to become what they please – 'I am large, I contain multitudes.' Now I understand the distinction between those who draw a style from a text and those who impose one on it – the difference is vast, and separates as clearly as Coleridge's definition of imagination and fancy – imagination orders, fancy associates. In these 'imaginers', there is always the fanciful at work, but they know the relative ease of having an idea against the difficulty of profoundly embodying a seminal text. What you get with Stein is the reality of each line spoken, the revelation of a text. It seems as if each line is spoken for the first time.

Brook comes well out of this, with his 'rough' style and his low-budget productions. Brook has his economics right. But Brook is twelve years older than Stein and at a different part of his journey. Stein is in something of a gilded cage, the Social Democratic luxury of subsidy, and this accounts for the violent rejection of him by parts of the left-wing press – they claim that he has let his skill be bought.

I liked Stein, because he seemed to me genuinely true to himself, and if he passes out of style, he'll come back in again. He is not an eclectic in the Brook way, and not susceptible to faddishness, neither does he become possessive of his 'boys and girls' (as he calls his actors) like Mnouchkine does. He keeps them. He lost Bruno Ganz, however. He confesses he has never found anyone like him and this clearly saddens Stein – he describes him as irreplaceable. When you are close to Stein, he gives the impression of a dominator. He has a ruthlessness voluntarily tempered by his choice of a collaborative medium.

That day, he was reeling from having lost the vote on wishing to introduce ten new actors and designers from Bremen. The company said 'No'. As he took me round his theatre, he was huffing and puffing over little details – no-one he encountered worried too much. The atmosphere is close and easy. This is the paradox that he admits – you work your balls off to keep who you have, but it's good for everyone when there's a change. He has films of most productions, and I could have watched them all had I wanted to.

(With support from the Goethe Institute, Stein invited me to be his assistant on Genet's Les Negres in January 1983. ATC were on at The Warehouse at the same time and, sadly, I was unable to take up this unique opportunity.)

13 November 1980
TRAIN TO WARSAW

The next day I tore myself away from West Berlin, before I failed to go anywhere else. But I regretted, and still do, not seeing the DDR East Berlin History Museum, which a frantic museum worker told me about in a West Berlin museum (called 'The Berlin Museum') that has nothing in it after 1920. 'No Adolf Hitler, no Holocaust. You'll find that only in the DDR,' he said, and then, turning round nervously all the while, '... this country is, you must understand me, sick.. do you see... Franz-Josef Strauss (right-wing Bavarian politician) very nearly got in... the Checkpoint Charlie Museum? Oh no! You're on the wrong track altogether... Stein? Yes, but SPD... there is no freedom here either...'. There was nothing unsound or extreme about the way he spoke.

I can't help liking this country. Maybe I mean loving this country. There is a seriousness and an honesty in its young people, that comes across all the time.

Long, restless journey spent with a pleasant young Pole who lives in London. He shouts abuse at a Russian soldier he sees guarding an army vehicle train. Arrive Warsaw, totally dark at 7.00pm, and Margaret Myewska, Director of the Polish ITI meets me on the platform.

Warsaw is easily the most scheduled and arranged of all the cities for me. I'm off the train, and directly into a play at the Palace of Art. Margaret shoos me up the steps to get me to hand in my coat, for the first of many times, before the bells ring and it starts.

FREDERICK THE GREAT

The evening begins with placards, and an applauded announcement about Solidarność (Solidarity). Solidarity is the first free trade union, set up only 3 months ago in the Lenin shipyard in Gdańsk and led by Lech Wałęsa. The play is *Frederick the Great*, and the set is a not very successful replica of 'Sans Souci' with big areas of black wings (curtains) still prominent amongst the golden cherubs and perspective. Not exactly a modern play about Solidarność, I think – I want to know what is happening now in Poland.

I am in for a surprise. If a line has an applicability to today or to Solidarność, the lead actor turns and plays to the audience, without it causing a single hiccup in the line of his performance. He actually leaves the actor he is talking to and walks straight down to the thrust and speaks the line directly to us.

Solidarity banner

"You Polish people are only capable of little acts of heroism and death," he says when a character shoots himself. Applause.

"You need money to have authority". Loud applause

"You Poles should save your money if you want to eat". Very loud applause.

If he felt a line would work better by addressing it to us (while at the same time addressing it to someone else) he raised his eyebrows, he winked and teased and paused – but he returned, without minutely denting the smooth line of the dialogue with the other, carried on and was answered – so that you thought, did that really happen or did I imagine that? Surely he can't … but he had… and he did it again and again and everything he 'ghost-asided' like this was something appropriate to the current circumstances in Poland.

His command and humour were awesome. It was the complete political integration of actor and play and audience; in this small community every nuance was understood. His use of his talents to bind trade unions, the audience, the play, himself and Frederick the Great together into a single strong statement, made with grace and humour, took my breath away. I've just seen the theatre, through the words of an historical text, say modern things that can't be stated in a newspaper or on television. How does a censor stop that?

The applause was abundant after this great performance, and as in the DDR, everyone then queued for twenty minutes for their coats in near silence, then went home. Margaret tells me it is considered rude to laugh in a Polish theatre, unless

Kantor's *Dead Class*

everyone really cannot help it. How loud the English laugh! Laughter is all right in England, because it doesn't matter if somebody hears you. In Poland, she says, it is bad form for an individual to laugh out loud.

I wandered Warsaw for two hours that night, and everything was dark, though some young people made a din on the streets; otherwise, a lot of drunks wandering about, and a feeling that a society will always rebel against an inert status quo, sooner or later. To me, in this moment, Kantor's *Dead Class* is an accurate representation of Poland, of people moving to orders, giving away nothing on the face, then resisting orders imperceptibly, and going another way.

14 NOVEMBER 1980
LIFE IN WARSAW

Warsaw: no newspapers, you have to queue early in the morning to buy one; no bread till 4pm; little food in the shops, only apples, cabbages, carrots, not much in the way of potatoes; chocolate shops with huge glass shelves with one packet of biscuits on each; butchers with no fresh meat, just some tins on the shelves; hot dogs stuffed with mushrooms, there are no sausages. Yet, in a little city bar, a sour cream soup of mushrooms was the best thing I tasted anywhere.

The film in the Warsaw museum of the Nazi destruction of Warsaw took my breath away – everything that I see, everywhere that I walk in the centre of old Warsaw has been re-constructed from the ruins of itself. The pride in the monuments, the packed trams, the crooked hotel bars, the sad dance floors, the dollar-buyers, the unfriendliness on the street, the sourness of Pole to Pole; the very astute common sense of the student leader I went to talk to in Warsaw University; the loveliness of the women, the little dome battle-hats they all wear so well, the well-dressed and proud carriage of the bourgeoise in the city, the utter forlorn-ness of people in groups as soon as you go further out of the centre – till you reach just-lit rooms in just-functioning stations, full of poor people in bad clothes, sitting, still, in large groups, saying nothing to each other, queuing for the one telephone, buying beer from a counter, beer with no label, and no glass for it; and through all this, everyone's acute respectability and tidiness – until you come to the peasant class, who give you a fright because you've never seen people as impoverished as that before…

Warsaw has two levels of existence. At the conscious, the life and images are conservative, obedient, tidy, dignified, proper, religious by habit and necessity; at the unconscious, they live those violent and bloody images so strange to the British, those visual shows full of anthems, and wheels, and heroism, and of hands appearing out of a pile of junk on stage, headless statues, and terrible wanton destruction, tableaux of hate and senseless violence, and people determinedly surviving. No wonder the vast majority of the country go to church, and crosses are everywhere. No Pole would be a believer in reason, or a simple humanitarian;

he could be an atheist or an absurdist – yet it seems here that even the young believe in the institution of the church. The Roman Catholic Church has an attendance far greater than Solidarity's ten million.

If Warsaw was ever made free, and it became rich, what a city it would be. As it is, it is a half-lit, impoverished, unstable, sandwiched backwater, with more good theatre than any other capital in the world. For its size, it is preposterously over-endowed artistically and intellectually. And so many paradoxes – television is very good, the Poles excel in music, graphic art, mathematics, science, not to mention realistic revolutionary thinking – and they have a rural economy that is centuries out of date. In Edinburgh, as I have said earlier, I'd seen the work of the Polish director Tadeusz Kantor and his 'Theatre of Death' captures his homeland like no one else.

15 November 1980
Chekhov's *PLATONOV*

Platonov is the best production I saw in Poland, and without doubt the most jubilant and spontaneous piece of work I've seen on the whole tour.

I didn't like the set much, although the garden setting was a clever simulation of gigantic bushes and Chinese lanterns, allowing action down-, middle-, and up-stage. The grouping of the first long scene was laboriously illustrative and fair. But the performance of Platonov by Zdzislaw Wardejn was insouciant, apparently reckless, and utterly seductive – from quite an unremarkable-looking man, slight and squarely-built. He is the character all the women fall for, and he convinced us entirely because he seemed so careless of himself, so un-egotistic. How difficult to play a complete charmer without appearing in the least conceited – though pleased at times with your successes. He did it naturally, and at times he achieved an astonishing intimacy with an enormous audience, opening himself up, allowing himself to look gauche, certainly not caring that towards the end of the play he looked ghastly. A complete 'giver', like the actor Wardejn, actually becomes the character in question...

The women were very distinct from each other, and the character of Sofia was desirable, ironic and glamorous in defeat. The moment before she is to grab Platonov and kiss him was held so deftly that you could hear the audience's collective heartbeat. Then she kissed him, and Platonov slid away, and punctured all tension as if it had never been there.

Perhaps the performance became too reckless, but the audience – the usually quiet Polish audiences – were roaring him on. He was incandescent, and could have got away with far more liberties than he took. He looked delighted with the five minutes of applause, which is always good to see – and I clapped, as I had *Frederick The Great*, so that Platonov could hear my claps above the rest and feel my delight – which, when you hear the phrase 'thunderous applause', is a collective phenomenon taking place, with each spectator wanting their applause to be heard over everyone else's.

16 November
SEEING PLAYS IN A FOREIGN LANGUAGE

I hadn't read this play before I saw it, and I didn't understand a word; though by the end I understood everything. It is an extraordinary thing, that; at the point where language is utterly alive on stage, and the actions clear, you hit a receptive plane that assimilates meaning over the course of the performance, so that by the end you catch up with the audience. The beginning is entirely dependent on the set, rate of change of grouping, and the animation or beauty of characters – or the frequency with which new ones arrive. As such, I, who am a worker in the theatre, become the model of the 'floating spectator', the last member of the various 'audience groups' within the audience to be stirred. I am a model of passive receptivity, unable to follow a nuance or make a distinction, appreciative or otherwise, until the performance is unmistakably fine. Conversely, if it is bad, and visibly slack or uninteresting, as a practitioner in the theatre I can study, with cruelly clear focus, the working to rule, working to idea, the not-working, the degree of dumb obedience, thoughtless or clumsy movement, vapid ranting and so on – to a degree terrifying to the actors, if my thoughts were broadcast over on their tannoy. Little about an acting company escapes the scrutiny of a 'deaf' director watching a performance; by the same token, nothing astonishes him more than to find, if the playing is good enough, that he finally grasps the whole packet of heart, ideas, character and plot.

So – a dangerous fellow is the next Polish director who stutteringly thanks me for his complimentary ticket to see an ATC production, though he could not 'follow it all'. Talk to him and see what he found true and what he found false. He's probably right, if he lasted the 2 hours …

17 November 1980
PRAGUE

My train arrives in Prague at 9.00am, a 14-hour journey. I can't sleep, but read a lot of Musil.

Read a history of Warsaw. Doze. A blood-red sunrise. I meet a man who makes marionettes in the carriage. He buys me a Czech breakfast of goulash and beer, takes me to the ITI – we speak French. I spend a very wide-awake day in Prague.

The city is an enormous shock. After re-constructed Berlin and re-constructed Warsaw, you walk about the most beautiful of European cities – a complete 14th–18th century paradise of architecture, gorgeous bridges with sculptures lining your path, palaces, castles, churches, monuments, squares, opera houses, open bright cafes, noisy beer halls, candle-lit vineries, well-dressed men and women – you pinch yourself that this is not the Vienna that you dreamt about. The lack of advertising, the trains, the sparkling new metro, the permanence and charm in every direction you look – and this is Socialism?! Why, it does work; look at these people – they look well, friendly, content, even better-dressed than Warsaw. A gorgeous American Embassy, a huge Monet exhibition packed. To my astonishment, people queue to look at pictures! Entrance is 1 krone (3p); parties going round the castle, sunset seen over Prague quite gorgeous as wood-smoke rises, people who speak French as well as German, even English, meat in shop windows, fewer queues, some loving couples, everything kept clean – what a picturesque, unspoilt little city – except for the massive, red Soviet banners everywhere you look, statements as concise and terminal as 'SOVIET UNION FOREVER'.

After eight hours' exposure to this, and a steak in a pretty restaurant, I meet Marta K– of Radio Prague, my friend-of-a-friend there. Yes, of course it's like this, it lulls everything… but – and then a list of the fears of everyday life, the restrictions, the endless petty corruption everywhere, the loathing – phlegmatic and quiet – of the Soviets, the marshalled red flag days when no-one cheers, and they put a 'cheering tape' onto TV and radio, the Lenin birthday rituals in schools, the run-down, unrestored suburbs, the impossibility of even being able to hire a car, let alone buy one, the packed trams, but really packed, so that you need to get out and walk when you're in a hurry. The impossibility of getting money changed to go abroad, or a visa without endless bribe demands. The Czechs, with their history of defeat, yet with their city intact. Their terrible, involved Soviet jokes. What Maria says tumbles out with the same sobriety and clarity that Margaret in Warsaw spoke.

I see two productions; one is awful, Bulgakov's *Molière*, the other worse still, a Russian 'philosophical comedy'. Both in packed small theatres with small stages. The over-employment of actors in 'wallpaper' parts was the worst I've ever seen – genuine loitering around the edges, miming surprise, sorrow or delight. One of these extras in the second play was stout, with a huge beard, another about 7 foot tall; as the sentimentality of the production became heightened, and the show moved to its climax in the breathy death of an acrobat, it really became a large-scale coarse acting sketch, fully subsidised and encouraged by a passive bleating audience, who clapped them for a full four minutes. Marta K–, who was with me, thought it just as bad, and we rushed out on the final blackout, up the stairs, to see a figure at the top, a sour, short man in a raincoat who looked blankly at us. She could lose her job if she is seen to be unofficially talking English with a foreigner – and she exhorted me not to ever mention her name, in anything.

She says, 'I don't want to be involved in politics.' Politics, for her, mean conspiracy, secrecy, danger, corruption, repression. The statement bears no relation to an English person saying, 'I don't want to be involved in politics'.

Nevertheless, Marta is swingeing and outspoken against the regime. Last year, 150,000 Czechs escaped. She is divorced, has a son of six, teaches English, and lives with her parents. In Prague, restrictions as to what can be seen, what you can read, and so on, are much tighter than in Warsaw. No American movies, no foreign papers even in the press centre, only plays that do not criticise the state. 'Slandering the state', or even talking critically on a train or on a tram, can lead to imprisonment.

I visit the Prague ITI. Mme Gabrielova, the director, says the Russian production of *Hamlet*, with the extraordinary Russian actor Vysotsky, was the greatest theatre production she ever saw in her career. She's seen all the very best European work; the Rustaveli company, Brook's company, Théâtre du Soleil, much of the work of Peter Zadek and Peter Stein – and she says this *Hamlet* was the very best of the best. The actor died last year of 'a heart attack', in Moscow, having, a year before, married a Frenchwoman in Paris. Without him, the production was over.

She says that the tone of the production was quiet. It began with Hamlet in the middle of a great space playing guitar, very sweetly, very well – then people wandering on, large scale intimate grouping. Hamlet was 'the man outside'. As the production went on, the actor achieved the extraordinary feat of holding a mirror up to the whole audience; so quietly, truly did he talk that everyone becomes drawn in utterly to his bewilderment, and his efforts to grasp meaning. It is interesting that the further east one moves, the more the degree of soul and truth become essential. It is almost as if the more adverse a regime, the greater the desire to find truth in fiction. So, *Hamlet* in Moscow – the incongruity is so vast it becomes quite magical.

http://rus-shake.ru/criticism/ Bartoshevich/Russian_Hamlet

On the other hand, in Socialist countries, when a production is bad, it's really the pits – as in Czechoslovakia.

20 November 1980
VIENNA

Mme Gabrielova's description of *Hamlet* reminds me that one of the great motivators in the theatre are the spell-binding productions you missed – you hear so much about them and over time, you piece the whole experience together and they, too, become guiding stars in your work.

Get 3.00pm train to Vienna from Prague. Good journey, I smuggle money for a Czech. Vienna chaos on arrival, but I get a lucky lift, and find a student hostel for only £3. Finally go out at 11.00pm and have a meal in town, read the What's On, and then walk around the very brightly lit and empty piazzas till 2am, seeing 'Vienna by night', but it's so bright it virtually looks the same as in the day-time. What a change – so many goods in the shop windows! So much artificial light!

21 November 1980

Last day. Find Musil's 'Museum Café', and write final letters home. Stop in the Griensteidl Café near Michaelplatz, a gorgeous old Viennese coffee house, enormous, elegant, intellectual, friendly, and I write from 2.30 to 5.30. A good way to have experienced Vienna. Have Viennese Schnitzel, make calls, buy wine, bread, ham, cheese for journey, and Guardian. Board at 8.30. Begin diary at 9.00, go on till 1.30 in the morning, sleep well in the luxury German carriage with chair/beds, wake at 9, wash, shave, write, arrive Ostend at 1.55. A great trip, with theatre being the handle to understanding a little of political life in Europe.

End, November 1980

SOUTH AMERICA JOURNAL, 1981

The second journal is as director of ATC, touring South America with *The Tempest* and *Quixote*. This group was the longest-lasting ensemble within the eight-year life of my spell as director of ATC. I think of all these actors as the core group of the company. They all shared life on the road for over three years straight and, with one exception, went on to perform at the Donmar Warehouse and in New York at the Britain Salutes New York Festival in the winter of 1983.

OCTOBER – NOVEMBER 1981
***QUIXOTE* AND *THE TEMPEST* IN SOUTH AMERICA**

Rio, Sao Paulo, Buenos Aires, Lima, Santiago, Caracas

The Company

Russell Enoch – Don Quixote/Gonzalo
Chris Barnes – Sancho Panza/Trinculo
Valerie Braddell – Dulcinea/Prospero
Christine Bishop – Duchess/Ariel
Jack Ellis – Duke/Caliban
Raymond Sawyer – Carrasco/Stefano
Denise Black – Maritornes/Miranda
Susan Biggs – Guitar & Mandolin
Paul Elkins – Stage Manager
Eric Starck – Tour Manager

Brazil

The Company arrived in Rio on Friday, 18 September at dawn. Our first performance was not until Monday 21 September in the capital, Brasilia. In the intervening period, the Company acclimatised themselves to a point of impatience. Dennis Clare, the British Council representative warned the Company about the savage muggings in terms so vivid that it was some time before anyone stepped out of the hotel.

It was an unexpectedly hot September, even for Brazilians. What we saw was Copacabana Beach, and a lot – I mean, thousands of tanned joggers running along the esplanade. Most of the Company stayed on the terrace in front of the hotel; some walked further afield; some got up at 5am, others slept till 11 – everyone's

The Company leaves for Caracas from Lima. From l to r, back; Chris Barnes, Ray Sawyer, Denise Black, JR, Russell Enoch, Christine Bishop; front; Valerie Braddell, Paul Elkins, Eric Starck; Jack Ellis takes the picture and is the only missing actor.

time was out. But we all swam on Copacabana and climbed up to see the Christ The Redeemer statue. We drank a lot of pina coladas. All spoilt; all ready to work.

RIO DE JANEIRO

A reception arranged by Dennis Clare to start the week off – an exceptionally busy party with everybody in Rio connected to the theatre who was available to come attending. There were two rival producers of two other *Tempest*s! At one stage I found myself talking simultaneously with three Mirandas. The reception was held in the foyer of the Teatro dos Quatro, our venue in Rio.

The Tempest opened in Rio to a slow handclap, nearly 40 minutes late – disturbing, but Valerie was to become hardened to having to overcome various nightmares at the start of Prospero's long opening sequence: slow handclaps in Rio, blackouts in Sao Paulo, usherettes flashing torches in her eyes in Lima, children shouting from the street in Porto Ordaz – always having to wait to the end of a delay before she could begin. She became very good at dominating an empty stage without speaking...

The audience in Rio was also quite different from that in the other Brazilian cities; more affluent, older, more ex-patriate. It was easy to make them laugh, difficult to move them.

MACUNAIMA THEATRE COMPANY

From my own point of view the most memorable event of the Sao Paulo visit was meeting the Macunaima Company and its director, Antones Funes.

SOUTH AMERICA JOURNAL, 1981

Macunaima's new production was *O Etorno Retorno* by Brazilian playwright Nelson Rodrigues, playing at the Company's theatre in downtown Sao Paulo. I had already seen their first show *Macunaima* (after which the Company is named) in London; this show had taken them to Colombia, Venezuela, New York, Washington and several European cities – it had also been an enormous success in Brazil. The novel on which it is based is a blend of folk-tale, myth and modern urban Brazil, particularly the city madness of Sao Paulo. Using fluid upstage/downstage action for the three protagonists with environment and events occurring in tableau form across the stage on rigid parallel lines, the stagecraft alone marked it out as an original work of theatre.

O Etorno Retorno is different. It is three 40-minute plays, one a surreal tale about the media and the reportage of a story; the second is about a family over several generations; the third concerns a disintegrating relationship. Still the large groupings with even more startling use of the entrances and exits–one literally invading the other. But the subject matter is less funny, less popular. It is, otherwise, as dazzling a work as *Macunaima* and will probably cause as much excitement when it goes to Europe.

The Sao Paulo public has responded firmly by not going to see it. The Company receives little money, except when it goes abroad – and then from the host country. Antones Funes says, "I am understood everywhere except here, in Brazil". The real difference between the two companies is money. ATC is funded by its government and Macunaima is not.

A public joint workshop over two days between Macunaima and ATC would have brought a lot of people into their theatre. Here, with almost certainly the best current company – certainly the best director – in Latin America, we could have

Christine, Denise and Valerie take a cigarette break en route to Buenos Aires

had an exchange that really counted both in artistic terms and in those of the British Council.

Unofficially, it happened anyway. It was excellent that it did. On Sunday afternoon, ATC went to the Macunaima theatre en bloc and saw *O Etorno Retorno*. At 9.30 the same night, a dozen Macunaimans came to see *Quixote*.

After the show about 30 people occupied a series of interlinked tables in the restaurant. I talked for some time with Antonio the director and later to Dennis Clare; I suggested that some exchange between Macunaima and our Company would be desirable. He will think about it.

Argentina

BUENOS AIRES

The flight to Buenos Aires was so turbulent that even the neurotic had to laugh. Apparently the Rio del Plata always makes for a bumpy ride. We had been told that Buenos Aires was much cooler and everyone left the plane wearing sweaters. They soon removed them – the temperature had snapped back to 30 degrees. We were put into the British Caledonian VIP lounge and waited a long time while Customs checked our eleven matching aluminium trunks. As ever, those with locks on were singled out for a thorough search. Arthur Edmondson, the British Council man met us, and then Roberto Barry, the local impresario organising our visit, drove us into the city. Barry's involvement meant that we got a world-class theatre to play in, the back-up of an excellent theatre company – technicians, canteen, box office and all – a packed press conference. It was to be a very busy week's work and the most satisfying of the entire tour. And not a single workshop.

We drove into Buenos Aires on the military's new airport highway that, to the community's disgust, has flattened a highly populous section of the city. The change from Brazil was striking. Everyone is smart, the style is Paris or Madrid; it's Spanish-bourgeois, much more buttoned-up, more dignified, a lot more conventionally old-fashioned. In Brazil they dance the samba; here they watch the tango with music supplied by elderly violinists in suits. Everyone claims that Argentina is European – not only in style and culture, but racially too. When we are asked about Brazil, people expect a racist joke...

Nobody is polite here about the military government, but nobody insults it either. Money is crazy money –15000 pesos to a £1, 5000 pesos for a beer. Things are opening up now; there are bright, satirical cartoons on sale at the news stand, critiques of government policy are being written in the papers and the token opposition party is vociferous. The water is being tested, but a particularly fierce attack on the government in the English-language newspaper lost the editor his job in the week we were there. Dictatorships are usually shown up when there's a dramatic absence of consumer goods; since there is plenty of everything in

SOUTH AMERICA JOURNAL, 1981

Buenos Aires, it all looks fine – a charming, elegant European city, full of squares and fountains and cafés and flower shops – in the middle of South America.

Argentina's supply of good films is restricted, and television is poor. So dancing and the theatre become prime activities in the capital; one as a form of self-expression, the other as a discreet political forum. As we were to find later in Chile, it's not what is said – everyone knows what could be said, what should be said, what can't be said – it's how to say this thing that everyone knows, without saying it. So new metaphors, new forms have to be found to suggest what can't be said. Ideally this metaphoric technique should throw up works that say it more cuttingly and more universally than if the facts were just stated. Wajda's manipulation of the censors in Poland over the last twenty years has been an effective example of this art. But this does not exist in the theatre in Argentina, except in the Teatro Abierto (Open Theatre), which has put on a number of courageous, naturalistic plays. The theatre has been burned down once, and re-opened elsewhere: on the two nights, I visited a packed house applauded wildly, all on their feet. The relation to the audience was direct and in good faith. What it lacked was a greater range of theatre style and form in which to express itself – it was all very much down to the written word. Its conventions are in the *Look Back In Anger* epoch.

And this is where our two productions come in. Here are the things that were most remarked on in Buenos Aires: the freedom of the actor within the piece and his possession of the role psychologically while remaining in deference to the production structurally; the actor's physical freedom on a bare stage, while remaining adroit and disciplined in his movements; the ensemble nature of both productions suggesting a structured give-and-take that can be seen to work; and the sense of contact with the audiences. These factors affected the theatre people who saw it – this much freedom was theirs too, if they wanted it. There is no law against working harmoniously together. It was the spirit in which it was done that suggested personal liberty, spoke of freedom of expression.

In a country like Argentina, a lively sense of allegory is essential to the theatre; otherwise, audiences stop thinking and the mere presence of the censor over a long period of time prevents even the permissible things from being said. I think that both *The Tempest* and *Quixote* touched on this nerve and were responsible for the very moving reception the theatre gave to us on the last night in Buenos Aires.

The sense of occasion was strongly felt by the Company in this 19th century theatre built throughout in the Spanish style; partly because of the remarkable technical back-up we received from the stage-crew, partly because the theatre was called the 'Cervantes'. And here was an English version of *Don Quixote*, and here, in this most masculine society, was Prospero being played by a young woman of 29. These factors gave edge to our being in such a place; but everyone felt the exhilaration of playing upon such a fine stage – visually, acoustically and atmospherically, it inspired the actors.

Above all, we were fixed in one theatre for a week and the Company seized the opportunities this afforded. Excellent use was made of the auditorium for entrances and exits, and these had real shock value in such a house; but they integrated fully with the 'stage-as-an-island' metaphor of *The Tempest*. The theatre was built by two old actors; they must have known exactly what they wanted – the foyers, salons, cafés and galleries of the theatre are spacious and elegant as one enters the building – then one goes into the auditorium itself and it feels like a chamber; dark, velvet, at every point allowing the spectator to sit up and see what is going on up on the stage. A remarkable space; the best that we have ever played.

Throughout our residency the Cervantes company was rehearsing in another part of the building. They all watched our shows, many of them more than once. The two companies talked together and I attended their rehearsals of Molière's *Tartuffe*. On our last night at the Cervantes, the director, the staff and the company gave a party for us in the Moorish-style salon behind the dress circle. A folk group played, people danced the tango, actresses sang, speeches were made – first by them, then by us; we gave champagne to the technicians, the theatre gave us each a tile from the fabric of the building and a lamp ("to hang in your first theatre") – this was a relic of the day the stage burned down twenty years ago, one night when the company was in residence there. Victor Roo, the theatre manager, had been in charge then and had overseen the restoration of the stage area. Our visit prompted this remarkable generosity and was one of the very rare occasions when all of the theatre's company – from director to flyman – came together. Despite the rhetoric of all such occasions it was very much a recognition from within the trade, so to speak – and the thanks we gave were heartfelt.

The last night at the Cervantes Theatre, Buenos Aires

SOUTH AMERICA JOURNAL, 1981

Chile

SANTIAGO

Halfway through the tour, we flew to Santiago. The flight took three hours with an alarming descent to land.

Argentina and Chile have very high literacy rates; Argentina's is 95%, that of Chile not far behind. Santiago is a sophisticated town, dominated by a startlingly fashionable, liberal middle class – you might be in a smart North American city. Men are less 'macho' than elsewhere in South America, and an informal stylishness pervades throughout the city. Poetry and music are important, the theatre also – as in Buenos Aires, there is a heavy restriction on films and television doesn't excite anyone that we met. They don't dance as much as in Brazil, Argentina or Peru but there are a lot of fashionable bars and restaurants. Prices are very high. One cannot go anywhere to eat without somebody singing folksongs, playing guitar.

If in Buenos Aires everyone wants you to see how European their city is, in Santiago the recurrent theme is that the person you are speaking to doesn't represent the government, rather that it is imposed upon them. Sensibility hits one in such big doses that London scepticism gets to work and one asks, if everyone hates this government so much, why is it still there?

Chile is actually interested in bringing about change through artistic expression; new writing and plays are very important indeed to the country – as important as in Poland, the fervour is comparable. There, however, the comparison ends. Censorship is far more alarming in Chile than in Argentina or Poland. The technique of 'self-censorship' is practised – *you* decide how far you can go, then you find out if you've gone too far.

I visited Gregory Cohen – a young playwright – in prison; the police claimed he participated in a demonstration, but in fact his plays and his acting were becoming too popular. He presented too strong an image to university students. A 6ft-5inch, concave, gaunt, Christ-like figure, absolutely straightforward to meet; he's 22. His case is with UNESCO and the ITI. At a benefit show on the Monday night, the mention of his name produced wild cheering for two minutes. Recently, a director who employed the novelty of producing a show in a circus tent was detained after the first night – and still is. Directors and companies don't know when they will be visited.

We did a workshop to a packed house of 300 actors and students on the Thursday morning, presenting, as we had in Rio, the Ariel/Caliban/Prospero relationship and working the audience into making suggestions as to how it should be staged. The response was cautious, yet inventive and intellectual.

I asked if our production of *The Tempest* would have been permitted by a Chilean company. This was the reply:

> 'The statement is strong, but it wouldn't offend the censor – except at the end of the first half – when Caliban, Stefano and Trinculo march off roaring 'Freedom, Hi Day Freedom, Freedom, Freedom'. That would have to go.'

During the daytime I talked to many people connected with the theatre. Everyone seemed critical, pessimistic about the country, and yet patriotic – a strong sense everywhere that something more would be achieved if enough skilled theatre people really wanted it to happen. Yet the divisions and sophistications of smart city life seemed, in Santiago, to afflict corporate resolve and action as surely as they can in London or Paris. A sophisticated people, materially comfortable, but lacking essential freedom. Yet the extent of demoralisation is revealed by the fact that the people are more visibly embarrassed by the restrictions than angry about them.

The potential for change in the theatre and for a future political forum lies with the students. These were the least demoralised people I spoke to. It is very unusual in this kind of lecture/discussion to be peppered with questions as much as the company was in Santiago. I was repeatedly asked the same question: how do we find a theatre language such as we have seen in *The Tempest*? What is the reaction to your production in England?

The following day. I was invited to observe a 'movement session'. Paul Elkins and Ray Sawyer came with me.

The session began by locking the door, and drawing the blinds. Then a group of students showed us, and the rest of the class in turn showed us, a series of their own prepared exercises and images. These were part of their course but, as the tutor told me later, almost none of these would be seen by the university examiner. They were a series of violent images about living in a police state, all performed

Workshop with students in Santiago

with a memorable dignity and poise. The only brief was to use that studio space as creatively as possible. Water dripped, torches flashed, screams in the dark, ladders endlessly climbed, paint chucked onto naked backs, men suspended on ropes – it was like a classic slice of Polish avant-garde when you put it all together and certainly as imaginative and as well executed – except that they knew nothing about Polish theatre. Yet they had unswervingly found the same form. Viewed politically or theatrically, it was a small phenomenon. And their assurance is what I remember. And these were the same students who had played the willing school-chorus in a Calderon play I had seen the day before, and their tutor was that play's director. The theatre culture seemed almost schizophrenic.

Clearly the Chilean theatre would like to bring these two sides of its character together into an un-censorable form in its productions. Until they gain political freedom, they'll continue to lock the doors and draw the blinds.

The last night in Santiago was *Quixote*. I have never seen an audience cheer and clap so hard for anything we have done, not even in Sao Paulo or Buenos Aires – it was overwhelming – I was shaking as I left the stage. I wish we could have done more there.

I am in no doubt at all that visiting companies to Chile, far from endorsing the regime, can do much in the most officially innocent way, to undermine it. Our vote for the Chileans by going there meant a very great deal to them. I don't know what it meant to those who support the regime; we met nobody who admitted to that.

No doubt we met them, nevertheless.

Peru

LIMA

The flight from Santiago to Lima took nearly four hours. The Company was entering its sixth week of the tour. Lima is much poorer than the towns in other countries we had come from, and this was evident immediately on driving into the city. Most capitals do a window-dressing job on the road from the airport into the capital; not here. Everything grey, dusty, broken down – poverty evident everywhere. And if it looked like this here, one knew that there would be more away from the city centre. Big warnings about the water and the vegetables. And immediately one realised that there was not going to be that large middle-class theatre-going public which we had found in Buenos Aires and Santiago.

There is very little theatre in Lima, and a lot more entertainments: variety shows, folk singing, dancing, cock-fighting, bull-fighting – and so on. It is a place of public events and communal activity and much nearer to our preconceptions of a Latin American city before we had actually seen one: enormous markets in Chinatown selling everything from carpets to falcons; nightly demonstrations in the main square (water cannon parked there permanently), fading, crumbling baroque buildings, news-stands selling a whole range of gory police magazines (always a murdered corpse on the cover), churches full of effigies, thronged with promenading worshippers, beggars and cripples on every corner and throughout Lima quite a different cast of face, more indigenous than we had seen in Argentina and Chile.

Our pleasant, faded hotel was in the centre of the old city and most of the company went out wandering the streets within an hour or so of arrival. After a briefing on the five days ahead, the whole company went out for the evening, eating or dancing in different parts of the city. There was a press conference for the whole Company on Friday morning; as was now customary, Valerie Braddell, our interpreter as well as our Prospero, answered the first questions and then translated. Articles appeared the following day. The Teatro Segura is of the same period and basic design as the Cervantes theatre in Buenos Aires, but there the comparison stops – a very flat acoustic and a poorly furnished auditorium made it a difficult house in which to generate much energy.

We had a lot of workshops on the schedule. Everyone led one type of workshop or another. Ray has taken a great number on movement and mime, often with Valerie. Chris specialises in the art of clowning; Russell, who has taught for years at LAMDA, has taken a number of workshops on voice, and Jack and Paul have made an excellent combination in taking workshops on any given subject or theme, having worked as a unit with students of several nationalities. And being a permanent ensemble, the company is used to working together. With our own translator, we were able to break down barriers very quickly and to know what the students understood, what they found difficult and how far they would be prepared to go.

Russell Enoch leads a workshop with students in Lima

SOUTH AMERICA JOURNAL, 1981

I saw two plays in Lima, both poorly directed though with some good actors. I talked at length with one group and with their director, Aurora; they put on satirical plays about Lima life (there is no political censorship) and tour children's plays around the favellas. They talked very well about what they were doing and Aurora was formidably knowledgeable about European theatre. But they have no money and several of the actors actually live in the theatre. We met other student actors who were starting a women's theatre troupe – a radical step there – but they were six months away from production. It seemed to me that touring, agit-prop theatre is the future here, and that a number of groups will be active within the next year. What is exciting is the degree of politicisation in their attitude to theatre; it is a means to making a statement about the many inequalities and discomforts that exist in Peru. It is just poverty, illiteracy, ignorance – but where to start? Theatre is a luxury in a town like Lima. Our Shakespeare there was a shiny import, rather than the suggestive allegory that it was in Argentina and Chile.

Venezuela

Venezuela is so wealthy (no more wads of damp paper money – this was the first country in which coins had any value) that it frequently books international stars and companies into the capital. Glamour and 'the best' have an important role in Caracas culture, though I have never been anywhere where it felt more inappropriate to be playing Shakespeare. What it does mean is that Caracas has seen Kantor, Brook, Lindsay Kemp, Macunaima, Mnouchkine, etc? It is a true international venue.

The night of *The Tempest* I went to see the La Barraca Company do a new play called *Telaramas*; I thought it brilliant – about the upbringing of a Venezuelan boy, done in full grotesque comic style, with a strong expressionistic touch and a wild use of props. Watched by an audience of thirteen, the company of five played with complete commitment and evident professional skill. Talking afterwards to the director, I learned that the company had played at festivals in several European cities. Since ATC were scheduled to do a workshop with them the following morning, I was alarmed as to what we could show them! Remembering that this was the very kind of workshop we had always wanted, I decided it was the time to introduce Jarry's *Ubu* and to construct exercises around this figure, and use him to explore political themes. The La Barraca company (all unsubsidised and unpaid, of course) knew just what we meant and the two companies did some brilliant impros together.

Heathrow

The company, now a caravanserai of hand luggage and exotic trophies, fumbled up the stairs of a 747, bid goodbye to the British Council and picked up *The Times* and *Express* for the first time in eight weeks – some turned to the reviews, some to the sport, some to the news first – everyone delighted, high at seeing the familiar again – dinner followed – and the company for the most part slept all the way to Heathrow, arriving at 7am on Saturday morning. Through immigration and looking very brown, the company sniffed the cold November morning, already sunny, and ran into the arms of those waiting for them at the gate.

PRODUCTIONS, PERFORMANCES, PUBLICATIONS

ATC LONDON, 1977-1985
Don Juan (1977) by Byron [Upstream Theatre]
Don Juan (1978) by Byron [Edinburgh Festival Fringe First]
The Provoked Wife (1979) by Vanbrugh [Edinburgh and tour of Scotland and England]
Don Juan (1979) by Byron [Avignon Festival]
Don Quixote Part One (1980) adapted by the company with Richard Curtis
Don Quixote Part Two (1980) by Richard Curtis
Measure for Measure (1980) by Shakespeare [Edinburgh Festival; Oxford Union]
The Tempest (1980) [in rehearsal at BAC; national tour, including Highlands and Islands]
Berlin/Berlin (1981) adapted from Musil
Don Quixote Part One, Don Quixote Part Two and *Measure for* Measure (1981) [Greece and former Yugoslavia]
Berlin/Berlin (1981) [Oxford]
Quixote (1981) [now one show, in South America]
The Tempest (1981) [Oxford; South America]
Berlin/Berlin (1982) [in Berlin, and German tour]
Ubu Roi (1982) [Edinburgh and tour]
The Provoked Wife, Quixote, The Tempest (1982) [all three plays on English, Scottish and European tours]
Berlin/Berlin, Ubu Roi, The Provoked Wife, Quixote, The Tempest (January-April 1983) [season of all five plays at the Donmar Warehouse, London]
Quixote (April-May 1983) [Perry Street Theatre, New York]
The Provoked Wife (April-May 1983) [Perry Street Theatre, New York]
Twelfth Night (1984) by Shakespeare [English tour and The Bridge Theatre, London; New Zealand, Australia, Hong Kong]
Don Juan (1984) by Molière [English tour and The Bridge Theatre, London; New Zealand, Australia, Hong Kong]

The Vandalist (1985) adapted from Jarry's *Ubu in Chains* [English and Scottish tour]

OLDHAM COLISEUM REPERTOIRE, 1985-1988
Bouncers (Autumn 1985) by John Godber, directed by John Retallack
Clowns on a School Outing (Autumn 1985) by Ken Campbell, directed by John Retallack
Tartuffe (Autumn 1985) by Molière, directed by John Retallack
The Accrington Pals (Autumn 1985) by Peter Whelan, directed by Annie Castledine
Mother Goose (Autumn 1985) by Kenneth Alan Taylor

Gregory's Girl (Spring 1986) by Bill Forsythe, directed by Ian Forrest
Me Mam Sez (Spring 1986) by Barry Heath, directed by John Retallack
Mad Adventures of a Knight (Spring 1986) by Richard Curtis, directed by John Retallack
Cloud 9 (Spring 1986) by Caryl Churchill, directed by Barry McGinn
The Kiss of The Spider Woman (Spring 1986) by Manuel Puig, directed by Paul Elkins
Girlfriends (Spring 1986) by Howard Goodall, directed by John Retallack

Loving and Working Season
Harvest in the North (Autumn 1986) by James Lansdale Hodson, directed by John Retallack
Love on the Dole (Autumn 1986) by Walter Greenwood, directed by Paul Elkins
Spring and Port Wine (Autumn 1986) by Bill Naughton, directed by John Retallack
Dick Whittington (Autumn 1986) by Renata Allen, directed by John Retallack

Spring 1987 Centenary Season
A Night on the Tiles (Spring 1987) by Frank Vickery, directed by John Retallack
Y'shunta Joined (Spring 1987) by Barry Heath, directed by Paul Elkins
The Importance of Being Earnest (Spring 1987) by Oscar Wilde, directed by John Retallack
Wuthering Heights (Spring 1987) by Emily Bronte, directed by Paul Elkins
A Midsummer Night's Dream (Spring 1987) by Shakespeare, directed by John Retallack

Loot (Autumn 1987) by Joe Orton, directed by Paul Elkins
Hanky Park (Autumn 1987) by Walter Greenwood, directed by Paul Elkins
The Playboy of The Western World (Autumn 1987) by John Synge, directed by John Retallack
Aladdin (Autumn 1987) by Renata Allen, directed by Jeff Longmore
(*Girlfriends* plays in London, 1987)
Twelfth Night (Spring 1988) by Shakespeare, directed by John Retallack
Stage Fright (Spring 1988) by Peter Fieldson, directed by Paul Elkins
The Steamie (Spring 1988) by Tony Roper, directed by Renata Allen
Educating Rita (Spring 1988) by Willy Russell, directed by John Retallack
Threepenny Opera (Spring 1988) by Bertold Brecht, directed by Paul Elkins

OXFORD STAGE COMPANY, 1989-1999

As You Like It (1989)
King Lear (1989)
The Witch and the Magic Mountain (1989)
Measure for Measure (1990)
The Real Don Juan (1990)
Woza Albert (1990)
The Miser (1990)
The Princess and the Monkey Palace (1990)
The Tempest (1991)
The Price (1991)
The Seagull (1991)
Days of Hope (1991)
The Magic Storybook (1991) [TMA Award: Best Show for Children, 1991]
Much Ado About Nothing (1992)
Hot Italian Nights (1992)
Pig in a Poke (1992)
Pericles & Comedy of Errors (1993)
The Venetian Twins (1993)
Fooling About (1993) [for children]
Romeo and Juliet (1994)
All My Sons (1994)
Great Expectations (1994)
Twelfth Night (1995)
Making the Future 1: (1995) [for young people]
Mirad: Boy from Bosnia, Parts 1 & 2 (1995)
Hitler's Childhood (1995)

Grace (1995)
Love Is A Drug (1995)
Hamlet (1996)
The Provoked Wife (1996)
My Mother Said I Never Should (1996)
Mirad (1996) [film version]
All's Well That Ends Well (1997)
The Comic Mysteries (1997)
Making the Future 2 (1998) [for Young People]
Junk (1998) [TMA Award: Best Show for Children and Young People, 1991]
Johnny Blue (1998)
Roots (1998)
Midsummer Night's Dream (1998)

PLAYS WRITTEN AND DIRECTED FOR COMPANY OF ANGELS, 2001-2011

Hannah and Hanna (2001) [Company of Angels tour in UK and Edinburgh 2001-2003; Edinburgh Festival; Winner of Herald Angel Award; World Service radio broadcast 2002; TMA Award/Best New Show for Young People nominee; British Council tours to India, Malaysia and the Philippines 2004-2005; produced and translated into French, Swedish, German, Dutch, Portuguese, Hebrew and Japanese; over 200 performances in Sweden and 100 in Belgium]

Wild Girl (2002) [Company of Angels/Quicksilver tour 2002; Wederzijds tour of Holland & Belgium 2004; Runner-up, Hans Snoek Award, Amsterdam 2004; Bristol Old Vic tour in co-production with Theatre Royal, Bath, Dukes Playhouse, Lancaster and Theatre Iolo, Cardiff 2013; translated and produced in French and Dutch]

Club Asylum (2002) [Company of Angels tour of Scotland; Tron Theatre Glasgow; translated into French], Oberon

Sweetpeter (2004) collaboration with Usifu Jalloh [Company of Angels National Tour; Polka Theatre London; translated & performed in French], Methuen

Virgins (2005) [Company of Angels National Tour; Edinburgh Festival; translated and performed in French, Swedish, German; over 150 performances in Sweden], Oberon

Risk (2006) [Company of Angels Scottish and English tour; Tron Theatre Glasgow; translated and performed in French and German; Theater an der Parkaue Berlin 2008; Compagnie L'Interlude Tour of France

2012; Avignon Festival 2013; further French touring including Paris 2014-15; "Although it is performed by five young professional actor-dancers, the raw voices of those involved in the workshop process can be heard in every detail of Retallack's text … Risk is an energetic, thoughtful and likeable show, with one or two shuddering moments of truth" *The Scotsman*], Oberon and Les Solitaires Intempestifs

Apples (2009) adapted by John Retallack from the novel by Richard Milward [Company of Angels & Northern Stage Newcastle; National Tour; Edinburgh Festival; Winner of Herald Angel Award]

Arlo (2010) [public reading for Company of Angels Theatre Café; Southwark Playhouse; Afternoon Play on BBC Radio 4]

Truant (2011) [National Theatre of Scotland & Company of Angels; Glasgow tour]

PLAYS DIRECTED FOR BRISTOL OLD VIC

Pictures at an Exhibition (2012) [Bristol Old Vic Young Company]

Wild Girl (2013) [Bristol Old Vic and regional tour: a co-production between Bristol Old Vic and Theatr Iolo]

Good Clown Bad Clown (2013) by Renata Allen [Bristol Old Vic production]

The Last Days of Mankind (2013) with Toby Hulse, adapted from original text by Karl Kraus [Bristol Old Vic/Bristol Old Vic Theatre School]

Dido and Aeneas (2015-2016) opera by Henry Purcell [Bristol Old Vic and tour]

Pink Mist (2016-2018) by Owen Sheers [Bristol Old Vic, Bush Theatre, London and national tour]

FREELANCE WRITING

The Plague (2000) adapted by John Retallack from the novel by Albert Camus [Dundee Rep]

The Foundling (2003) [Brighton Theatre Company tour of South-East]

Common Ground (2003) [Cardboard Citizens tour for homeless people in London]

Ballroom (2004) [national tour; Riverside Studios London; translated into French; "*A play with dancing by John Retallack, Ballroom takes you in its firm-but-gentle embrace and spins you off into the strange sunset world of the seaside tea dance…It's funny. It's sad. It's an elating symbol of how differences of age and temperament can be fleetingly dissolved in dance*" Jeremy Kingston, *The Times*]

A Bridge to the Stars (2007) adapted by John Retallack from the novel by Henning Mankell [Cottesloe Theatre; National Theatre Connections Festival; Afternoon Play BBC Radio 4]
The Outsider (2013) adapted by John Retallack from the novel by Albert CAMUS [90 minute broadcast on BBC Radio 3 on the centenary of Camus' birth 3 November 2013]
Arlo (2013) [Afternoon Play on BBC Radio 4]
Hannah and Hanna in Dreamland (2016-2017) [UK Arts International/ HOUSE; Turner Gallery, Margate 2016; Edinburgh Fringe 2017]
The Good Companions (2017-2018) by JB Priestley, adapted for BBC Radio 4 by John Retallack [broadcast 3 February 2018]
Hannah and Hanna in Dreamland (2019) [performed at *Making Waves* festival in conjunction with the Turner Prize exhibition, Margate]
The Hummingbird (2022-2023) by Sandro Veronesi, adapted by John Retallack for BBC Radio 3 [nominated for Best Adaptation in BBC Audio Awards 2023]

KEY FREELANCE PRODUCTIONS

The Fair Day (1988) [Warrenpoint, Northern Ireland]
Hamlet (1988) [New Delhi, India]
Comedy of Errors (1993) [Washington, US, Shakespeare Theatre]
Romeo and Juliet (1994) [The Globe, Tokyo]
Rockabye and *Footfalls* (1999) [Bergen Festival, Norway]
The Plague (1999) [Dundee, Scotland]
The Clearing (1999) [Wederzijds, Amsterdam]
Junk (2000) [Den Nationale Scene, Bergen, Norway]
Hannah and Hanna (2003) [Theatre de Poche, Brussels]
Pink Mist (2015) [The Bush and National Tour]
Dido and Aeneas (2015) [Bristol Old Vic and tour]
Hannah and Hanna in Dreamland (2017) [Marlowe, Canterbury and tour]
Unicorns, Almost (2018) [Hay-on-Wye Festival]

MAIN PUBLISHED WORKS

Junk (1999) adapted from Melvyn Burgess' novel, Methuen
Hannah and Hanna (2002), English and Media
Hannah and Hanna (2004), French (acting edition)
Hannah et Hanna (2004), Editions Fontaine
Sweetpeter (2006) in *New Plays for Young People*, Methuen
Four Plays for Company of Angels (2008) by John Retallack [*Hannah and Hanna, Risk, Club Asylum, Virgins*], Oberon

Risque (2009), Editions Bleu
Apples (2012), Oberon
Hannah and Hanna in Dreamland (2019), Oberon

ACKNOWLEDGEMENTS

Above all, thanks to Stephen Brown for editing this book and giving me so much crucial advice at a stage when I very much needed it. His comments and questions are always critical, illuminating and helpful. Profound thanks also to Heather Kay who proof-read the manuscript with customary precision. Thanks to Karl James for his original design of the cover and to Maia Adelia for her stylish amendments to this edition. I especially want to thank Janet Taylor, Nick Marston and Michael Boswood for the time they gave to reading the book and offering invaluable advice at an early stage. Emma Balch, Jack Ellis, Prue Skene, Tony Graham, Nicola Russell, Roy Blatchford, Patch Connolly, Alain Arbibe, Stuart Wood and Dick McCaw all had very helpful things to say and I am grateful to them all. Lastly, thanks to Toby Matthews and Ben Burrows at Holywell Press for their patience and detailed engagement with the book from first to last.